A SHORT-TITLE CATALOGUE OF MUSIC PRINTED BEFORE 1825 IN THE FITZWILLIAM MUSEUM, CAMBRIDGE

Edited by

VALERIE RUMBOLD *and* IAIN FENLON

CAMBRIDGE
UNIVERSITY PRESS

Published by the Press Syndicate of the University of Cambridge
The Pitt Building, Trumpington Street, Cambridge CB2 1RP
40 West 20th Street, New York, NY 10011-4211, USA
10 Stamford Road, Oakleigh, Victoria 3166, Australia

First published 1992

Printed in Great Britain at the University Press, Cambridge

A catalogue record for this book is available from the British Library

Library of Congress cataloguing in publication data
Fitzwilliam Museum.
A short-title catalogue of music printed before 1825 in the
Fitzwilliam Museum, Cambridge/edited by Valerie Rumbold and Iain Fenlon.
p.   cm.
Includes bibliographical references.
ISBN 0 521 41535 7 (hardback)
1. Music – Bibliography – Catalogs.   2. Fitzwilliam Museum –
Catalogs.   I. Rumbold, Valerie.   II. Fenlon, Iain.   III. Title.
ML 136.C212F58   1992
016.78′026′3–dc20   91-29977   CIP MN

ISBN 0 521 41535 7   hardback

CONTENTS

ILLUSTRATIONS

Joseph Wright of Derby: *The Hon. Richard Fitzwilliam*, 1764 *frontispiece*

Between pages 138 and 139

FOREWORD

THIS SHORT-TITLE catalogue of the Museum's holdings of early printed music has been produced as a first step towards replacing J.A. Fuller-Maitland and A.H. Mann's 1893 *Catalogue of the Music in the Fitzwilliam Museum, Cambridge*. Over the last century the collections have changed in various ways: many items, both printed books and manuscripts, have been added; but in 1926 some printed books deemed to be suitable for student use were transferred to the Pendlebury Library of the Faculty of Music (although the best and rarest part of the collection, including the personal music library of the Founder, Viscount Fitzwilliam, remained intact). A new catalogue was thus long overdue, and its first stage is completed in this catalogue of the early printed material.

That this first step has been possible is due to the imaginative generosity of the Faculty Board of Music in making available from the John Stuart of Rannoch Sacred Music Fund means to cover the cost of twelve months' work. First and foremost I thank Professor Alexander Goehr who so readily and effectively appreciated, and led others to appreciate, the importance and benefit of the project. Thanks to Dr Iain Fenlon, the Fitzwilliam's Honorary Keeper of Music, the cataloguer was chosen and the work went ahead. Dr Valerie Rumbold completed the task well on time; and she has contributed with Dr Fenlon the Introduction to this volume. We are also grateful to Mr O.W. Neighbour, formerly of the British Library, for advice about cataloguing procedures and for other bibliographical assistance.

The Fitzwilliam is fortunate indeed in such friends and helpers. The University at large, its students and its visitors gain by their happily combined effort.

Michael Jaffé

This publication has been generously supported by the Faculty Board of Music, University of Cambridge.

INTRODUCTION:
VISCOUNT FITZWILLIAM,
COLLECTOR OF ANCIENT MUSIC

RICHARD FITZWILLIAM, 7th Viscount Fitzwilliam of Merrion and of Thorncastle (1745–1816), whose personal collection forms the core of the collection of early printed music now in the Fitzwilliam Museum, was the eldest son of Richard the 6th Viscount and his wife Catherine, née Decker.[1] Her father, Sir Matthew Decker Bt, had arrived in England from Holland in about 1700, and had rapidly risen to a position of considerable financial influence: it has been estimated that at his death Sir Matthew was probably the richest of the Dutch mercantile settlers gathered around the Dutch Church at Austin Friars in the heart of the City of London.[2] Catherine, born in about 1710, married the 6th Viscount Fitzwilliam in 1744 from the Decker house at 8 St James Square, an address which provides clear proof of the family's position in the highest reaches of London society. As the eldest of four daughters, Catherine inherited a substantial fortune which in turn was passed to her eldest son, born one year after her marriage. It was this inheritance that enabled him to cultivate the connoisseurship for which he was principally known to the public:

His lordship possesses . . . feelings alive to the sufferings of his fellow beings, with a warmth of sincerity which an excellent heart alone could dictate . . . with a liberality which we would gladly see more generally imitated [he] readily permits every respectable person to view his noble library and capital collection of valuable pictures, setting a good example to those connoisseurs who, like misers, hoard their curiosities for their own private amusement, without benefitting or enlightening in the public in any shape whatever.[3]

Fitzwilliam's education followed the traditional pattern of an eighteenth-century gentleman, first at Charterhouse, and then, from 1761, at Trinity Hall, Cambridge, where he was to develop a network of musical acquaintances which was to help shape his noticeably antiquarian tastes.[4] Here, for example, he met the organist Joah Bates: in later years they would be associated through their roles in the Concert of Ancient Music, founded in 1776, of which Bates was to be conductor, and Fitzwilliam a director.[5] A mutual friend was William Lobb, fellow of Peterhouse, who in 1764 presented Fitzwilliam with a manuscript copy of his setting for solo voice and strings of Petrarch's 'Ohime, il bel viso'; and it was in Lobb's rooms that another friend of Fitzwilliam's, Norton Nicholls (who was later to assist him by translating French libretti for the Concert of Ancient Music), met the poet Thomas Gray in 1762.[6] In 1764 Nicholls further recorded that Gray 'has Fitzwilliam's Harpsichord, and we sing Duetts, Marcello's Psalms, in great privacy, an hour or two'.[7] In addition to studying the keyboard (he was taking lessons on both the organ and the harpsichord during these years), Fitzwilliam was also pursuing formal musical studies in composition, as is shown by a manuscript of exercises in figured bass in which he notes that he was taking lessons with John Keeble, in whom he had a link with the older keyboard tradition represented by Keeble's teachers and associates Thomas Kelway, Johann Christoph Pepusch and Thomas Roseingrave.[8]

Having received the degree of MA in 1764, Fitzwilliam embarked in earnest on his career as collector and connoisseur of music. By 1765 he had moved to Paris (the first of many lengthy visits abroad not only to France but also to Spain, Italy and the Low Countries): in the French capital he studied the harpsichord with the eminent teacher Jacques Du Phly (1715–89), who also instructed him in figured bass. Du Phly's exercises for Fitzwilliam survive, neatly written out in a small commonplace book inscribed 'R. Fitzwilliam, Paris 1765'.[9] Whereas as an undergraduate he had selected his few purchases of printed music from the standard repertories of the recent past (Bononcini, Handel, Geminiani), he now started to buy more extensively in this area and, in addition, to develop that less conventional taste for French music, especially of the seventeenth and early eighteenth centuries, that is such a distinctive feature of his collection. Fitzwilliam's practice of signing and dating books as he bought them allows us to trace his acquisition, remarkable by the standards of English taste, of a sizeable collection of French works of the seventeenth and eighteenth centuries during the many months spent in Paris during the late 1760s and early 1770s. In 1765 he bought the score of Rameau's *Pigmalion*, the first of a large number of the composer's works that he was eventually to own, and the following year he purchased a copy of Dieupart's *Suittes de clavessin*. The next year saw large-scale purchases of folio full scores of French operas published by Ballard, including six works by Lulli, Charpentier's *Medée*, Desmarets's *Circé* and Elisabeth Claude Jacquet de la Guerre's *Cephale et Procris*. This pattern was continued by his acquisition, still in 1767, of a number of manuscript scores originally produced by Foucault, whose shop (which went out of business about 1730) maintained a team of copyists to make manuscripts for wealthy clients: Fitzwilliam's volumes include scores of eight ballets by Lulli as well as works by Desmarets and Colasse.[10] Towards the end of that decade, Fitzwilliam added to his collection a magnificent find, Boivin's elegantly printed full scores of motets by Lalande, originally issued in 1729, as well as two books of *Pieces de clavecin* by his old teacher Du Phly; on the verso of the title-page they bear a manuscript note giving instructions about fingering.[11] As might be expected, Fitzwilliam also bought harpsichord music in some quantity: during these same years he acquired Couperin's *L'Art de toucher le clavecin* (1717), and Rameau's *Pieces de clavecin en concerts* (1741) among other volumes. As with his purchases of opera and ballet scores, Fitzwilliam's taste in keyboard music clearly encompassed the past as well as the present. The latter received further impetus in 1771 when Du Phly presented him with two books of keyboard pieces which were then bound, together with his earlier two sets, in a Parisian binding. Although he still spent time in the

French capital during the 1770s, Fitzwilliam's purchases of French music now slackened off, though they never ceased. Even in London he still sought out pieces by French composers, above all music for the harpsichord: the Walsh edition of Rameau's five concertos (the *Pieces de clavecin en concerts*) as well as the same composer's *Pieces de clavecin* and *Nouvelles suites de pieces de clavecin* which Walsh issued as Rameau's Op. 2 and 3 were acquired in this way.

It was during his residence in Paris that Fitzwilliam met the dancer known as 'Mademoiselle Zacharie', who became his mistress in the mid-1780s.[12] The experience of living in Catholic France is also relevant to his *Lettres d'Atticus*, which reflect on a variety of subjects, principally on the relations between religion and society. (First published anonymously as separate letters, then issued in a collected French edition, still anonymous, in 1811, they were printed under his own name in an English translation only in 1825, ten years after his death.) With his pronounced taste for the spectacles of the *ancien régime*, indicated not only by his purchases of French baroque opera but also by his collection of sumptuous volumes of engravings of royal festivities, Fitzwilliam's reaction to the French Revolution was presumably negative. Certainly he patronised the émigré book-binder the Comte de Caumont, and it has been suggested that it was from émigrés that he acquired in 1791 a recently copied set of Rameau scores in manuscript.[13] In his role as a director of the Concert of Ancient Music Fitzwilliam sponsored in this year a performance of part of Rameau's *Castor et Pollux*, no doubt wishing to insist, in a context where Handel – whom he also collected avidly – had come to be accepted as the staple of the 'ancient' repertory, that the French music of the *ancien régime* should also have its place in the celebration of past musical splendours.[14]

In effect, Fitzwilliam's bias towards 'ancient' music is quite as striking as the taste for things French in the purchases that he began to make in the late 1760s. His French acquisitions were entirely typical of his collection in favouring the productions of the first half of the eighteenth century and before, at the expense of contemporary music. As can be seen from the chronological list of his collection of printed music, his greatest passion of all among the baroque composers was for Handel, who had died when Fitzwilliam was in his early teens, and who was to become the object of an aristocratic cult which found expression in two movements to which Fitzwilliam was to serve as director: the Concert of Ancient Music and the Handel Commemoration. In the list of his accessions for 1767, for example, his early determination to build up as complete a collection as possible of Handel's published works is obvious: although his purchase of a dozen French scores in that year is remarkable in itself, it is dwarfed for sheer bulk by the acquisition of nearly thirty Handel items. The acquisition of Handel's music was to remain a lifelong interest, though unfortunately nothing is known of how he came to own the greatest prize of his entire music collection, the mass of fragments and sketches in Handel's autograph, some of which came into his possession as early as 1778.[15] Throughout his collecting career he was eager to support the publication of new editions of Handel's works: in 1799, for example, a score of Handel volumes, many bearing Fitzwilliam's name as subscriber, were added to the collection; and he was also a subscriber for two sets of Samuel Arnold's complete edition (1787–97). It was also clear that, quite apart from his special love of Handel, Fitzwilliam was generally supportive of the editing and publication of early music: he subscribed to William Boyce's *Cathedral Music* (1760–73), H. Hargraves's edition of Clari's madrigals (c. 1765), John Stafford Smith's *Collection of English songs . . . composed about the year 1500* (1779), John Parry's *British Harmony* (1781) and Benjamin Goodison's projected Purcell edition (c. 1788–90); and he was probably also a subscriber to William Hawes's incomplete edition of Thomas Morley's *Triumphs of Oriana* (1814).[16]

If the two most striking lines of interest in Fitzwilliam's collection of printed music are the Handelian and the French, a third is also worth noting: music for his own instrument, the harpsichord. Not surprisingly, in this area too the baroque appealed particularly to him: it is significant that his teacher, John Keeble, was noted for an old-fashioned approach to composition for the instrument, and that his friend Joseph Kelway (who may also have given him lessons) was an enthusiast for the works of Domenico Scarlatti.[17] In 1772 Fitzwilliam demonstrated his commitment to this element in the baroque keyboard tradition by taking the extreme step of travelling to Spain to search out works by Scarlatti, the climax of the journey being a meeting with Scarlatti's pupil Antonio Soler, who also made him a present of his own works in manuscript: Fitzwilliam later made these new sources of both composers available for publication in England.[18] The printed edition of the Soler pieces which finally took its place in Fitzwilliam's collection thus possessed all three of the qualifications which, singly or in combination, account for most of the relatively few contemporary and near-contemporary works included among his printed music: a connection with a revered master, personal acquaintance with the composer and relevance to Fitzwilliam's own instrument. Despite his primary enthusiasm for the baroque keyboard, he even allowed himself to be sufficiently interested by modern keyboard developments to purchase in 1805 two collections arranged by Clementi specifically for students of the piano,[19] although whether he actually played the new instrument is not clear. Yet, even if he had experimented, his apparent lack of response to the most characteristic music being written in his lifetime must have limited his appreciation of the new medium. For it is the astonishing truth that, as it has come down to us, his printed music collection includes not a single work by Haydn or Mozart or Beethoven – an omission which suggests just how far this musical antiquarian had separated himself from current taste.

It seems clear that Fitzwilliam, who never married, made his activities as collector and connoisseur of music and the fine arts the principal business of his life. Yet, as the chronological list of his collection shows, there were years when little or no printed music was acquired, and in one case at least the lull can be related to other demands on his time: in 1776 his father died, and he succeeded to the family honours.[20] The new responsibilities brought by his wealth and position probably account for the check to the growth of the printed music collection at this time. Other activities outside the field of musical connoisseurship testify to his participation in the usual privileges and sinecures of his rank: he was elected a fellow of the Royal Society in 1789, was also Vice Admiral for Leinster and from 1790 to 1806 sat as MP for Wilton, a position to which he was preferred by his cousin, Henry 10th Earl of Pembroke.[21] He apparently sought election not out of any interest in affairs of state – in fact he was rarely present, even for major votes – but out of a desire to advance his prospects of gaining the English titles he felt were his by right. It seems to have rankled with him that his Viscountcy was merely Irish, and he devoted much fruitless energy to petitioning for the grant of the Earldom of Warrington and the Barony of Vaux, both of which he held to be his by descent.

On his death in 1816, Fitzwilliam left the bulk of his property not to the two brothers who were to succeed him in title but to his cousin the Earl of Pembroke. To his University, however, he left his pictures, books and manuscripts, with financial provision for a museum to house them. Unfortunately, the University was not quick either to catalogue or to house the collections adequately, and it is possible that some items were lost. Further confusion in the printed music collection was made possible by the steady addition of further items from other sources, so it is fortunate that Fitzwilliam's habit of inscribing and dating his books enables at least the core of his music library to be identified today – although there remains a problematic group of uninscribed volumes associated with inscribed volumes only by binding.[22] Despite such difficulties, however, Fitzwilliam's printed music collection remains a uniquely valuable example of the musical interests of a connoisseur of antiquarian inclinations in the second half of the eighteenth century.

Iain Fenlon
Valerie Rumbold

NOTES

1 G[eorge] E[dward] C[okayne], *The Complete Peerage of England, Scotland, Ireland, Great Britain and the United Kingdom*, edited by Vicary Gibbs and others, 12 vols. (London, 1910–40), 7th Viscount Fitzwilliam.

2 This account is based on the introduction by Charles Wilson to *The Dutch Connection: The Founding of the Fitzwilliam Museum* (Cambridge, 1988), pp. 5–15.

3 William Playfair, *British Family Antiquity* (London, 1810), vol. v.

4 Charles Cudworth, 'Fitzwilliam and French Music of the Baroque', in *French Music and the Fitzwilliam* (Cambridge, 1975), 7–11 (p. 7); Richard Andrewes, 'Viscount Fitzwilliam, Musical Antiquarian', in *Gainsborough, English Music and the Fitzwilliam* (Cambridge, 1977), 7–10 (p. 7).

5 Stanley Sadie (ed.), *The New Grove Dictionary of Music and Musicians*, 20 vols (London, 1980), 'Joah Bates'; Andrewes; 'Viscount Fitzwilliam', p. 8.

6 Andrewes, 'Viscount Fitzwilliam', p. 7; Lobb's autograph, now MU. MS IIIK, is inscribed on the first leaf 'From the author to R. Fitzwilliam 1764'. For Norton Nicholls see Cudworth, 'Fitzwilliam and French Music', p. 11; R.W. Ketton-Kremer, *Thomas Gray: A Biography* (Cambridge, 1955), p. 190.

7   Ketton-Kremer, *Thomas Gray*, p. 205; for Fitzwilliam's own set of Marcello's *Estro poetico-armonico*, not acquired until 1778, see MU. 409.

8   MU. MS 93: see J.A. Fuller-Maitland and A.H. Mann, *Catalogue of the Music in the Fitzwilliam Museum, Cambridge* (Cambridge, 1893); Andrewes, 'Viscount Fitzwilliam', p. 7; Sadie (ed.), *The New Grove*, 'John Keeble'.

9   MU. MS 100; see Fuller-Maitland and Mann, *Catalogue of the Music*, p. 40, where the inscription is not recorded and the book is consequently misdated c. 1780.

10 MU. MSS 80–4; see Fuller-Maitland and Mann, *Catalogue of the Music*, pp. 35–6. All five volumes, which are bound in a similar style, are the work of the same scribe, and are inscribed and dated 1767 by Fitzwilliam on their title-pages.

11 This volume is bound in a standard contemporary trade binding together with the *Second livre de pièces de clavecin* (signed and dated 'R. Fitzwilliam 1769 – de la part de l'auteur'); and the *Troisieme livre de pièces de clavecin* (signed and dated 'R. Fitzwilliam 1771 – de la part de l'auteur'); and the *Quatrieme livre de pièces de clavecin* (signed and dated 'R. Fitzwilliam 1772 – de la part de l'auteur') as MU. 429. See *French Music and the Fitzwilliam*, p. 42, where Du Phly's handwritten instructions 'Du Doigter' are transcribed.

12 John Huskinson, 'Mademoiselle Zacharie: La Fidelle Amie et l'Amie la Plus Tendre et Sincere', in *French Music and the Fitzwilliam*, pp. 39–40, 460.

13 For Caumont bindings, see the three volumes of Boyce's *Cathedral Music* (MU. 411 A–C), which carry Caumont's ticket bearing his name and address at 39 Gerrard Street, Soho; the bindings are entered in Caumont's account book under the date 1802. For other examples of his work and a note on his life see Maggs Bros Ltd Catalogue 966, *Bookbinding in Great Britain: The Sixteenth to the Twentieth Century* (London, 1975), pp. 202–3. For the Rameau scores, see Cudworth: 'Fitzwilliam and French Music', p. 11. The scores in question, uniformly bound in contemporary French bindings, are now MU. MSS 59–65. They contain *Hippolyte et Aricie, Les Indes Galantes, Castor et Pollux, Les Fêtes d'Hébé, Dardanus, Zoroastre* and *Les Paladins*, are copied on paper watermarked 'Auvergne 1785', and are signed and dated 'Fitzwilliam 1791'. See Fuller-Maitland and Mann, *Catalogue of the Music*, pp. 31–2.

14 For the score used in the performance of *Castor et Pollux*, now MU. MS 176, see Fuller-Maitland and Mann, *Catalogue of the Music*, p. 121. The volume which is signed and dated 'Fitzwilliam 1797' but also bears a note of the dates of the 1791 performances, contains the libretto in both English and French written on the flyleaf in Fitzwilliam's hand.

15 For the Handel fragments, part of a larger collection the remainder of which is now in the British Library, see Charles Cudworth, 'Fitzwilliam and Handel', in *Handel and the Fitzwilliam* (Cambridge, 1974), pp. 7–9; see Fuller-Maitland and Mann, *Catalogue of the Music*, pp. 159ff ('Manuscripts and sketches by G.F. Handel catalogued by A.H. Mann') and, for the British Library material, Alec Hyatt King, *Handel and his Autographs* (London, 1967).

16 For the evidence regarding this subscription, see the entry under Morley in the main catalogue, below p. 84.

17 Gerald Gifford, 'Viscount Fitzwilliam and the English "Scarlatti Sect"', in *Italian Music and the Fitzwilliam* (Cambridge, 1976), 10–13 (pp. 11–12); Sadie (ed.), *The New Grove*, 'Joseph Kelway'.

18 The meeting with Soler is recorded in an inscription in Fitzwilliam's copy of Soler's *XXVII Sonatas para clave* (London) (MU. 418), which was printed by the publisher Birchall from the manuscript given to Fitzwilliam by the composer: 'The originals of these harpsichord lessons were given to me by Father Soler, at the Escurial, the 14th February, 1772.' The Scarlatti manuscript (MU. MS 147) also acquired on this visit was

the basis for Birchall's edition of *Thirty sonatas* (MU. 423). For a note on the relationship of manuscript and printed volume see Fuller-Maitland and Mann, *Catalogue of the Music*, p. 89. The manuscript, which is made up of fascicles copied by a number of different hands, is completed by a thematic index (pp. 124–5) in Fitzwilliam's own handwriting.

19 MU. 416, MU. 430.

20 G[eorge] E[dward] C[okayne], *Peerage*, 7th Viscount Fitzwilliam.

21 R.G. Thorne (ed.), *The House of Commons 1790–1820, The History of Parliament*, 5 vols. (London, 1986), III, pp. 774–5.

22 For guidance on these items, see the headnote to the 'Chronological list' and the entries in the main catalogue.

PREFACE

THIS CATALOGUE supersedes the account of the printed music given in the 1893 *Catalogue of the Music in the Fitzwilliam Museum, Cambridge* by J.A. Fuller-Maitland and A.H. Mann. Although as a short-title catalogue the present work makes no claim to add significantly to the sum of bibliographical knowledge, it offers the user of the collection several advantages over the nineteenth-century catalogue. Items are now arranged by composer rather than in shelf order; more information is given, including transcription of the Founder's inscriptions and those of other owners likely to be of interest to musicologists; and for the first time the numerous accessions of early printed music over the last century are brought into the catalogue. In addition, the 'Numerical list' sets out the collection in shelf order, and the 'Chronological list of the Founder's collection' shows, as far as surviving evidence permits, how his musical library grew over the years.

Entries in the main catalogue are arranged by composer, or, where none is given, by title. Anonymous songs, however, form an exception to this rule, and are placed under first line, unless they are described as coming from a larger work, in which case that title provides the heading. In arranging the entries in alphabetical order, preference is given to words denoting the kind of piece: *The Professional Collection of Glees*, for example, appears under 'Glees'. Where it would be cumbersome to arrange the works of exceptionally well-represented composers in one alphabetical sequence, numbered subdivisions are set out in a headnote.

Titles are given in abbreviated form without internal capitalisation. In the main catalogue they are italicized only where it is necessary to distinguish the title of a song from the first line which provides the heading: for example, the form 'What beauties does Flora disclose? *Charming Moggy*' shows that the first line is not part of the title but has been supplied from the underlay.

Pagination and foliation are not exhaustively described, and mild irregularities are ignored. Where a sequence or its last page is unnumbered, square brackets indicate that the number is editorially supplied. Imprints are usually abbreviated, only foreign or more complex imprints being given in full. The dates given in square brackets for undated items are for the most part derived from the works listed below, and no independent authority is claimed for them.

Throughout the entries brackets are used as follows: round brackets in titles transcribe round brackets in the source; angle brackets, wherever found, enclose material out of sequence, either from the title or from elsewhere in the publication (notably variations between the titles of the first and subsequent volumes); and square brackets enclose material supplied by the compiler.

Cross-references between articles are placed at the end of each article (in articles with numbered subdivisions they form a separate 'Appendix'). Cross-references to other parts of the same article are placed in sequence within the article, marked *'see above'* or *'see below'* as appropriate. For convenience, all single songs arranged by composer or title of a larger work are also cross-referenced under first line.

This catalogue would have been impossible to compile without constant access to reserved books and other facilities in the Department of Manuscripts and Printed Books of the Fitzwilliam Museum, and my thanks are due to the Keeper, Mr Paul Woudhuysen, for his patient cooperation. Dr Iain Fenlon, Honorary Keeper of Music, has provided invaluable support and Mr O.W. Neighbour has given generous assistance in solving a wide range of problems. Finally, I wish to thank Linda Randall for the exemplary patience and rigour with which she has edited the typescript.

Valerie Rumbold

WORKS CONSULTED

The British Union-Catalogue of Early Music Printed before the Year 1801, edited by Edith B. Schnapper, 2 vols. (London, 1957)

The Catalogue of Printed Music in the British Museum to 1980, 62 vols. (London, 1981)

Fitzwilliam: A Cambridge Collection of Music (catalogue of exhibition held in Zurich in 1986)

French Music and the Fitzwilliam: A Collection of Essays and a Catalogue of an Exhibition of French Music in the Fitzwilliam Museum in May and June 1974 (Cambridge, 1975)

Fuller-Maitland, J.A., and Mann, A.H., *Catalogue of the Music in the Fitzwilliam Museum, Cambridge* (Cambridge, 1893)

Handel and the Fitzwilliam: A Collection of Essays and a Catalogue of an Exhibition of Handeliana in the Fitzwilliam Museum in May and June 1974 (Cambridge, 1974)

Humphries, Charles, and Smith, William C., *Music Publishing in the British Isles from the Beginning until the Middle of the Nineteenth Century* (Oxford, 1970)

Neighbour, O.W., and Tyson, Alan, *English Music Publishers' Plate Numbers in the First Half of the Nineteenth Century* (London, 1965)

Sadie, Stanley (ed.), *The New Grove Dictionary of Music and Musicians*, 20 vols. (London, 1980)

Smith, William C., *A Bibliography of the Musical Works Published by John Walsh during the Years 1695–1720* (London, 1968)

Smith, William C., and Humphries, Charles, *A Bibliography of the Musical Works Published by the Firm of John Walsh during the Years 1721–1766* (London, 1968)

Handel: A Descriptive Catalogue of the Early Editions, second edition with supplement (Oxford, 1970)

ABBREVIATIONS

f.	folio
fol.	upright folio format
obl. fol.	oblong folio format
no.	number
s. sh.	single sheet
WM	date from watermark
4°	quarto
8°	octavo
12°	duodecimo

CATALOGUE

ABEL (CARL FRIEDRICH)

Sei sonate a solo per il flauto traversa e basso . . . Opera sesta. [Score]. pp.24.
Printed for the Author . . . by R. Bremner: London, [1765] fol.
MU. 1374

see THE SUMMER'S TALE

ABRAMS (HARRIETT)

Crazy Jane, a favorite ballad . . . for three voices. [Begins: 'Why fair maid in ev'ry
feature']. pp.5. *L. Lavenu: London,* [c.1799] fol. [This is the first item in a volume
made up of separate songs with printed title-page 'A Collection of miscellaneous
music, by various authors. Sold by G. Walker . . . Duets'].
MU. 1211[1]

The last time I came o'er the moor, a favorite duett . . . with an accompaniment
for the harp or piano forte. pp.3. *L. Lavenu: London,* [c.1800] fol.
MU. 1211[19]

ADIEU

Adieu! my Fernando *see* KREUTZER (R.)

Adieu thou lovely youth *see* ARTAXERXES

THE AGREEABLE AMUSEMENT *see* BRETT

AH

Ah! prithee ask me not *see* HAIGH (T.)

Ah! proteggete o Dei *see* SARTI (G.)

Ah tell me softly *see* STORACE (S.), [The Prize]

Ah! where can fly my soul's true love? *see* PLEYEL (I.J.)

I

AIRS

Aires & symphonys for ye bass viol . . . out of the late operas . . . also some excellent lessons. pp.14. *J. Walsh . . . & J. Hare: London*, [c.1710] obl. fol.
MU. 1172

Recueil d'airs de contredanses, menuets et vaudevilles nouveaux. [Melody]. pp.271. *Chez M^l. Boivin . . . M^r Le Clerc . . . Mlle Castagnery . . . Duchêne Libraire: Paris*, [c.1760] 8°.
MU. 1205

ALBERTI (DOMENICO)

VIII Sonate per cembalo. Opera prima. pp. 27. *I. Walsh: London*, [1748] obl. fol. [Inscribed 'R. Fitzwilliam 1768'].
MU. 484^1

ALBINONI (TOMMASO GIOVANNI)

⟨Cantate à voce sola . . . Opera quarta⟩. pp.101. [Imperfect: wants title and first gathering]. [*Sala: Venice*, 1702] obl. 4°. [Title supplied from running foot. Not Op. 6 as recorded in some bibliographies].
MU. 521

Under ye gloomy shade. *A cantata*. ff.[2]. [*London*, c.1720] fol.
MU. 1190^{55}

see THOMYRIS

ALCOCK (JOHN, THE ELDER)

Six and twenty select anthems in score: for one, two, three, four, five, six & eight voices. To which are added a burial service . . . and part of the last verse of the 150th: psalm in Latin, for eight voices and instruments, in twenty-one parts. pp.iv, 210. [Imperfect: wants pp.1–136]. [*London*], 1771 fol. [Contains contemporary newspaper cuttings].
MU. 1203

see AMUSEMENT

ALCOCK (JOHN, THE YOUNGER)

Eight easy voluntarys, for the organ. pp.17. *Longman, Lukey & Co., London*, [c.1775] obl. fol. [Some MS bass figuration].
MU. 1370

see AMUSEMENT

ALL

All hail to the King. *Bellisle March or the Review.* [Song]. [*London*, c.1763] s.sh. fol.
MU. 1197²³

All in the downs *see* CAREY (H.), Sweet William's farewell to black-ey'd Susan;
see STEVENS (R.J.S.)

L'ALLEGRO

Let me wander not unseen. Sung in . . . 'L'Allegro e Penseroso'. [Music by G.F.
Handel. Words adapted from Milton by C. Jennens]. [*London*, c.1745] s.sh. fol.
MU. 1197⁵⁰

ALMAHIDE

Songs in the new opera, call'd Almahide. The songs done in Italian & English.
pp.64. *I: Walsh . . . P. Randall . . . and I. Hare: London*, [1710] fol.
MU. 1277

see BABELL (W.), The 3ᵈ. [altered in MS to 4ᵗʰ] book of the ladys entertainment

ALMIGHTY GOD *see* STEVENS (R.J.S.), The collect for the first Sunday
in Advent

AMUSEMENT

Amusement for the ladies, being a selection of the favorite catches, canons, glees,
and madrigals . . . composed by Mornington [i.e. G.C. Wellesley, Earl of], Arne,
Arnold, Alcock, Cooke, Dupuis, Hayes, Harington, Atterbury, Callcott, Danby,
Norris, Paxton, Smith, Stevens, Webbe. Vol: II [number in MS]. 3 vols.
[Imperfect: wants vols. I and III. Title as in vol. II]. *Longman & Broderip:
London*, [c.1785–93] obl. fol.
MU. 1228

AND

And must we part for ever. [Duet]. pp.220–1 *of a collection. J. Bland, London*,
[c.1790] fol.
MU. 1211¹⁷

ANTHEMS

Six select anthems in score (never before engraved) for two and three voices with
a thorough bass for the harpsichord or organ composed by Dr. Croft, Dr. Blow,

Mr Henry Purcell and Jeremiah Clarke. pp.51. *Wm Randall: London*, [1769] fol.
[With minor alterations in MS].
MU. 1470

APOLLO AND DAPHNE

The sun from the east tips the mountains with gold. *A Hunting Song . . . in
Appollo and Daphne*. [Music by J.E. Galliard. Words by P. Whitehead]. [*London*,
c.1765] s.sh. fol.
MU. 1197^2

APOLLO'S FEAST

Apollo's Feast, or the harmony of ye opera stage . . . out of the latest opera's
compos'd by M^r: Handel done in a plain & intelligable character with their
symphonys for voices and instruments. pp.231. *I: Walsh . . . and Ioseph Hare:
London*, [1726] fol. [With frontispiece].
MU. 1458

2^d. Book. Apollo's Feast or the harmony of the opera stage . . . out of the latest
operas composed by Bononcini, Attilio [i.e. A. Ariosti] & other authors done in a
plain & intelligible character with their symphonys for voices and instruments
. . . Book the second, pp.226. *I: Walsh . . . and Ioseph Hare: London*, [1726] fol.
[With frontispiece].
MU. 1459

3^d. Book. Apollo's Feast or the harmony of the opera stage . . . out of the latest
operas compos'd by Mr: Handel. done in a plain & intelligible character with
their symphonys for voices and instruments . . . Book the third. pp.209. *I: Walsh
. . . and Ioseph Hare: London*, [1729] fol. [With frontispiece].
MU. 1460

ARIANNA

How is it possible. *A favourite minuet in Ariadne*. [Song set to air from overture
to G.F. Handel's 'Arianna']. [*London*, c.1740] s.sh. fol.
MU. 1197^{32}

ARIOSTI (A.) *see* APOLLO'S FEAST; *see* POCKET

ARNE (MICHAEL)

[Almena]. The overture, songs, & duets in the opera of Almena . . . . adapted for
the voice & harpsichord. [Words by R. Rolt]. pp.49. *The Author: London*, [1764]
obl. fol. [One number re-texted in MS].
MU. 1177^2

The Lass with the delicate air. [Song, begins: 'Young Molly who lives at the foot of the hill']. [*London*, c.1760] s.sh. fol.
MU. 1197[19]

Thro' the wood lassie, or Sawny's Return. [Song, begins: 'Oh Nelly na longer thy Sawny now mourn'. An answer to 'O Sandy why leaves thou thy Nelly']. [*London*, c. 1765] s.sh. fol.
MU. 1197[56]

The Thrush. [Song, begins: 'Sweet thrush that makes the vernal year']. ff.[2]. [Imperfect: wants f.2]. *J. Simpson:* [*London*, c.1765] fol.
MU. 1197[84]

ARNE (THOMAS AUGUSTINE)

Arrangement: 1. Cantatas, operas, oratorios
2. Collections of songs
3. Single songs
4. Instrumental works
5. Appendix

1. Cantatas, operas, oratorios

Alfred *see below*: The Judgment of Paris; Rule Britannia [single songs]

Arcadian Nuptials *see below*: Vocal Melody, Book XIV [collections of songs]

Artaxerxes. An English opera. [Text translated from P. Metastasio by the composer]. [Score]. pp.196. *John Johnson, London*, [1762] fol. [With cast list in contemporary MS].
MU. 1357

[Blind Beggar of Bethnal Green]. The songs and duetto, in the Blind Beggar of Bethnal Green . . . with the favourite songs . . . in the Merchant of Venice . . . to which will be added, a collection of new songs and ballads. [The words of 'The Blind Beggar' by R. Dodsley; those of 'The Merchant' after Shakespeare]. pp.28. *Printed by William Smith and sold by the Author, London*, [c.1742] fol.
MU. 1182[1]

[Comus]. The musick in the masque of Comus. Written by Milton . . . Opera prima. [Score]. pp.47. *J. Simpson, London*, [c.1750] fol. [A few comparisons with the version of this work by Henry Bishop in later MS].
MU. 1366

Cymon and Iphigenia. A cantata. pp.9. *Printed by authority and sold by Jo*[n]. *Johnson, London*, [c.1760] fol.
MU. 1197[33]

[Elfrida]. The songs, duets and chorusses in Elfrida . . . with the overture

adapted for the harpsi^{d}.. [Words by W. Mason]. pp.61. *Iohn Iohnston . . . and Longman Lukey and Co: London*, [1772] obl. fol.
MU. 1260

Eliza. An English opera. [Words by R. Rolt]. [Score]. pp.105. *I. Walsh: London*, [c.1758] fol.
MU. 1367

[The Guardian Outwitted]. The overture, songs and duets in the opera call'd the Guardian outwitted, for the voice and harpsichord . . . No. 1. pp.54. [Imperfect: wants vol. 11]. *R: Bremner, London*, [1764] fol.
MU. 1184 A

[The music in the Judgment of Paris, consisting of all the songs, duettos and trio, with the overture, in score . . . To which . . . are added the celebrated ode . . . call'd Rule Britannia [from Alfred], and Sawney & Jenney . . . Opera sesta]. [Words of 'The Judgment of Paris' by W. Congreve]. pp.66. [Imperfect: wants title and pp. 64–6]. *Henry Waylett: [London, c.1745]* fol.
MU. 1365^{1}

Judith, an oratorio. [Words by I. Bickerstaff]. [Score]. pp.97. *I. Walsh: London*, [1761] fol.
MU. 1181

[Another copy]
MU. 1363

[Judith]. Vain is beauty's gaudy flow'r. *A favourite song in Judith*. ff. [2]. *[London*, c.1765] fol.
MU. 1197^{6}

Love and Resentment *see below*: Summer Amusement [collections of songs]

Merchant of Venice *see above*: The Blind Beggar of Bethnal Green

Thomas and Sally, or the Sailor's Return, a dramatic pastoral . . . with the overture in score. [Words by I. Bickerstaff]. pp.51. [Imperfect: wants pp. 47–51]. *I. Walsh: London*, [1765] fol.
MU. 1184 E

see below: Thomas & Sally [single songs]

[The Way to Keep Him]. Ye fair marri'd dames. Sung . . . in The Way to Keep Him. [Words by D. Garrick]. *[London*, c.1765] s.sh. fol.
MU. 1197^{17}

2. Collections of songs

Lyric Harmony. Part I ⟨II⟩ . . . for the voice, harpsichord, and violin. 2 vols. Plate nos. 20–4 of 'The New Musical Magazine'. *Harrison & Co: London*, [1784] obl. fol.
MU. 1248$^{3-4}$

Summer Amusement, a collection of lyric poems, with the favourite airs set to them . . . with the new cantata, call'd Love and Resentment. pp.40. *Printed for the Author: London*, [c.1760] fol.
MU. 1184 B

The Syren. A new collection of favorite songs. pp.33. *Longman and Broderip: London*, [1777] fol.
MU. 1184 C

The Vocal Grove, being a collection of favorite songs. pp.37. *Longman, Lukey and Co: London*, 1775 fol.
MU. 1184 D

[Vocal Melody. Book XI]. No. XI. British Melody. A favourite collection of English songs and a cantata. pp.19. *I. Walsh: London*, [1760] fol.
MU. 1184 F

[Vocal Melody. Book XIII]. A collection consisting of favourite songs and cantatas. pp.40. [Imperfect: wants pp.39–40). *I. Walsh: London*, [c.1765] fol.
MU. 1182³

[Vocal Melody. Book XIV]. A favourite collection of songs, with the dialogue in the Arcadian Nuptials . . . Book XIV. pp.14. *I. Walsh: London*, [1764] fol.
MU. 1182²

3. Single songs

Elegy on the death of M^r. Shenstone. [Song for four voices, begins: 'Come shepherds we'll follow the hearse']. pp.3. *J. Dale:* [*London*, c.1790] fol.
MU. 1365²

Excuse for a love slip. [Song, begins: 'What means that tender sigh my dear?'].
[*London*, c.1760] s.sh. fol.
MU. 1197⁴⁶

Lotharia. [Song, begins: 'Vainly now ye strive to charm me']. [*London*, c.1775] s.sh. fol.
MU. 1189⁴³

Rule Britannia, verse and chorus. [Song, begins: 'When Britain first by heaven's decree'. From 'Alfred']. ff.[2]. *H. Andrews: London*, [1804^{WM}] fol.
MU. 1171

see above: The Judgment of Paris [cantatas, operas, oratorios]

Sawney & Jenney *see above*: The Judgment of Paris [cantatas, operas, oratorios]

Thomas & Sally. [Song, begins: 'When late I wander'd o'er the plain'. From 'Thomas and Sally'. Words by I. Bickerstaff]. [*London*, c.1770] s.sh. fol.
MU. 1197²¹

4. Instrumental works

Six favourite concertos, for the organ, harpsichord, or piano forte: with instrumental parts. [Keyboard only]. *Harrison & Co: London*, [c.1787] fol.
MU. 1182[4]

5. Appendix

see AMUSEMENT

see ARTAXERXES

see COMUS

see DAWN

see IN, In infancy our hopes & fears

see MY, My banks they are furnish'd

see THE SACRIFICE OF IPHIGENIA

see THE SUMMER'S TALE

see THOMAS AND SALLY

see WOU'D

ARNOLD (JOHN)

The Essex Harmony: being a choice collection of the most celebrated songs and catches . . . for one, two, three, four, and five voices. Volume I. The third edition, with additions. pp.160. *Printed by A. Rivington and J. Marshall, for J. Buckland, B. Law, and S. Crowder: London*, 1786 8°
MU. 1270

The Essex Harmony: being an entire new collection of the most celebrated songs, catches, canzonets, canons and glees, for two, three, four, five, and nine voices. From the works of the most eminent masters . . . Vol. II. The second edition with large additions. pp.154. *Printed by G. Bigg, and sold by J. Buckland, and S. Crowder: London*, 1777 8°.
MU. 1271

ARNOLD (SAMUEL)

Little Bess the ballad singer . . . the words by S.J. Arnold. [Song, begins: 'When first a babe upon the knee']. [Score]. pp.4. *The Author: London*, [c.1794] fol. [Inscribed 'A.M. Jeffery': later Mrs R.J.S. Stevens].
MU. 1287[24]

[The Mountaineers]. Faint and wearily the way-worn traveller, sung . . . in the Mountaineers. [Duet]. pp.4. *Preston & Son, London*, [c.1795] fol.
MU. 1211[10]

Peeping Tom of Coventry, a comic opera in two acts. [Words by J. O'Keefe]. pp.40. *Harrison & Co: London*, [1800^WM] 8°. [Vol. II, no.3, of 'The Piano-Forte Magazine'].
MU. 1402

[Twelve sonatas. Op.XII, part 2]. [Keyboard]. pp.60. [Imperfect: wants title]. [c.1785] obl. fol.
MU. 1403

[The Spanish Barber]. [The Fandango overture, airs, &c. in the Spanish Barber. Op. XVII]. [Words from 'Le Barbier de Seville' by Beaumarchais, adapted in part by G. Colman]. pp.29. [Imperfect: wants title]. [*J. Bland: London*, 1778] obl. fol.
MU. 1254³

[Surrender of Calais]. Pauvre Madelon, a favorite song & duett . . . in the Surrender of Calais. [Begins: 'Could you to battle march away?'. Words by G. Colman the younger]. pp.4. *Preston & Son, London*, [1801^WM] fol.
MU. 1211²¹

see AMUSEMENT

see HANDEL (G.F.) [Arnold's edition]

see THE SUMMER'S TALE

ARSACE

Figurati estinte / My charmer! come bless me! *A favourite song in the opera of Arsaces*. [Music by G.H. Orlandini. Words by P.A. Rolli]. ff.11–12 *of a collection*. [*London*, c.1721] fol.
MU. 1190⁵⁶

ARSACES *see* ARSACE

ARTAXERXES

Adieu thou lovely youth. *Sung . . . in Artaxerxes*. [Music by T.A. Arne]. ff.[2]. [*London*, c.1765] fol.
MU. 1197⁴⁸

Fair Aurora prithee stay. *Sung . . . in Artaxerxes*. [Music by T.A. Arne]. *S. Phillips: London*, [c.1762] s.sh. fol.
MU. 1197²⁶

Thy father, away. *Sung . . . in Artaxerxes*. [Music by T.A. Arne]. [*London*, c.1770] s.sh. fol.
MU. 1197³⁷

AS

As blyth as the linnet sings in the green wood. *Robin Hood*. [Song]. [From 'Robin Hood'. Music by C. Burney. Words by M. Mendez]. [*London*, 1750] s.sh. fol.
MU. 1197[55]

As Cupid one day roving saw *see* MARCHANT

As I saw fair Clora *see* HAYDEN (G.); *see* TURN

As Jockey was walking one midsummer morn. *The Sex*. [Song]. [Words by Mr Rolt]. [*London*, c. 1750] s.sh. fol.
MU. 1189[38]

ASTARTO

Mio caro ben / Dear pritty maid. *Mio caro ben. A favourite aire in Astartus. The English words by Mr Sunderland*. [Music by G.B. Bononcini]. [*London*, c.1721] s.sh. fol.
MU. 1190[71]

ASTARTUS *see* ASTARTO

ASTIANASSE

[Ascolsa o figlio]. Observe, observe you tuneful charmer. *Sung . . . in Astynax. Translated by Mʳ. Carey*. [Music by G.B. Bononcini]. [*London*, c.1727] s.sh. fol.
MU. 1190[51]

ASTYNAX *see* ASTIANASSE

AT

At eve when Silvan's shady scene *see* BRETT

At Polwart on the green. *The Kind Lass of Polwart*. [Song]. [*London*, c. 1725] s.sh. fol.
MU. 1190[43]

At St. Osyth *see* HOWARD (S.), The Lass of St. Osyth

At the brow of a hill *see* HOWARD (S.), The Lass of the Hill

ATTEND ALL YE FAIR *see* THE WAY TO KEEP HIM

ATTERBURY (L.) *see* AMUSEMENT

ATTILIO [i.e. A. Ariosti] *see* APOLLO'S FEAST, 2ᵈ. Book; *see* POCKET

ATTWOOD (THOMAS)

In peace love tunes the shepherd's reed, glee for three voices, the words from the Lay of the Last Minstrel, by Walter Scott. pp.9. Plate no. 108 Vocal English. *Monzani & Co., London*, [1807^WM] fol.
MU. 1211^26

O! Thou who thro' the silent air, a duett, with an accompaniment for the harp or piano forte, the words translated from the German of Kleist by Walpole. pp.3. Plate no. 105 Vocal English. *T. Monzani:* [London, c.1805] fol.
MU. 1211^11

AVISON (CHARLES)

Twelve concertos (divided into two sets) for two violins, one alto-viola, and a violoncello. This work is also adapted to the practice of the organ or harpsichord alone, or these to serve as an accompanyment to the parts in concert . . . Opera nona. Set I ⟨II⟩. 2 vols. [Keyboard only]. *R. Johnson for the author: London*, 1766 fol. [Each set inscribed 'R. Fitzwilliam 1771'. With a subscribers' list].
MU. 488^1–2, bound with MU. MS. 208

AYRTON (EDMUND)

An anthem for voices and instruments in score . . . perform'd . . . as an exercise previous to his being admitted to the degree of Doctor in Music . . . & afterwards . . . on the . . . day of general thanksgiving appointed for ye peace. Dedicated to the Honorary President, & Honorary Vice Presidents of the Royal Society of Musicians. pp.58. *The Author:* [London, 1788] fol. [Inscribed 'R. Fitzwilliam 1788'. With a subscribers' list].
MU. 369

B. (R.) [i.e. Robert Broderip]

A collection of duets, rotas, canons, catches & glees . . . inscribed to . . . the Bristol Catch Club and the Cecilian Society. pp.iv, 133. [Bristol, 1795] obl. 4°.
MU. 1332

BABELL (WILLIAM)

The 3^d. book of the ladys entertainment or banquet of musick, a choice collection of the most celebrated aires & duets in the opera's of Pyrrhus & Clotilda. [The music of the former by A. Scarlatti; of the latter by F. Conti]. Curiously set and fitted to the harpsicord or spinnet. ff.22. *J. Walsh . . . P. Randall . . . & J. Hare: London*, [1709] fol.
MU. 1180^1

The 3^d. [altered in MS to 4th] book of the ladys entertainment . . . in the opera's of Hydaspes & Almahide. [Music of the former by F. Mancini]. pp.31. *J. Walsh . . . & J. Hare: London*, [c.1716] fol.
MU. 1180^2

Suits of the most celebrated lessons. pp.77. *Sold by John Young* [pasted over Walsh and Hare imprint]: *London*, [c.1718] fol.
MU. 1180^3

[Another issue]. *I: Walsh: London*, [c.1730] fol. [Inscribed 'R. Fitzwilliam 1768'].
MU. 488^3, bound with MU. MS 208

BACH (JOHANN CHRISTIAN)

Six overtures . . . addapted for the harpsichord. [Arranged from Six symphonies, Op.3]. pp.27. *Welcker: London*, [c.1770] fol. [This is the first item in a volume inscribed 'H.M. Thrale', presumably Hester Maria, eldest daughter of Hester Lynch Thrale (Mrs Piozzi). A child's drawings of people in eighteenth-century dress occupy the blanks between items. Stamped 'W. Laubach', with matching repagination throughout the items].
MU. 1400^1

Six sonatas for the piano forte or harpsichord . . . Opera 5. pp.34. *Welcker: London*, [c.1768] obl. fol. [Inscribed 'R. Fitzwilliam 1768. From the author'].
MU. 362 E

Six sonatas for the harpsichord or piano-forte . . . Opera XVII. [Previously published as Op.12]. pp.41. *John Preston: London*, [c.1780] obl. fol.
MU. 1244^2

Six symphonies, Op.3 *see above*: Six overtures

see THE SUMMER'S TALE

BACH (JOHANN SEBASTIAN)

Johann Sebastian Bachs vierstimmige Choralgesänge. [Erster] ⟨–vierter⟩ Theil. [Edited by C.P.E. Bach]. pp.218. [Imperfect: wants title to Part 1 (that to Part 2 has been bound in its place) and pp.217–18 (supplied in MS)]. *Bey Johann Gottlob Immanuel Breitkopf: Leipzig*, [1784]–7 4°.
MU. 1223

Exercices pour le clavecin . . . Œuv. III. [The final two strokes in MS]. [Clavierübung Teil 3]. pp.63. Plate no. 307. *Au bureau de musique de C.F. Peters: Leipzig*, [reprint after 1815 from plates c.1804] obl. fol. [Stamped 'R. Cocks & Co. 20 Princes St Hanover Squ.'].
MU. 482^2

Die Kunst der Fuge. [Part of 'Musikalischer Kunstwerke in strengen Style, von J.S. Bach u. andern Meistern']. [Score with keyboard reduction]. pp.183. *Bey Hans Georg Nägeli: Zürich*, [1802] obl. fol.
MU. 482[1]

BAILDON (JOSEPH)

[The Laurel, a collection of English songs . . . 2 bk, Book I. No.2]. If love's a sweet passion. [c.1760] s.sh. fol.
MU. 1189[8]

[The Laurel, a collection of English songs . . . 2 bk, Book I. No.3]. Beauty's bright standard. [Song, begins: 'How pleasing is beauty']. [c.1760] s.sh. fol.
MU. 1189[9]

The Union of love and wine. [Song, begins: 'With woman and wine I defy ev'ry care']. [*London*, c.1770] s.sh. fol.
MU. 1197[67]

UN BANDEAU *see* GRÉTRY (A.E.M.), Richard Coeur de Lion

BANISTER (JOHN)

A ⟨2ᵈ.⟩ collection of the most celebrated song tunes with their symphonys taken out of the choicest opera's and fitted to the violin. [Melody]. 2 vols. *Printed for I: Walsh . . . and I: Hare: London*, [c.1717] Single sheets, originally stab-stitched.
MU. 1334[1–2]

BARNARD

[Love in a Village]. In love shou'd there meet a fond pair. *A song in Love in a Village*. [*London*, c.1775] s.sh. fol.
MU. 1197[60]

BARRET (J.) *see* HARPSICHORD MASTER

BARRYMORE (R.), LORD *see* WHERE, Where ah where shall I my shepherd find

BARSANTI (F.) *see* GEMINIANI (F.), [Sonatas Op.1. Nos. 7–12]

BARTHELEMON (FRANÇOIS HIPPOLYTE)

Durandarte and Belerma. A pathetic Scotch ballad, with an accompanyment for the harp. [Begins: 'Sad and fearful is the story'. Words from 'The Monk' by M.G. Lewis]. pp.4. *Rt. Birchall: London*, [c.1800] fol.
MU. 1287[31]

see PEEP

BASSANI (GIOVANNI BATTISTA)

Harmonia festiva, being the eighth opera of divine mottetts . . . for a single voice with proper symphonies. pp. 84. *William Pearson, for John Cullen . . . and John Young: London*, [1708] fol.
MU. 491[3]

Harmonia festiva, being the thirteenth opera of divine mottetts . . . for a single voice with proper symphonies. pp. 30. *William Pearson, for John Cullen . . . and John Young: London*, [1710] fol.
MU. 491[2]

see ZIANI (P.A.)

BE

Be hush'd ye rude tempests. *Arcas and Rosetta*. ff.[2]. [*London*, c.1770] fol.
MU. 1197[41]

BEETHOVEN (L. VAN) *see* THOMSON (G.)

BEFORE THE URCHIN WELL COU'D GO *see* WORGAN (J.), The Thief

BELLISLE MARCH *see* ALL HAIL TO THE KING

BENEATH

Beneath a green shade. *Peggy's Mill*. [Words by A. Ramsay]. [*London*, c.1730] s.sh. fol.
MU. 1190[49]

BERTON (PIERRE MONTAN) and TRIAL (JEAN CLAUDE)

Silvie. Opéra . . . dediée a son Altesse Sérénissime Monseigneur le Prince de Conty . . . Les paroles sont de Mr Laujon. [Score]. pp.332. *Chez M. Trial . . . M. De la Chevardiere: Paris*, [c.1767] fol. [Inscribed 'R. Fitzwilliam 1771'].
MU. 489

BICKHAM (GEORGE)

The musical entertainer. [Edited by R. Vincent]. Engrav'd by George Bickham jun^r. Vol: I. 2 vols. [Imperfect: wants vol. II]. Plate nos. I–XXV. *Geo: Bickham: London*, [1737] fol.
MU. 1191^1

[Another copy]. [Imperfect: wants vol. II and numerous pp. from vol. I].
MU. 1194

[Another issue]. [Imperfect: sections of both volumes miscombined, wanting numerous pp.] *Charles Corbett:* [*London*, c.1740: p.51 of vol. II bears the date 1737]. [Contains several names and children's drawings].
MU. 1193

BIGGS (EDWARD SMITH)

Come my bonny love. A duett with an accompaniment for the piano forte. pp.3.
Rt. Birchall: London, [c.1798] fol.
MU. 1211^{29}

BEI MÄNNERN *see* MOZART (W.A.), The manly heart

THE BILLET DOUX *see* SHIELD (W.)

THE BIRD THAT HEARS *see* SNOW (J.)

BISCHOFF (JOHANN GEORG)

Six sonates à violoncelle, et basse . . . Oeuvre premiere. pp.25. *Chez J. Schmitt: Amsterdam*, [c.1780] fol.
MU. 1192^1

BLAKE (BENJAMIN)

Six duets. For a violin, and tenor. [2 parts]. *Willm: Napier: London*, [1781] fol.
[The pieces are numbered 25–30 in MS].
MU. 1446–7

BLEST

Blest as th'immortal gods is he. *A Hymn to Venus*. [Music by J. Morgan. Words translated from Sappho by A. Phillips]. [*London*, c.1725] s.sh. fol.
MU. 1190^{44}

BLOW (JOHN)

Amphion Anglicus. A work of many compositions, for one, two, three and four voices: with several accompagnements. pp.216. *William Pearson, for the author; and . . . sold . . . by Henry Playford: London*, 1700 fol. [Acquired by J.R.S. Stevens in 1796].
MU. 1305

An Ode on the death of Mr. Henry Purcell . . . The words by Mr. Dryden. pp.30. *J. Heptinstall, for Henry Playford: London*, 1696 fol.
MU. 375²

see ANTHEMS

see CATCH CLUB

see HARPSICHORD MASTER

BLOW BLOW THOU WINTER WIND *see* STEVENS (R.J.S.)

BONONCINI (GIOVANNI BATTISTA)

The Anthem which was performed . . . at the funeral of . . . John, Duke of Marlborough. The words taken out of Holy Scripture. [Score]. pp.19. Plate no. 631. *I. Walsh: London*, [c.1738] fol. [Inscribed 'R. Fitzwilliam 1765'].
MU. 495

[Another copy].
MU. 515²

Astartus. An opera. [Words by A. Zeno]. [Score]. pp.81. *Iohn Young* [pasted over imprint of I. Walsh . . . and I. Hare]: *London*, [1721] fol.
MU. 500

[Cantate et duetti dedicati alla Sacra Maestà di Giorgio Rè della Gran Bretagna]. pp.99. [Imperfect: wants title]. [*London*, 1721] obl. fol. [Inscribed 'R. Fitzwilliam 1769'. With a subscribers' list, with MS additions].
MU. 302

[Another issue]. *London*, 1721. [Inscribed 'R. Fitzwilliam 1763'. From the same plates as the previous copy, but with title omitting dedication and without subscribers' list].
MU. 437

Divertimenti da camera, tradotti pel cembalo da quelli composti pel violino, o flauto. pp.40. *Sold onely at M^rs. Corticelle's House: London*, 1722 obl. fol. [Inscribed 'R. Fitzwilliam 1799']
MU. 361 F

[Another copy].
MU. 1256

see APOLLO'S FEAST, 2ᵈ. Book

see ASTARTO

see ASTIANASSE

see BONONCINI (M.A.)

see CAMILLA

see OVERTURES

see POCKET

see THOMYRIS

BONONCINI (MARCO ANTONIO)

Songs in the new opera of Camilla . . . more correct than the former edition. [Music actually by G.B. Bononcini. Words translated from the Italian of S. Stampiglia by O. MacSwiney]. ff.47. *John Cullen: London*, [1707] fol.
MU. 1278

see CAMILLA

BOYCE (WILLIAM)

Fifteen anthems, together with a Te Deum, and Jubilate, in score for 1, 2, 3, 4, & 5 voices, composed for the royal chapels. [Edited by P. Hayes]. pp.3, 141. *Printed for the Author's widow and family: London*, 1780 fol. [Inscribed 'R. Fitzwilliam 1799'. With a subscribers' list].
MU. 364

Cathedral Music: being a collection in score of the most valuable and useful compositions for that service, by the several English masters of the last two hundred years. 3 vols. *Printed for the Editor: London*, 1760–73 fol. [Inscribed 'R. Fitzwilliam 1767' (vol. I), 'R. Fitzwilliam 1768' (vol. II), 'R. Fitzwilliam 1773' (vol. III). With a subscribers' list. Bound in gilt vellum, with label of the Comte de Caumont (39 Gerrard Street, Soho) in vol. I].
MU. 411 A–C

An ode perform'd in the Senate House at Cambridge, on the first of July, 1749, at the installation of his Grace the Duke of Newcastle, Chancellor of the University. The words by William Mason, M.A. To which is added an anthem perform'd yᵉ following day. [Score]. pp.67, 70. [*London*, 1749] fol. [Inscribed 'R. Fitzwilliam 1771'].
MU. 363 A

The Pleasures of the Spring Gardens at Vaux-hall. The words by Mʳ. Lockman. [Song, begins: 'Flora goddess sweetly blooming']. [*London*, c.1740] s.sh. fol.
MU. 1189²

Rail no more & c. [Song]. [*London*, c.1750] s.sh. fol.
MU. 1197^{35}

[The Secular Masque]. The Song of Diana, in M^r. Dryden's Secular Masque. [Begins: 'With horns and with hounds']. ff.[2]. [c.1750] fol.
MU. 1197^{74}

Solomon. A serenata, in score, taken from the canticles. [Words arranged by E. Moore]. pp.101. *I. Walsh: London*, [1760] fol. [Inscribed 'R. Fitzwilliam 1771'].
MU. 363 B

Twelve sonatas for two violins with a bass. [3 parts]. *I. Walsh: London*, [1747 or later] fol.
MU. 318 A^8, 318 B^8, 318 D^8

Eight symphonys in eight parts. Six for violins, hoboys, or German flutes, and two for violins, French horns and trumpets, with a bass for the violoncello and harpsicord . . . Opera seconda. [8 parts, with a second copy of bass]. *I. Walsh: London*, [1760] fol.
MU. 320 C^2, 320 G^{14}, 320 H^{14}, 320 I^{14}, 320 J^{14}, 320 K^{14}, 320 L^3, 320 M^{14}, 320 N^{14}

Tell me, lovely shepherd, where. A favourite song. [From Solomon]. pp.3. *Longman and Broderip: London*, [c.1790] fol. [Inscribed 'A.M. Jeffery': later Mrs R.J.S. Stevens].
MU. 1287^{29}

see THE SUMMER'S TALE

BRAHAM (JOHN)

The English Fleet in 1342, a celebrated historical comic opera . . . arranged for the piano forte by D. Corri, the words by T. Dibdin. pp.110. *M.P. Corri & Co.* [deleted, and replaced in MS by 'J. Hill']: *London*, [1805^{WM}] fol.
MU. 1186^5

see REEVE (W.)

BRETT

A new song on Sadler's Wells. [Begins: 'At eve when Silvan's shady scene'. Plate II of 'The Agreeable Amusement']. [*London*, c.1750] s.sh. fol.
MU. 1189^{40}

BRODERIP (R.) *see* B. (R.)

BRYAN (JOSEPH)

Dorus & Cleora. A favourite cantata. [Begins: 'Cleora sat beneath a shade']. ff.2. [*London*, c.1770] fol.
MU. 1197[76]

BURNEY (CHARLES)

La musica che si canta annualmente nelle funzioni della settimana santa, nella cappella pontificia ... Raccolta e pubblicata da Carlo Burney. pp.iv, 42. *Stampata per Roberto Bremner: London*, 1771 fol. [With a frontispiece. Inscribed 'R. Fitzwilliam 1772'].
MU. 366[1]

see AS, As blyth as the linnet

see TO, To an arbour of woodbine

BURTON (JOHN)

Ten sonatas for the harpsichord, organ, or piano forte. pp.55. *Printed for the Author: London*, [1766] obl. fol. [Inscribed 'R. Fitzwilliam 1769'].
MU. 485[1]

BY

By a pratt'ling stream on a Midsummer's Eve. *Sweet William*. [Song]. [*London*, c.1755] s.sh. fol.
MU. 1197[25]

BYRD (W.) *see* THE CARMAN'S WHISTLE

CAESAR (W.) *see* PLAYFORD (J.), Select musicall ayres and dialogues

 CALLCOTT (JOHN WALL)

A collection of glees, canons, and catches ... selected, and arranged with an accompaniment for the piano-forte ... by William Horsley ... Volume the first ⟨second⟩. 2 vols. *Published, for the Author's widow, by Birchall, Lonsdale, and Mills: London*, 1824 fol. [With a frontispiece].
MU. 1219 A–B

Thyrsis. A glee for four voices. Also adapted as a duett. [Begins: 'Thyrsis when he left me']. pp.7. *Longman and Broderip: London*, [c.1795] fol.
MU. 1211[33]

see AMUSEMENT

CALLIOPE

Calliope, or English Harmony. A collection of . . . English and Scots songs . . . with the thorough bass and transpositions for the flute . . . Vol: the first. [Compiled by Henry Roberts]. 2 vols. [Imperfect: wants vol. II]. *Engrav'd & Sold by Henry Roberts: London*, 1739 8°. [With a frontispiece].
MU. 1329

CAMILLA

The opera of Camilla, with the overture, symphonyes and accompanyments, to be perform'd either vocally or instrumentally. [Music by G.B. Bononcini, though often attributed to A.M. Bononcini, words translated from the Italian of S. Stampiglia by O. MacSwiney]. [3 parts]. *I: Walsh . . . and I: Hare: London,* [c.1717] fol.
MU. 1421 A

CARBONELLI (GIOVANNI STEFANO)

Sonate da camera, a violino, e violone, o cembalo, dedicate all'illustrissimo ed eccellentissimo signore il Sig". Duca di Rutland. pp.65. [*London*, 1729] fol.
MU. 1176

CAREY (GEORGE SAVILLE)

The Sailor's Allegory. [Song, begins: 'Life's like a ship'. The attribution to Carey is doubtful]. ff.[2]. *Longman and Broderip: London,* [c.1790] fol. [Inscribed 'A.M. Jeffery': later Mrs R.J.S. Stevens].
MU. 1287[3]

CAREY (HENRY)

[Cephalus and Procris]. The hunting song in Cephalus and Procris. [Begins: 'Hark away tis ye merry ton'd horn']. [*London*, c.1731] s.sh. fol.
MU. 1189[48]

[A choice collection of six favourite songs]. ff.6. [Imperfect: wants title and f.1]. [*Printed for the Author: London*, 1742] fol.
MU. 1190[1–5]

In these groves. *A two part song*. [*London*, c.1730] s.sh. fol.
MU. 1189[45]

[The Provoked Husband]. Stand by! Clear the way! Sung . . . in ye Provokd Husband. Words & music Mr. Careys. [Begins: 'What tho' they call me country lass']. [*London*, c.1735] s.sh. fol.
MU. 1197[57]

Sweet William's farewell to black-ey'd Susan. [Song, begins: 'All in the downs the fleet was moor'd'. Words by J. Gay]. p.75 *of a collection*. [*London*, c.1720] fol.
MU. 1197[27]

see THE CONTRIVANCES

see WHAT, What Cato advises

CARISSIMI (G.) *see* PRATT (J.)

THE CARMAN'S WHISTLE

The Carman's Whistle. Then [i.e. John] come kiss me now. [Two pieces for keyboard by William Byrd taken from MU. MS 168, the Fitzwilliam Virginal Book]. [c.1790]. ff.[7]. [Inscribed, 'From Queen Elizabeth's Virginal Book', as MU. MS 168 used erroneously to be known].
MU. 1237

CARTER (CHARLES THOMAS)

Oh Nanny wilt thou fly with me. [Score]. pp.3. *Rt. Birchall: London*, [c.1805] fol. [Inscribed 'A.M. Jeffery': later Mrs R.J.S. Stevens].
MU. 1287[11]

CATCH CLUB

The Catch Club or merry companions. A collection of favourite catches for three and four voices, compos'd by M[r]. Henry Purcell, D[r]. Blow, and the most eminent authors. Book I. 2 vols. [Imperfect: wants vol. II]. *I. Walsh: London*, [c.1762] obl. fol. [Inscribed 'R. Fitzwilliam 1799'].
MU. 357 D

CAVENDISH (GEORGIANA, DUCHESS OF DEVONSHIRE)

I have a silent sorrow here. *The favorite song, sung . . . in the Stranger, the words by B.B. Sheridan*. [Music arranged by Mr Shaw]. [Score]. pp.[4]. *Longman, Clementi & Comp[y].: London*, [c.1800] fol. [Initialled A.M.J., i.e. A.M. Jeffery, later Mrs R.J.S. Stevens].
MU. 1287[14]

CEASE

Cease my Cloe. *A song by an eminent master*. ff.[2]. [*London*, c.1730] fol.
MU. 1190[10]

CECILIA VOLGI UN SGUARDO *see* HANDEL (G.F.) [selections and arrangements: songs, arias and cantatas]

CHARMING

Charming to love is morning's hour. Cheerful glee for five voices. Poetry by M^{rs}. Cowley. [Music by R.J.S. Stevens, who has signed the copy]. pp.22–6 *of a collection. The Author:* [*London*, c.1800] obl. fol.
MU. 1288 A^5

CHARPENTIER (MARC ANTOINE)

Medée. Tragedie. [Words by T. Corneille]. [Score]. pp.lxiv, 350. *Par Christophe Ballard: Paris*, [1694] fol. [Inscribed 'R. Fitzwilliam 1767'].
MU. 339

CIAMPI (L.V.) *see* THE SUMMER'S TALE

CLARI (GIOVANNI CARLO MARIA)

Sei madrigali . . . Parte prima. Edited by H.H[argrave]. [Italian words, prefaced by English translation. The madrigals are dated 1740–5]. pp.ii, 2, 62. [*London*, c.1765] fol. [Inscribed 'R. Fitzwilliam 1791'. With a subscribers' list].
MU. 479

see PRATT (J.)

CLARKE (JEREMIAH)

Choice lessons for the harpsichord or spinett, being the works of the late famous M^r. Jeremiah Clarke . . . carefully corrected by himself, being what he design'd to publish. ff.36. *Charles King . . . J^n: Young . . . J^n: Hare: London*, 1711 obl. 4°. [Inscribed 'R. Fitzwilliam 1767'].
MU. 420 A

see ANTHEMS

see HARPSICHORD MASTER

CLARKE (JOHN) *see* HANDEL (G.F.), [selections and arrangements: vocal works]

CLAYTON (THOMAS)

Songs in the new opera, call'd Arsinoe Queen of Cyprus. [Words from the Italian of T. Stanzani]. pp.49. *I: Walsh . . . and I. Hare* [the latter name added later]: *London*, [c.1706] fol. [Bookplate of Arthur F. Hill, 1905].
MU. 1283

Songs in the new opera call'd Rosamond. [Words by J. Addison]. ff.47. *I. Walsh . . . and P. Randall: London*, [1707] fol.
MU. 1284

CLEMENTI (MUZIO)

Clementi's introduction to the art of playing on the piano forte: containing the elements of music; preliminary notions on fingering with examples; and fifty fingered lessons . . . by composers of the first rank, ancient and modern: to which are prefixed short preludes by the author. pp.63. *Clementi, Banger, Hyde, Collard & Davis: London*, [1804^WM] fol. [Inscribed 'Fitzwilliam 1805'].
MU. 430

Clementi's selection of practical harmony for the organ or piano forte . . . by the most eminent composers. To which is prefixed an epitome of counterpoint by the editor. 2 vols. *Clementi, Banger, Hyde, Collard & Davis: London*, [1805: watermarks range from 1797 to 1803] obl. fol. [Inscribed 'Fitzwilliam 1805'].
MU. 416

CLEORA SAT BENEATH A SHADE *see* BRYAN (J.)

CLOTILDA

[Songs in the opera call'd Clotilda]. [Music by F. Conti. Some songs with Italian words, some English, some both]. ff.51. [Imperfect: wants title]. [*L. Pippard: London*, 1709] fol.
MU. 1279

see BABELL (W.), The 3^d. book of the ladys entertainment

COBSTON ( ) *see* JUPITER AND EUROPA

COCCHI *see* THE SUMMER'S TALE

COLASSE (PASCAL)

Achille et Polixene. Tragedie, dont le prologue & les quatre derniers actes ont esté mis en musique par P. Colasse . . . et le premier acte par feu Mre J.B. de Lully. [Words by J.G. de Campistron]. [Score]. pp.xxxviii, 316. *Par Christophe Ballard: Paris*, 1687 fol. [Inscribed 'R. Fitzwilliam 1767'. Some corrections in MS].
MU. 328

Enée et Lavinie. [Words by B. Le Bovier de Fontenelle]. [Score]. pp.lii, 234. [The original pp.xix–xx have been replaced by an engraved sheet in eighteenth-century

style]. *L'Academie Royalle de Musique ... et ... chez l'auteur: Paris,* 1710 [apparently a misprint for 1690] fol. [Inscribed 'R. Fitzwilliam 1767'].
MU. 338

Thetis et Pelée. [Words by B. Le Bovier de Fontenelle]. [Score]. pp.344. [Imperfect: wants pp.193–210 (supplied in MS)]. *Par Christophe Ballard: Paris,* 1689 fol. [Inscribed 'R. Fitzwilliam 1767'].
MU. 337

COLLASSE (P.) *see* COLASSE (P.)

COLMAN (C.) *see* PLAYFORD (J.), Select musicall ayres and dialogues; *see* Select ayres and dialogues for one, two, and three voyces

COLMAN (E.) *see* PLAYFORD (J.), Select musicall ayres and dialogues

COME

Come dear Philada, let us haste away. *The Happy Pair. A dialogue.* [Song]. [*London,* c.1725] s.sh. fol.
MU. 1190³⁴

Come Delia *see* POPELEY (W.)

Come fair nymphs *see* GREENE (M.), The Happy Shepherd

Come follow follow me. *The Fairy Queen. A song.* [*London,* c.1720] s.sh. fol.
MU. 1190²⁸

Come let us prepare. *The Free Mason's Health.* [Song, words by Burkhead]. [*London,* c.1720] s.sh. fol.
MU. 1190¹⁹

Come my bonny love *see* BIGGS (E.S.)

Come shepherds *see* ARNE (T.A.), Elegy on the death of Mʳ. Shenstone [single songs]

Come sweet lass, let's banish sorrow. *Love and a Bumper or Fanny's Delight. A new medley song adapted to the German flute.* [*London,* c.1750] s.sh. fol.
MU. 1189²⁶

Come unto these yellow sands *see* PURCELL (H.), The Tempest [vocal music: dramatic music]

Come zephyrs *see* ECCLES (J.), [Semele]

COMUS

[Comus]. O thou wert born to please me, a favorite duet . . . in the Masque of Comus. [Masque by T.A. Arne. This number adapted from 'Pace caro mio sposo' in Martin y Soler's 'Una Cosa Rara']. ff.[2]. [c.1790] fol.
MU. 1211⁹

CONTI (F.) *see* BABELL (W.), The 3ᵈ. book of the ladys entertainment; *see* CLOTILDA

THE CONTRIVANCES

Genteel in personage. *The Maid's Husband . . . in yᵉ Contrivances*. [Song by H. Carey]. [c.1730] s.sh. fol.
MU. 1189⁴⁷

COOKE (BENJAMIN)

A collection of glees, catches and canons, for three, four, five and six voices. pp.68. *The Author: London*, [1775] obl. fol. [With MS figured bass].
MU. 1252¹

Nine glees and two duets, (never before printed) composed by the late Dr. Benjamin Cooke. Published from the original manuscripts by his son, Robert Cooke . . . Opera V. pp.64. *Longman & Broderip, and may be had of The Editor: London*, 1795 obl. fol. [With a subscribers' list].
MU. 1252²

see AMUSEMENT

see GALLIARD (J.E.), The Morning Hymn

CORELLI (ARCANGELO)

Arrangement: 1. Collected works
  2. Concertos
  3. Sonatas

1. Collected works

The score of the four setts of sonatas . . . for two violins & a bass. Dedicated to Sʳ. Richard Corbet . . . Barᵗ. Vol Iˢᵗ. ⟨The score of the twelve concertos . . . for two violins & a violoncello, with two violins more, a tenor & thorough bass for ripieno parts . . . Dedicated to Ralph Tenison . . . Vol. IIᵈ.⟩ The whole carefully corrected by several most eminent masters, and revis'd by Dr. Pepusch. 2 vols. *Benjamin Cooke: London*, [1732] fol. [With a frontispiece to each volume].
MU. 1195–6

The score of the four operas, containing 48 sonatas . . . for two violins and a bass ⟨The score of the twelve concertos . . . for two violins and a violoncello, with two violins more, a tenor, and thorough bass for ripieno parts⟩ . . . The whole revis'd and carefully corrected by Dr. Pepusch. Vol. I. ⟨II⟩. 2 vols. Plate nos. 550–1. I. *Walsh: London*, [1735] fol. [Both volumes inscribed 'R. Fitzwilliam 1765'. With a frontispiece to vol. I].
MU. 305–6

[Another copy]. [Without frontispiece. Between title and text are gathered several engravings of the composer].
MU. 1198^1, 1198^3

2. Concertos

Concerti grossi con duoi violini, e violoncello di concertino obligati, et duoi altri violini, viola, e basso di concerto grosso . . . Opera sesta. XII great concertos . . . being the sixth and last work of Arcangelo Corelli. [With a second title-page following no. VIII: 'Preludii, allemande, gighe, corrente, sarabande, gavotte e minuetti. Parte seconda per camera'. [7 parts]. I: *Walsh: London*, [c.1740] fol. [With a frontispiece to violin I].
MU. 320 G^8, 320 H^8, 320 I^8, 320 J^8, 320 K^8, 320 M^8, 320 N^8

3. Sonatas

Opera prima. XII sonatas of three parts for two violins and a bass with a through bass for ye organ, harpsicord or arch lute. [4 parts]. Plate no. 364. I. *Walsh: London* [1740 or later] fol.
MU. 318 A^3, 318 B^3, 318 C^1, 318 D^3

[Sonatas Op.1. no.9] *see below* [Sonatas Op.3], in the concerto grosso arrangement by Geminiani

Opera secunda. XII sonatas of three parts for two violins and a bass with a through bass for ye organ, harpsicord or arch lute. [3 parts, with a second copy of bass]. Plate no. 365. I. *Walsh: London*, [1730 or later] fol.
MU. 318 A^4, 318 B^4, 318 C^2, 318 D^4

Opera terza. XII sonatas of three parts for two violins and a bass with a through bass for ye organ, harpsicord or arch lute. [4 parts]. Plate no. 366. I. *Walsh: London*, [1730 or later] fol.
MU. 318 A^5, 318 B^5, 318 C^3, 318 D^5

[Sonatas Op.3]. *Concerti grossi con due violini, viola e violoncello di concertino obligati, et due altri violini e basso di concerto grosso. Composti delli sei sonate del'opera terza d'Arcangelo Corelli per Francesco Geminiani.* [7 parts]. Plate no. 569. I. *Walsh: London*, [1735] fol. [Comprises nos. 1, 3, 4, 9 and 10 of Op.3 and no.9 of Op.1].
MU. 320 G^{11}, 320 H^{11}, 320 I^{11}, 320 J^{11}, 320 K^{11}, 320 M^{11}, 320 N^{11}

[Sonatas Op.4]. Suonate da camera, a tre, doi violini, violoncello, e cimbalo . . . Opera quarta. Prima parte. Nuovamente ristampata. [1 part only]. *Da Henrico Aertssens: Antwerp*, 1692 fol.
MU. 1265

Opera quarta. XII sonatas of three parts for two violins and a bass with a through bass for ye organ, harpsicord or arch lute. [3 parts, with a second copy of bass]. Plate no. 367. *I. Walsh: London*, [c.1730 or later] fol.
MU. 318 A^6, 318 B^6, 318 C^4, 318 D^6

[Sonatas Op.5]. XII solos for a violin with a thorough bass for the harpsicord or violoncello . . . Opera quinta [With a second title-page following p. 38: 'The second part']. [Score]. pp.68. *I. Walsh: London*, [1740] fol. [Inscribed 'R. Fitzwilliam 1765']
MU. 307

[Another copy]
MU. 1198^2

[Sonatas Op.5. Nos.1–6]. Concerti grossi con due violini, viola e violoncello di concertino obligati, et due altri violini e basso di concerto grosso da Francesco Geminiani composti delli sei soli della prima parte dell'opera quinta d'Arcangelo Corelli. [7 parts]. *I: Walsh and Ioseph Hare: London*, [1726] fol.
MU. 1286 A^3, 1286 B^3, 1286 C^3, 1286 D^3, 1286 E^3, 1286 F^3, 1286 G^3

[Another issue]. [7 parts]. *I: Walsh: London*, [c.1735] fol.
MU. 320 G^9, 320 H^9, 320 I^9, 320 J^9, 320 K^9, 320 M^9, 320 N^9

[Sonatas Op.5. Nos.7–12]. Concerti grossi con due violini, viola e violoncello di concertini obligati, et due altri violini e basso di concerto grosso . . . composti della seconda parte dell'opera quinta d'Arcangelo Corelli per Francesco Geminiani. [7 parts]. *I: Walsh and Ios: Hare: London*, [1729] fol.
MU. 1286 A^4, 1286 B^4, 1286 C^4, 1286 D^4, 1286 E^4, 1286 F^4, 1286 G^4

[Another issue]. Concerti grossi . . . da Francesco Geminiani composti delli sei soli della seconda parte dell'opera quinta d'Arcangelo Corelli. [7 parts]. *I. Walsh: London*, [1734] fol.
MU. 320 G^{10}, 320 H^{10}, 320 I^{10}, 320 J^{10}, 320 K^{10}, 320 M^{10}, 320 N^{10}

CORRI (DOMENICO)

A select collection of the most admired songs, duetts, &c., from operas . . . and from other works . . . in three books . . . The music . . . divided into phrases . . . and to each are appropriated its graces, cadences, &c . . . A proper accompaniement is also arranged . . . to enable any harpisicord [*sic*] player to accompany himself with ease, although unacquainted with the rules of thorough bass. 3 vols. *John Corri: Edinburgh*, [c.1799] fol. [With a frontispiece].
MU. 1224 A–C

Donald. A favourite song to the original Scotch tune. The accompanyment by Sigr: Corri. [Begins, 'When first you courted me']. pp.3. *Printed by R. Birchall: London*, [c.1795] fol. [Inscribed 'A.M. Jeffery': later Mrs R.J.S. Stevens].
MU. 1287[17]

see BRAHAM (J.)

COU'D

Cou'd a man be secure. *A favorite duet.* [By Starling Goodwin]. ff.2. *Printed for A. Bland: London*, [c.1790] fol.
MU. 1211[8]

COULD YOU TO BATTLE MARCH AWAY? *see* ARNOLD (S.), The Surrender of Calais

COUPERIN (FRANÇOIS)

L'Art de toucher le clavecin . . . Dedié a sa Majesté. pp.71. *Chés L'Auteur . . . Le Sieur Foucaut: Paris*, 1717 fol. [Inscribed 'R. Fitzwilliam 1769']
MU. 424

Pieces de clavecin . . . Premier livre. pp.75. *Chés L'Auteur . . . Le Sieur Foucaut: Paris*, 1713 fol. [Inscribed 'R. Fitzwilliam 1769'].
MU. 425

Second livre de pièces de clavecin. pp.86. *Chés L'Auteur . . . Le Sieur Foucaut: Paris*, [1717] fol. [Inscribed 'R. Fitzwilliam 1769'].
MU. 426

COURTEVILLE (R.) *see* HARPSICHORD MASTER

CRABBED AGE *see* STEVENS (R.J.S.)

CRESO *see* HANDEL (G.F.), [12 Arias] [selections and arrangements: songs, arias and cantatas]

CROFT (WILLIAM)

Musicus apparatus academicus, being a composition of two odes . . . perform'd in the theatre at Oxford on Monday July the 13th. 1713. The words by M[r]. Joseph Trapp A.M. pp.64, 27. *The Author: London*, [1720] fol. [Inscribed 'R. Fitzwilliam 1771'].
MU. 412

see ANTHEMS

see HARPSICHORD MASTER

CROSBY (B.) *see* ENGLISH; *see* IRISH

DALAYRAC (NICOLAS)

La Soirée orageuse. Comédie en un acte et en prose, par M. Radet . . . Œuvre XII. [Score]. pp.143. *Chez Le Duc: Paris,* [c.1790] fol. [Preliminary pages are uncut sheets of edicts of 1791].
MU. 1188

DAMON (WILLIAM)

The second booke of the musicke of M. William Damon . . . conteining all the tunes of Dauids Psalmes . . . composed into 4. parts. [Imperfect: altus only]. *Published . . . by W. Swayne . . . Printed by T. Este, the assigné of W. Bird: [London],* 1591 4°. [Bound in a sheet of vellum MS].
MU. 1468

DANBY (J.) *see* AMUSEMENT

DAVIES (RICHARD)

Hobbinol, a new song. Set for two German flutes. [Begins: 'Young Hobbinol (the blithest swain)']. [*London,* c.1750] s.sh. fol.
MU. 1189[13]

The Irish Lassie. Set for the German flute. [Song, begins: 'No Highland lad, or dear pantin']. [*London,* c.1755] s.sh. fol.
MU. 1189[11]

DAVY (J.) *see* REEVE (W.)

DAWN

A dawn of hope my soul revives. *A Dawn of Hope. A New Song.* [By T.A. Arne]. [*London,* c. 1745] s.sh. fol.
MU. 1197[63]

[Another issue]: [*London,* c.1750].
MU. 1189[39a]

DEAR

Dear Cloe is my sole delight. *To Cloe. A song by an eminent master.* [*London,* c.1720] s.sh. fol.
MU. 1190[57]

Dear Cupid smile thou god of love. *Sung at Sadlers Wells.* [*London*, c.1730] s.sh. fol.
MU. 1190[26]

DEAREST CREATURE *see* GIARDINI (F.)

DEFESCH (WILLEM)

VIII Concerto's in seven parts . . . Dedicated to His Royal Highness the Prince of Wales. [4 parts only]. *I. Walsh: London*, [c.1745] fol.
MU. 1430

Hail England! Old England! *An Occasional Ode on the Dawn of the Success of our Arms . . . The words by M*[r]. Boyce. [*London*, c.1759] s.sh. fol.
MU. 1197[24]

Mutual Love. A new song. [Begins: 'Wer't thou fairer than thou art']. [*London*, c.1750] s.sh. fol.
MU. 1189[27]

Polly of the Plain . . . The words by M[r]. Boyce. [Song, begins: 'Let others sing in loftier lays']. [*London*, c.1753] s.sh. fol.
MU. 1189[19a]

X. Sonata's for two German flutes or, two violins; with a thorough bass. Dedicated to William Huggins . . . Opera settima. [2 parts only]. *Engrav'd and Sold by Benj*[n]. *Cooke: London*, [1733] fol.
MU. 1439

To Lysander. Sung at Marybon-Gardens. [Begins: 'Why shine those charming eyes so bright']. [*London*, c.1750] s.sh. fol.
MU. 1189[15]

To make me feel a virgins charms. [Song]. [*London*, c.1755] s.sh. fol.
MU. 1189[17]

see O, O lovely maid

see TO, To woo me and win me

DE LA GUERRE *see* JACQUET DE LA GUERRE

DEMETRIO

Demetrio. [Pasticcio, arranged by G. Cocchi]. Overture. [Keyboard]. pp.5. [c.1770] fol.
MU. 1400[10]

DESMARETS (HENRI)

Circé. Tragedie. [Words by L. Gillot de Saintonge]. [Score]. pp.lvii, 288. *Chez Christophe Ballard: Paris*, 1694 fol. [Inscribed 'R. Fitzwilliam 1767'].
MU. 329

DIBDIN (CHARLES)

The Padlock. A comic opera . . . The words by the author of the Maid of the Mill [i.e. I. Bickerstaff]. pp.[42]. *Printed for the Author & sold by J. Johnston: London*, [1768] obl. fol.
MU. 1254¹

see LIONEL AND CLARISSA

DID

Did you see e'er a shepherd. *A new song*. [By J. Worgan]. [*London*, c.1760] s.sh. fol.
MU. 1197⁵²

DIDO AND ENEAS

Hear me mourning princess. *A song in the Mask of Dido and Eneas*. [Music by J.C. Pepusch, words by B. Booth]. [*London*, c.1716] s.sh. fol.
MU. 1190⁷⁶

DIETZ (JOSEPH)

XII Variations pour le clavecin sur le rondeau favori de Mʳ: [J.C.] Fischer. pp.7. *Welcker: London*, [c.1770] obl. fol.
MU. 1404¹

DIEUPART (CHARLES)

Select lessons for the harpsicord or spinnett . . . plac'd on five lines in yᵉ English cliff. ff.10. *I. Walsh . . . and I. Hare: London*, [1731] obl. fol.
MU. 420 B

[Six suittes de clavessin . . . pour un violon & flûte avec un basse de viole & un archilut, dediés a Madame la Comtesses de Sandwich]. [Imperfect: wants title. Keyboard only]. [*Chez Estienne Roger . . . Sold by Francis Vaillant: Amsterdam*, c.1705] fol. [Inscribed 'R. Fitzwilliam 1766'].
MU. 435

DIGNUM (CHARLES)

Fair Rosale, a favourite song. [Begins: 'On that lone bank where Lubin dy'd'. Other editions give the heroine's name as 'Rosalie']. [Score]. pp.3. *Messrs Thompson: London*, [c.1795] fol. [Inscribed 'A.M. Jeffery': later Mrs R.J.S. Stevens].
MU. 1287²⁵

DITTERS (C.D.) *see* DITTERSDORF

DITTERSDORF (CARL DITTERS VON)

The favorite sinfonie [in C major] ... Disposed for the piano forte or harpsichord. Composed by Sig^r. Carlo Ditters. pp.6. *T. Skillern: London*, [c.1780] obl. fol.
MU. 1410

DIXON (W.) *see* HARMONIC SOCIETY OF CAMBRIDGE

DON'T YOU REMEMBER *see* MOULDS (J.)

DOUBT THOU THE STARS ARE FIRE *see* STEVENS (R.J.S.)

LA DOUCE CLARTÉ DE L'AURORE *see* KREUTZER (R.)

DRAGHI (GIOVANNI BATTISTA)

Six select suites of lessons for the harpsicord in six severall keys. ff.35. Plate no. 199 [added in MS]. *I. Walsh ... and I. Hare ... and P. Randall: London*, [1707] fol.
MU. 488⁴, bound with MU. MS 208

DU PHLY (JACQUES)

Pieces ⟨second–quatrieme livre de pièces⟩ de clavecin. *Chez L'Auteur.* ⟨Vol. IV *Au Bureau D'abone^mt. Musical*⟩: *Paris*, [c.1769], 1769, 1771, [1772] fol. [The composer's instructions 'Du Doigter' in MS on verso of title to vol. I. Vol. I inscribed 'R. Fitzwilliam 1769 – de la part de l'auteur'. Vols. II–IV have the same inscription, except that the dates are respectively 1769, 1771 and 1772. The composer was Fitzwilliam's teacher: for his MS book of Du Phly's exercises, dated 1765, see MU. MS 100].
MU. 429

THE DUENNA

The Duenna or Double Elopement, a comic-opera . . . for the voice, harpsichord, or violin. [Music composed and selected by T. Linley the elder and T. Linley the younger. Words by R.B. Sheridan]. pp.58. *C. and S. Thomson: London,* [1775] obl. fol.
MU. 1251²

DUPORT (JEAN PIERRE)

Six sonatas pour le violoncelle . . . dediées à Messire Fitzwilliam. pp.33. *Imprimé pour l'auteur, et vendu par Mr. Bremner: London,* [c.1770] fol. [Inscribed 'R. Fitzwilliam 1770'].
MU. 308

DUPUIS (T.S.) *see* AMUSEMENT

DURANTE (FRANCESCO)

⟨Sonate per cembalo, divise in studii e divertimenti⟩. pp.xxiv. [Imperfect: wants title, supplied from dedication]. [*Philippus de Grado: Naples,* 1732] obl. fol.
MU. 1261

ECCLES (JOHN)

The Iudgment of Paris or the Prize Music . . . The words by Mʳ Congreve. pp.71. *I. Walsh: London,* [c.1702] fol. [Inscribed 'R. Fitzwilliam 1768'].
MU. 378¹

[Semele]. Come zephyrs come. *Air in the opera of Semele, the words by Mʳ Congreve.* ff.2. [*London,* c.1730] fol.
MU. 1190⁶⁷

[Semele]. O sleep why do'st thou leave me. *Air in the opera of Semele, the words by Mʳ Congreve.* ff.[2]. [*London,* c.1730] fol.
MU. 1190³³

[Semele]. See after the toils of an amorous fight. *Air in yᵉ opera of Semele, the words by Mʳ Congreve.* [Score]. ff.[3]. [*London,* c.1710] fol.
MU. 1190⁸⁰

ECCLES (JOHN) *and* PURCELL (DANIEL)

A collection of lessons and aires for the harpsicord or spinnett. Compos'd by Mr: J: Eccles Mr: D: Purcell and others. ff.10. *I. Walsh . . . and I. Hare: London,* [1702] obl. fol. [Inscribed 'R. Fitzwilliam 1766'].
MU. 361 C

EGVILLE (J. D') *see* MARIAGE

ENGLISH

The English Musical Repository: a choice selection of esteemed English songs. pp.288. *B. Crosby & Co: London*, 1807 8°. [With a frontispiece].
MU. 1207

FAINT AND WEARILY *see* ARNOLD (S.), The Mountaineers

FAIR

Fair Aurora *see* ARTAXERXES

Fair Hebe I left with a cautious design. [Song. Words by Viscount Cantelupe]. [*London*, c.1750] s.sh. fol.
MU. 1197[29]

Fair Sally *see* SHIELD (W.), [The Wandering Melodist]

FAIREST IF THOU CAN'ST BE KIND *see* GALLIARD (J.E.), [Circe]

FIGURATI ESTINTE *see* ARSACE

A FILLET *see* GRÉTRY (A.E.M.), Richard Coeur de Lion

FINE

Fine songsters apologies too often use. *The Thing*. [Song]. [*London*, c.1765] s.sh. fol.
MU. 1197[14]

FISCHER (J.C.) *see* DIETZ (J.)

FISHER (F.E.)

Six sonatas for two violins with a thorough bass for the harpsichord. Dedicated to the Musical Society at Cambridge . . . Opera prima. [3 parts]. *J. Johnson: London*, [c.1755] fol.
MU. 1371

FISIN (JAMES)

[Six songs. Op.8. No.5]. Only tell him that I love. pp.18–21 *of a collection. Smart's Music Warehouse: London*, [c.1800] fol. [Inscribed 'A.M.J.', i.e. A.M. Jeffery: later Mrs R.J.S. Stevens].
MU. 1287[12]

A FLAXEN HEADED COW BOY *see* **SHIELD (W.)**, The Farmer

FLORA GODDESS SWEETLY BLOOMING *see* **BOYCE (W.)**, The Pleasures of the Spring Gardens

FLOREAT AETERNUM *see* **STEVENS (R.J.S.)**

FLORIDANTE

O lovely charmer. [O cara spene]. *Favourite minuet in the additional songs of Floridant.* [Music by G.F. Handel, words by P.A. Rolli]. ff.[2]. [*London*, 1722] fol. [From plates of 'The Monthly Mask of Vocal Musick'].
MU. 1190[63]

FOOLISH WOMAN *see* **RAVENSCROFT (J.)**

FORBID

Forbid me not enquire. *The answer to Pinks and Lillies or Damon nonplus'd.* [Song]. [*London*, c.1725] s.sh. fol.
MU. 1190[85]

FORD (THOMAS)

There is a lady sweet & kind, madrigal for four voices. [Presumably arranged by R.J.S. Stevens, who has signed the copy]. pp.3. *Printed & Sold for Mr. Bartleman by Messrs. Birchall & Co: London*, [c.1820] fol.
MU. 1288 B[27]

see **SINCE**

FORGIVE

Forgive ye fair, nor take it wrong. *Miss Stevenson's advice to her own sex.* [Song]. [*London*, c.1750] s.sh. fol.
MU. 1189[10]

FORTH

Forth from my dark and dismall cell. *Tom A Bedlam*. [*London*, c.1720] s.sh. fol.
MU. 1197[4]

FRISCHMUTH (L.) *see* TARTINI (G.), II Concerti . . . accommodati per il cembalo

FROBERGER (JOHANN JACOB)

10. suittes de clavessin . . . mis en meilleur ordre et corrigée d'un grand nombre de fautes. pp.38. *Chez Pierre Mortier: Amsterdam*, [c.1710] obl. fol.
MU. 361 E

FROM

From night till morn *see* SHIELD (W.)

From Oberon *see* STEVENS (R.J.S.)

From silent shad's *see* PURCELL (H.), Bess of Bedlam [vocal music: songs]

From sweet bewitching tricks of love. *The blind eat many a fly*. [Song]. [*London*, c.1740] s.sh. fol.
MU. 1197[64]

FULL FATHOM FIVE *see* PURCELL (H.), [The Tempest] [vocal music: dramatic music]

GALILEI (VINCENTIO)

Fronimo. Dialogo . . . sopra l'arte del bene intavolare, et rettamente sonare la musica negli strumenti artificiali si di corde come di siato, & in particulare nel liuto. Nuovamente restampato, & dall'autore istesso arrichito, & ornato di novità di concetti, & d'essempi. pp.182. [Imperfect: wants pp.179–82 (supplied in MS)]. *Apresso l'Herede di Girolamo Scotto: Vineggia*, 1584 4°.
MU. 1321

GALLIARD (JOHANN ERNST)

[Circe]. Fairest if thou can'st be kind. *A song . . . in the opera of Circe. p.9 of a sequence which also includes MU. 1190[21]*. [*London*, c.1720] fol.
MU. 1190[22]

The Hymn of Adam and Eve, out of the fifth book of Milton's Paradise-Lost. [Cantata for 2 voices]. pp.30. [*London*], 1728 obl. 8°. [Inscribed 'R. Fitzwilliam 1768'. With a subscribers' list].
MU. 523

[A revised version]. The Morning hymn, taken from the fifth book of Milton's Paradise Lost. Set to music by the late John Ernest Galliard. The overture, accompanyments & chorusses added by Benjamin Cooke. pp.70. [Score]. *Printed by Welcker . . . And may be had at Mr. Cooke's: London*, [1773] fol. [Inscribed 'Fitzwilliam 1782'].
MU. 494[1]

Six sonatas for the bassoon or violoncello with a thorough bass for the harpsicord. pp.27. *Iohn Walsh: London*, [c.1740] fol. [Inscribed 'R. Fitzwilliam 1767'].
MU. 487

see APOLLO AND DAPHNE; *see* JUPITER AND EUROPA

GAMBALL (JAMES)

Cynthia. A song. [Begins: 'O blest abode and envyed seat']. [*London*, c.1720] s.sh. fol.
MU. 1190[61]

GAY

The gay dragoons on Wellands banks. *Stocking Hall or the Gay Dragoons*. [Song, parody of 'All in the downs' or *Black-eyed Susan*]. [*London*, c.1720] s.sh. fol.
MU. 1190[74]

GEMINIANI (FRANCESCO)

The art of playing on the violin, containing all the rules necessary to attain to a perfection on that instrument, with great variety of compositions . . . Opera IX. pp.8, 51. *Preston & Son: London*, [c.1790] fol.
MU. 311[5]

Concerti grossi, con due violini, violoncello, e viola di concertino obligati, e due altri violini, e basso di concerto grosso ad arbitrio . . . Dedicati a sua eccellenza Henrietta, Duchessa di Marlborough . . . Opera seconda. [7 parts]. [*London*], 1732 fol.
MU. 1286 A[2], 1286 B[2], 1286 C[2], 1286 D[2], 1286 E[2], 1286 F[2], 1286 G[2]

[Another issue]. [7 parts]. *I. Walsh: London*, [c.1740–9] fol.
MU. 320 G[5], 320 H[5], 320 I[5], 320 J[5], 320 K[5], 320 M[5], 320 N[5]

Concerti grossi, con due violini, viola e violoncello di concertino obligati, e due altri violini e basso di concerto grosso . . . Opera terza. [7 parts]. *Iohn Walsh: London*, [c.1730] fol.
MU. 1286 A[1], 1286 B[1], 1286 C[1], 1286 D[1], 1286 E[1], 1286 F[1], 1286 G[1]

[Another issue]. [7 parts]. *I. Walsh: London*, [c.1740–9] fol.
MU. 320 G⁶, 320 H⁶, 320 I⁶, 320 J⁶, 320 K⁶, 320 M⁶, 320 N⁶

Concerti grossi composti a 3, 4, 5, 6, 7, 8 parti reali . . . Dedicati alla celebre Accademia della buona ed antica musica. Opª. VII. [8 parts]. *Printed for the Author by J: Johnson: London*, [1748] fol.
MU. 320 A², 320 G⁷, 320 H⁷, 320 I⁷, 320 J⁷, 320 K⁷, 320 M⁷, 320 N⁷

Concerti grossi . . . dedicati all'Altezza Reale di Federico Prencipe di Vallia *see below*: [Sonatas Op. IV]

Pieces de clavecin, tirees des différens ouvrages de Mʳ. F. Geminiani adaptées par luy meme à cet instrument. pp.35. *Printed for the Author by J. Johnson: London*, 1743 [actually a reprint of c.1755] fol.
MU. 304³

The second collection of pieces for the harpsichord. Taken from different works of F. Geminiani, and adapted by himself to that instrument. pp.59. *Printed for the Author by Mrs. Johnson: London*, 1762 fol.
MU. 304⁴

[Sonatas Op.1]. XII solo's for a violin with a thorough bass for the harpsicord or bass violin. [Score]. pp.35. Plate no.378. *I: Walsh: London*, [c.1730] fol. [With MS additions, ornaments, fingering and phrasing].
MU. 311⁴

[Sonatas Op.1]. Le prime sonate a violino, e basso . . . nuovamente ristampate, e . . . corrette . . . Dedicate all'illustrissima ed eccellentissima signora Dorotea Contessa di Burlington. pp.41. *London*, 1739 fol. [Inscribed 'R. Fitzwilliam 1763'].
MU. 304¹

[Sonatas Op.1. Nos. 7–12]. Sonatas of three parts. For two violins with a thorough bass for the harpsicord or violoncello. Made from the solos of Francesco Geminiani. [Arranged by F. Barsanti]. [3 parts]. *I. Walsh: London*, [c.1742] fol.
MU. 318 A⁷, 318 B⁷, 318 D⁷

[Sonatas Op.4]. Sonate a violino e basso . . . dedicate all'illustrissima ed eccellentissima signora Margarita Contessa d'Orrery. Opera IV. [Score]. pp.48. *Printed for the Author by John Johnson: London*, 1739 [actually a reprint of 1745] fol.
MU. 304²

[Sonatas Op.4]. Concerti grossi a due violini, due viole e violoncello obligati con due altri violini, e basso di ripieno . . . dedicati all'Altezza Reale di Federico Prencipe di Vallia . . . composti dalle sonate a violino e basso dell opera IV. [8 parts]. *Printed for the Author by I. Iohnson: London*, 1743 fol. [With a frontispiece. Owing to later rebinding this now appears as the first item of a large set of orchestral music assembled by Viscount Fitzwilliam (see 'Numerical list'). Originally the first item would have been *Handel's Overtures* (MU. 320 G¹, etc.)].
MU. 320 A¹, 320 G⁴, 320 H⁴, 320 I⁴, 320 J⁴, 320 K⁴, 320 M⁴, 320 N⁴

The Tender Lover. The words by Prior. [Song, begins: 'In vain you tell your parting lover']. [*London*, c.1750] s.sh. fol.
MU. 1197⁷¹

see CORELLI, [Sonatas Op.3] [sonatas]

see CORELLI, [Sonatas Op.5] [sonatas]

see HANDEL (G.F.), Handel's celebrated Water Musick compleat [instrumental works: Water Music]

GENTEEL IN PERSONAGE *see* THE CONTRIVANCES

GENTLE

Gentle love this hour befriend me. *A song, the words by a gentleman.* [i.e. A. Hill]. [*London*, c.1720] s.sh. fol.
MU. 1190⁷³

THE GENTLE SHEPHERD

The overture, songs, & duetts, in the pastoral opera of the Gentle Shepherd. [Music arranged and composed by T. Linley the elder, words arranged from A. Ramsay by R. Tickell]. pp.25. *S.A. & P. Thompson, London*, [1781] obl. fol.
MU. 1258²

GERARD (JOHN)

On Friendship. [Song, begins: 'The world, my dear Myra']. [Imperfect: title badly torn]. [*London*, c.1765] s.sh. fol.
MU. 1197⁴⁹

GIARDINI (FELICE)

Voi amante, or rondeau. [Song, with an English version beginning 'Dearest creature']. [*London*, c.1760] s.sh. fol.
MU. 1197⁵⁸

see THE SUMMER'S TALE

GIBBS (JOSEPH)

Eight solos for a violin with a thorough bass for the harpsicord or bass violin. pp.41. *Printed for the Author, and sold by Peter Thompson: London*, [1746] fol. [With a subscribers' list].
MU. 1285

GIORDANI (TOMMASO)

Queen Mary's Lamentation . . . The instrumental parts by Sig[r]: Giordani. [Song, begins: 'I sigh and lament me in vain']. [Score]. pp.4. *Preston & Son: London*, [c.1790] fol. [Inscribed 'A.M. Jeffery': later Mrs R.J.S. Stevens].
MU. 1287[21]

GLADWIN (THOMAS)

Eight lessons for the harpsichord or organ, three of which have an accompanyment for a violin. pp.47. *Welcker: London*, [c.1770] obl. fol.
MU. 1244[3]

GLEES

[The Professional Collection of Glees . . . by . . . Callcott, Cooke, Danby, Hindle, Stevens and Webbe]. pp.54. [Imperfect: wants all but pp.22–3 (2 copies), 42–5, which comprise pieces by R.J.S. Stevens extracted by him and kept in his personal archive]. [*Printed for the Authors, & sold by Longman & Broderip: London*, c.1791] obl. fol.
MU. 1230[2–3], 1288 A[6]

GO ROSE *see* GREENE (M.)

GOD

God save great George our King. For two voices. ['The National Anthem', with a verse relating to Wade's expedition against the Jacobites]. p.29 *of a collection*. [*London*, c.1745] fol.
MU. 1197[80]

GOOD

Good wine in a morning. *The pleasure of drinking in season. A song*. [*London*, c.1720] s.sh. fol.
MU. 1190[25]

GOODWIN (S.) *see* COU'D

GORTON (WILLIAM)

A choice collection of new ayres, compos'd and contriv'd for two bass-viols. [2 parts]. *John Young: London*, 1701 obl. 8°. [In contemporary MS are added twelve variations on a ground and one other piece for the same instruments].
MU. 1002–3

GRANO (GIOVANNI BATTISTA)

No more Florilla when I gaze. *Song.* p.10 *of a collection which also includes MU. 1190²²⁻⁴.* [*London*, c.1720] fol.
MU. 1190²¹

GRAVES (JAMES)

Tis he's an honest fellow. [Song, also called *The Boon Companion*]. [*London*, c.1720] s.sh. fol.
MU. 1190⁴⁰

A song on His Majesty King George yᵉ second being proclaim'd. [Begins: 'To proclaim King George the second, the drums did beat']. [*London*, 1727] s.sh. fol.
MU. 1190⁵⁰

GREAT

Great Cecil rais'd a stately pile. *A poem to the Right Honᵇˡᵉ. Lady E. Cecil on her Ladyship's birth-day.* [Song]. [*London*, c.1720] s.sh. fol.
MU. 1190⁷⁹

GREENE (MAURICE)

Forty select anthems in score, composed for 1, 2, 3, 4, 5, 6, 7, and 8 voices . . . Volume First ⟨Second⟩. 2 vols. *J. Walsh: London,* 1743 fol. [Inscribed 'R. Fitzwilliam 1768'. With a subscribers' list].
MU. 368

Go Rose. A favourite song. [Begins: Go rose my Chloe's bosom grace']. ff.[2]. [*London*, c.1760] fol.
MU. 1197⁴⁰

The Happy Shepherd. [Song, begins: 'Come fair nymphs to this sweet grove']. *T. Wright: London,* [c.1735] s.sh. fol.
MU. 1189⁷

A collection of lessons for the harpsichord. pp.73. *John Johnson: London,* [c.1750] obl. fol. [Inscribed 'R. Fitzwilliam 1768'].
MU. 485²

A collection of lessons for the harpsicord . . . 2ᵈ. book. [The first book as issued by Walsh may have been 'Six overtures for the harpsicord or spinnet']. pp.24. *I. Walsh: London,* [c.1755] obl. fol. [Inscribed 'R. Fitzwilliam 1768'].
MU. 485³

GRÉTRY (ANDRÉ ERNEST MODESTE)

Richard Coeur de Lion. Comédie en 3 actes . . . par M. Sedaine . . . Dediée a Madame des Entelles. Mise en musique par M. Gretry . . . Œuvre XXIV. [Score]. pp.144. *Chez Houbaut . . . chez Castaud: Paris and Lyons*, [1785] fol.
MU. 1364

The favorite duett . . . in Richard Coeur de Lion. [Begins: 'Un bandeau couvre les yeux'. With an English version, beginning: 'A fillet blinds that subtle god']. pp.[3], *including pp.10–11 of a collection. Preston: London*, [c.1795] fol.
MU. 1211[36]

GRIFFES (EDWARD)

Arabel. [Song, begins: 'Whilst you to lovely Arabel']. [Imperfect: wants top RH corner]. [*London*, c.1755] s.sh. fol.
MU. 1197[83]

THE GROVES, THE PLAINS *see* VANBRUGHE (G.), Lesbia's reproach

GUGLIELMI (PIETRO ALESSANDRO)

Il Desertore. Overture. [Keyboard]. pp.5. [*London*, c.1770] fol.
MU. 1400[8]

GUIGOU

La nouvelle Valentine. Stances elegiaques. Paroles de Mad[me]. P*** de Lyon . . . Dediées à S.A.R. Mademoiselle, avec l'agrément de son auguste mère, S.A.R. Madame la Duchesse de Berry. [Song, begins: 'Sous le ciel doux et pur']. pp.4. *Chez Frere fils . . . chez Cartoux: Paris and Lyons*, [c.1820] fol.
MU. 1440[2]

GWILT (G) *see* WARREN (T.), Index to a collection of vocal harmony; A general index to Warren's collection

HAGUE (CHARLES)

A collection of songs . . . the words selected and revised by the Rev[d]. James Plumptre . . . the music adapted and composed by Charles Hague. pp.viii, 200. *Printed by Francis Hodson. Sold by Preston: Cambridge and London*, 1805 4°. [With a subscribers' list].
MU. 1222

HAIGH (THOMAS)

Ah! prithee ask me not, a favorite ballad, with an accompaniment for the piano forte . . . The words from J.H. Hendley's Persian Relyes. pp.3. *Clementi, Banger, Hyde, Collard & Davis: London,* [c.1805] fol. [Initialled 'A.M.J.', i.e. A.M. Jeffery: later Mrs R.J.S. Stevens. With MS figured bass].
MU. 1287[13]

HAIL ENGLAND! *see* DEFESCH (W.)

HANDEL (GEORG FREDERIC)

Arrangement: 1. Arnold's edition
             2. Selections and arrangements
             3. Church music
             4. Operas and other stage works
             5. Oratorios, odes and other choral works
             6. Instrumental works
             7. Appendix

1. Arnold's edition

[The Works of Handel, in score . . . under the immediate direction and inspection of Dr. [Samuel] Arnold . . . Subscriptions received by Dr. Arnold . . . Messrs. Longman and Broderip . . . Messrs. Birchall and Co.]. [Title from wrapper in Royal College of Music]. [*London*: 1787–97] fol. Issued in 180 nos. [Imperfect: represented are nos.1–37, 39–56, 60–121, 131–9, 146–72. With some subscribers' lists. The present collection consists of parts of at least three sets, distinguished by bindings, bookplates, etc. See also individual works as set out below].
MU. 345, 352, 443–72, 1433–8

2. Selections and arrangements

Anthems
Eight anthems . . . dedicated to . . . the Princess of Wales. Arranged for voices, with an accompaniment for the organ or piano forte, by William Sexton . . . and John Page. pp.108. *The Editors: London,* 1808 fol. [Inscribed, 'R.J.S. Stevens, Charterhouse, 1817'. With a subscribers' list].
MU. 1294

Chorusses
Six grand chorusses from M[r]: Handel's Oratorios. Adapted for the organ or harpsichord by M[r]. Hook. 3 vols. *W[m]: Randall: London,* [1778–81] fol. [With a frontispiece to each volume. Each volume inscribed 'Fitzwilliam 1799'].
MU. 354 A[1–3]

Duets

Thirteen celebrated Italian duets, accompanied with the harpsichord or organ. pp.91. *W^m: Randall: London*, [1777] fol. [Inscribed 'Fitzwilliam 1799'. With a subscribers' list. With a frontispiece].
MU. 395

Twelve duets for two voices with a thorough bass for the harpsicord or bass violin, collected out of all the late operas compos'd by M^r. Handel, to which is added the celebrated trio in the opera of Alcina. [Score]. pp.46. Plate no.557. *I. Walsh: London*, [c.1755] fol. [Inscribed 'R. Fitzwilliam 1775'].
MU. 354 B

Fitzwilliam Music

The Fitzwilliam Music, never published. Three hymns, the words made by the late Rev^d. Charles Wesley . . . set to music by George Frederick Handel, faithfully transcribed from his autography in the Fitzwilliam Museum, Cambridge, by Samuel Wesley . . . presented to the Wesleyan Society at large. pp.4. *To be had of M^r: S. Wesley*, [1826] fol.
MU. 499

Minuets

Handel's favourite minuets from his operas & oratorios, with those made for the balls at court, for the harpsichord, German flute, violin or guitar. pp.80: *4 vols, with only the first title-page, continuously paginated. I: Walsh: London*, [1726] 8°.
MU. 1273

When I survey Clarinda's charms. *A song made to a favourite minuet.* [*London*, c.1730] s.sh. fol. [The air appears on p.29 of the above collection].
MU. 1189^46

Overtures

Handel's overtures from all his operas & oratorios for violins &c. in 8 parts. [8 parts]. *Printed for I. Walsh: London*, [1760] fol. [Inscribed 'Fitzwilliam 1799'].
MU. 320 G^1, 320 H^1, 320 I^1, 320 J^1, 320 K^1, 320 L^1, 320 M^1, 320 N^1

Handel's overtures from all his operas and oratorios set for the harpsicord or organ. pp.277. *H. Wright: London*, [c.1785] fol. [The address in the imprint has been altered in MS. Inscribed 'Fitzwilliam 1801'].
MU. 355^1

The overtures to the ten anthems composed chiefly for the chapel of his Grace the late James Duke of Chandos . . . adapted for the organ, harpsichord, or piano forte. pp.25. *H. Wright: London*, [1787] fol. [Inscribed 'Fitzwilliam 1801'].
MU. 355^2

Songs, arias and cantatas
Cecilia volgi un sguardo. [Title supplied in MS]. [Score]. pp.168–93. [*John Walsh: London*, 1738 or later] fol. [Although advertised as a cantata, this was originally published at the end of Alexander's Feast. Inscribed 'Fitzwilliam 1801'].
MU. 514

Handel's songs selected from his latest ⟨ ⟩ oratorios. For the harpsicord, voice, hoboy or German flute ⟨Vol II–V⟩. The instrumental parts . . . may be had separate. [Volume nos. added in MS]. 5 vols. *I. Walsh: London*, [1749–59] obl. fol.
MU. 1239–43

Handel's songs, selected from his oratorios, for the harpsichord, voice, hautboy, or German flute, in 5 vols. Vol 1ˢᵗ ⟨–5ᵗʰ⟩. [Volume nos. added in MS]. *H. Wright: London*, [1786] obl. fol. [Inscribed 'Fitzwilliam 1805'].
MU. 1232–6

[12 Arias from 'Siroe', 'Ariodante', 'Il Pastor Fido', 'Teseo', 'Muzio Scevola', 'Creso', the last of which is a pasticcio to which Handel is not known to have contributed. Some arias are from plates used in 'Apollo's Feast']. pp.26. [Imperfect: wants title]. [*John Walsh: London*, c.1730] fol.
MU. 1356²

Vocal works
The vocal works composed by G.F. Handel, arranged for [i.e. with an accompaniment for] the organ or piano forte by Dʳ: John Clarke. 4 vols. *Button & Whitaker: London*, [1805–9] fol. [The arranger is also known as Clarke-Whitfeld. With a subscribers' list. With a frontispiece to each volume. Proposal for Clarke's 'Twelve Glees' loose in vol. 1].
MU. 439–42

3. Church music

Anthems: Chandos
The complete score of ten anthems composed chiefly for the chapel of his Grace the late James Duke of Chandos . . . in three volˢ. Vol.I ⟨–III⟩. 3 vols. *Wright & Wilkinson: London*, [1784] fol. [Each volume inscribed 'Fitzwilliam 1799'. With a frontispiece to each volume].
MU. 351 A–C

Anthem, in score, composed at Cannons, for his Grace the Duke of Chandos, between the year's 1718 & 1720. [12 anthems, each with this title-page, beginning: 'I will magnify thee', 'Let God arise', 'Let God arise' (a longer variant), 'Have mercy upon me', 'O come let us sing', 'O sing unto the Lord', 'My song shall be alway', 'As pants the hart', 'The Lord is my light', 'In the Lord put I my trust', 'O praise the Lord with one consent', 'O praise the Lord, ye angels' (not in fact a Chandos anthem)]. Nos.72–84 of Arnold's edition (see 1. above): [c.1790] fol.

[pp.43–6 of 'In the Lord put I my trust' are misplaced, at the beginning of 'O praise the Lord with one consent'].
MU. 460 A$^{1-6}$, 460 B$^{1-6}$

see above: selections and arrangements: overtures

Anthems: coronation
Handel's celebrated coronation anthems in score, for voices & instruments. Vol.I. pp.98. *William Randall: London*, [1769] fol. [Vol. II is 'The anthem . . . perform'd . . . at the funeral of . . . Queen Caroline'; vol. III is 'Te Deum et Jubilate' [Utrecht]; vol. IV is 'Handel's grand Dettingen Te Deum'. Inscribed 'Fitzwilliam 1799'. With a frontispiece].
MU. 396

Anthem. For the coronation of George II^D. Composed in the year, 1727. [Begins: 'Let thy hand be strengthened']. No.157 of Arnold's edition (see 1. above): [c.1795] fol.
MU. 1435

Anthem. For the coronation of George II^D. Composed in the year, 1727. [Begins: 'Zadok the priest']. No.158 of Arnold's edition (see 1. above): [c.1795] fol.
MU. 1436

Anthem. For the coronation of George II^D. Composed in the year, 1727. [Begins: 'My heart is inditing']. Nos.158–9 of Arnold's edition (see 1. above): [c.1795] fol.
MU. 1438

Anthem. For the coronation of George II^D. Composed in the year, 1727. [Begins: 'The King shall rejoice']. Nos.171–2 of Arnold's edition (see 1. above): [c.1796] fol.
MU. 1437

The Coronation anthem. [Keyboard arrangement of 'Zadok the priest']. Plate no.57 of 'The Piano-Forte Magazine'. pp.9. *Harrison & Co: London*, [c.1797] 8°.
MU. 501^5

Anthems: Dettingen
Anthem. For the victory at Dettingen. Composed in the year, 1743. [Begins: 'The King shall rejoice']. Nos.156–7 of Arnold's edition (see 1. above): [c.1795] fol.
MU. 1433^2

Anthems: funeral of Queen Caroline
The anthem which was perform'd . . . at the funeral of . . . Queen Caroline . . . Vol.II. [Begins: 'The ways of Zion do mourn']. [Score]. pp.54. *William Randall: London*, [1769] fol. [Vol. I is 'Handel's celebrated coronation anthems'; vol. III is 'Te Deum et Jubilate' [Utrecht]; vol. IV is 'Handel's grand Dettingen Te Deum'. Inscribed 'Fitzwilliam 1799'. With a frontispiece].
MU. 393

Anthem. For the funeral of Queen Caroline. Composed in the Year, 1737. Nos.155–6 of Arnold's edition (see 1. above): [c. 1795] fol.
MU. 1434

Anthems: wedding of Frederick Prince of Wales
Anthem. For the wedding of Frederick Prince of Wales and the Princess of Saxa-Gotha. Composed in the Year, 1736. [Begins: 'Sing unto God']. Nos.153–4 of Arnold's edition (see 1. above): [c. 1795] fol. [Inscribed 'Fitzwilliam 1801'].
MU. 352

Te Deum: Chandos
Te Deum, in score, composed for his Grace the Duke of Chandos (in the year 1719). Nos.14–15 of Arnold's edition (see 1. above): [1788] fol.
MU. 461³

Te Deum, in score, composed for his Grace the Duke of Chandos (in the year 1720). No.20 of Arnold's edition (see 1. above): [1788] fol.
MU. 461¹

Te Deum: Dettingen
Handel's grand Dettingen Te Deum in score. For voices and instruments . . . Vol. IV. pp.92. *William Randall: London*, [1769] fol. [Vol. 1 is 'Handel's celebrated coronation anthems'; vol. 11 is 'The anthem . . . perform'd . . . at the funeral of . . . Queen Caroline'; vol. 111 is 'Te Deum et Jubilate' [Utrecht]. Inscribed 'Fitzwilliam 1801'. With a frontispiece].
MU. 353

Te Deum, composed in the year 1743 for the victory at Dettingen. Nos.17–19 of Arnold's edition (see 1. above): [1788] fol.
MU. 461⁶

Te Deum: Queen Caroline
A short Te Deum, in score, composed for her late Majesty Queen Caroline, in the year 1737. No.13 of Arnold's edition (see 1. above): [1788] fol. [The work was more probably composed c.1714].
MU. 461²

[Another copy].
MU. 1433¹

Te Deum and Jubilate: Utrecht
Te Deum et Jubilate, for voices and instruments, perform'd before the Sons of the Clergy. [Utrecht Te Deum and Jubilate]. [Score]. pp.71. *Iohn Walsh: London*, [c.1731] fol.
MU. 476¹

Te Deum et Jubilate for voices and instruments, perform'd before the sons of the

clergy . . . Vol.III. [Score]. pp.71. *W. Randall: London*, [1769] fol. [Vol. I is 'Handel's celebrated coronation anthems'; vol. II is 'The anthem . . . perform'd . . . at the funeral of . . . Queen Caroline'; vol. IV is 'Handel's grand Dettingen Te Deum'. Inscribed 'Fitzwilliam 1799'. With a frontispiece].
MU. 398

A grand Te Deum, composed in the year 1713 for the Peace of Utrecht. Nos.15–16 of Arnold's edition (see 1. above): [1788] fol.
MU. 461[4]

A grand Jubilate, composed in the year 1713, for the Peace of Utrecht. Nos. 16–17 of Arnold's edition (see 1. above). [With introductory symphony supplied from no.20]: [1788] fol.
MU. 461[5]

4. Operas and other stage works

Admeto
The favourite songs in the opera call'd Admeto. [Words by N.F. Haym and P.A. Rolli, after A. Aureli]. [Score]. pp.36. *I. Walsh: London*, [c.1754] fol. [Inscribed 'R. Fitzwilliam 1767'].
MU. 385 A

Aetius
see below: Ezio

Agrippina
Agrippina, opera in tre atti, rappresentata . . . nell'anno 1709. [Words by V. Grimiani]. Nos.146–9 of Arnold's edition (see 1. above): [c.1795] fol. [Inscribed 'Fitzwilliam 1800'. With a frontispiece].
MU. 467

Alceste
Alcides, an English opera, in score. [Music for play by T. Smollett, with additional text by T. Morell]. Nos.84–5 of Arnold's edition (see 1. above): [c.1790] fol.
MU. 465[1]

The Alchemist
The music, in the Alchymist. [Music for play by B. Jonson]. No.64 of Arnold's edition (see 1. above): [c.1790] fol.
MU. 465[3]

Alcides
see above: Alceste

Alcina
Alcina. An opera. [Words by A. Marchi, after Ariosto]. [Score]. pp.91. Plate no.605. *I. Walsh: London*, [c.1737 or later] fol. [Inscribed 'R. Fitzwilliam 1767'].
MU. 391 A

see above: Twelve duets for two voices [selections and arrangements: duets]

Alessandro
A collection of the most celebrated songs in the opera of Alexander. [Words by P.A. Rolli, after O. Mauro]. ff.[27] [*Benjamin Cooke: London*, c.1727] fol.
MU. 1276

The Opera of Roxana, or Alexander in India. [Score]. pp.79. *Printed for & sould by I: Walsh: London*, [c.1748] fol. [Inscribed 'R. Fitzwilliam 1767'].
MU. 386 B

Alexander
see above: Alessandro

Ariadne
see below: Arianna

Arianna
Ariadne. An opera. [Words altered from P. Pariati]. [Score]. pp.88. Plate no.633. *I. Walsh: London*, [c.1750 or later] fol. [Inscribed 'R. Fitzwilliam 1767'].
MU. 382 A

Ariodante
The favourite songs in the opera call'd Ariodante. [Words by A. Salvi, after Ariosto]. [Score]. pp.25. *I. Walsh: London*, [1735] fol.
MU. 477 A²

see above: [12 Arias] [selections and arrangements: songs, arias and cantatas]

Arminio
Arminius. An opera. [Words altered from A. Salvi]. [Score]. pp.91. Plate no.605. *I. Walsh: London*, [1737] fol. [With a subscribers' list. Inscribed 'R. Fitzwilliam 1767'].
MU. 385 B

Arminius
see above: Arminio

Atalanta
[Atalanta. An opera]. [Words altered from B. Valeriani]. [Score]. pp.83. [Imperfect: wants title]. [*Walsh: London*, c.1755] fol. [Inscribed 'R. Fitzwilliam 1767'].
MU. 386 A

Berenice

Berenice. An opera. [Words by A. Salvi]. [Score]. pp.82. Plate no.619. *I. Walsh: London*, [1737] fol. [Inscribed 'R. Fitzwilliam 1767'].
MU. 391 B

Deidamia

Deidamia. An opera. [Words by P.A. Rolli]. [Score]. pp.89. *Jn°. Walsh: London*, [1741] fol. [Inscribed 'R. Fitzwilliam 1767'].
MU. 385 C

Ezio

Aetius. An opera. [Words from P. Metastasio, English words by S. Humphreys]. [Score]. pp.91. *I. Walsh: London*, [1732] fol. [Inscribed 'R. Fitzwilliam 1767'].
MU. 390 A

Faramondo

Faramondo. An opera. [Words altered from A. Zeno]. [Score]. pp.91. Plate no.633. *I. Walsh: London*, [1740] fol. [Inscribed 'R. Fitzwilliam 1767'].
MU. 384 A

Flavio

Flavius. An opera. [Text adapted by F. Haym from S. Ghigi, drawing on Corneille]. [Score]. pp.64. *Publish'd by the Author. Printed and Sold by I. Walsh: London*, [c.1731] fol. [Inscribed 'R. Fitzwilliam 1767'].
MU. 390 B

Floridante

Floridant. An opera. [Words by P.A. Rolli]. [Score]. pp.81. *Publish'd by the Author. Printed and Sold by I: Walsh . . . and In° & Ioseph Hare: London*, [c.1726 or later] fol. [Inscribed 'R. Fitzwilliam 1767'].
MU. 388 A

[All the aditional celebrated aires in the opera of Floridante]. ff.11. [Imperfect: wants title]. [*Rich^d. Meares: London*, c.1723] fol.
MU. 1356[4]

Giulio Cesare

Julius Caesar: an opera. [Words by N.F. Haym]. [Score]. pp.118. *Printed at Cluer's Printing-Office: London*, [1724] 8°.
MU. 1355

Venere bella per un instante. *A favourite song*. [From Giulio Cesare]. ff.[2]. [*London*, c.1725] fol.
MU. 1190[59]

[Giulio Cesare. Opera of Julius Caesar]. [Score]. pp.53. [Imperfect: wants title (given as supplied in MS, since no perfect copy of this issue is available)]. [*Walsh: London*, c.1750] fol. [Inscribed 'R. Fitzwilliam 1767'].
MU. 383 A

Giulio Cesare, opera in tre atti, rappresentata . . . nell'anno 1723. Nos.43–7 of Arnold's edition (see 1. above): [1789] fol.
MU. 469

Giustino
Justin. An opera. [Words altered from N. Beregani]. [Score]. pp.104. Plate no.609. *I. Walsh: London*, [1740 or later] fol. [Inscribed 'R. Fitzwilliam 1767'].
MU. 387 B

Hymen
see below: Imeneo

Imeneo
[Hymen]. [Score]. pp.32. [Imperfect: wants title (given as supplied in MS, since no perfect copy of this issue is available)]. [*Walsh: London*, c.1760] fol. [Inscribed 'R. Fitzwilliam 1767'].
MU. 384 B

[Another copy].
MU. 1356[1]

Julius Caesar
see above: Giulio Cesare

Justin
see above: Giustino

Lotario
[Lotharius. Opera]. [Words by A. Salvi]. [Score]. pp.45. [Imperfect: wants title (given as supplied in MS, since no perfect copy of this issue is available)]. [*Walsh: London*, c.1760] fol. [Inscribed 'R. Fitzwilliam 1767'].
MU. 381 A

Lotharius
see above: Lotario

Muzio Scevola
Aria nel Muzio Scaevola . . . Duetto nel Muzio Scaevola. [Words by P.A. Rolli]. [Score]. pp.6. [*Benjamin Goodison's Purcell subscription: London*, c.1787] fol.
MU. 341 B[7]

see above: [12 Arias] [selections and arrangements: songs, arias and cantatas]

Orlando
Orlando. An opera. [Words by G. Braccioli, after Ariosto. English words by
S. Humphreys]. [Score]. pp.90. Plate no.247. *I: Walsh: London*, [c.1750] fol.
[Inscribed 'R. Fitzwilliam 1767'].
MU. 389 A

Otho
see below: Ottone

Ottone
Otho. An opera. [Score]. pp.92. Plate no.223. *Publish'd by the Author. Printed and
Sold by I: Walsh: London*, [c.1740] fol. [Inscribed 'R. Fitzwilliam 1767'].
MU. 384 C

Partenope
Parthenope. An opera. [Words altered from S. Stampiglia]. [Score]. pp.99, [2].
[Imperfect: wants the additional song following p.99]. *I: Walsh . . . and Joseph
Hare: London*, [1731] fol. [Inscribed 'R. Fitzwilliam 1767'].
MU. 389 B

Il Pastor Fido
[A second collection of the most favourite songs in the opera call'd Pastor Fido].
[Words by G. Rossi, after B. Guarini]. pp.26: *pagination highly irregular*. Plate
no.283. [Imperfect: wants title]. [*In°. Walsh: London*, 1734] fol.
MU. 477 A^1

Masque, consisting of a prelude, airs, duettes, a chorus, and dances. Nos. 159–60
of Arnold's edition (see 1. above): [c. 1795] fol.
MU. 466^2

see above: [12 Arias] [selections and arrangements: songs, arias and cantatas]

Poro
Porus. An opera. [Words altered from P. Metastasio]. [Score]. pp.82. *I. Walsh:
London*, [1731] fol.
MU. 522

[Another issue]. Plate no.225 [on table of songs, not on title]. *I: Walsh: London*,
[c.1750] fol.
MU. 387 A

Ptolomy
see below: Tolomeo

Radamisto
Il Radamisto. Opera. [Words altered by N.F. Haym from an anonymous play
based on Tacitus]. [Score]. pp.121. *Publisht by the Author. Printed and Sold by*

Richard Meares . . . & by Christopher Smith: London, [1720] fol. [Inscribed 'R. Fitzwilliam 1767'].
MU. 388 B

Radamistus. An opera. [Score]. pp.71. Plate no.633. *I. Walsh: London*, [c.1740] fol.
MU. 475^1

Riccardo Primo
[Richard ye 1st. An Opera]. [In MS, in a printed frame]. [Words for the most part by P.A. Rolli]. [Score]. pp.23. [*I: Walsh: London*, c.1750] fol. [Inscribed 'R. Fitzwilliam 1767'].
MU. 381 B

Richard the First
see above: Riccardo Primo

Rinaldo
[Arie dell' opera di Rinaldo]. [Words by G. Rossi from A. Hill after Tasso]. [Score]. pp.67. [Imperfect: wants title]. [*Walsh and Hare: London*, 1711] fol. [Inscribed 'R. Fitzwilliam 1767'].
MU. 388 C

[Another issue]. *J: Walsh . . . & J: Hare: London*, [c.1714] fol.
MU. 475^2

Rodelinda
Rodelinda, an opera. [In MS, in a printed frame]. [Words by A. Salvi, adapted by N.F. Haym]. [Score]. pp.62. Plate no. 619. *I. Walsh: London*, [c.1750] fol.
MU. 1185^2

[Another copy]. [Imperfect: wants title (supplied in MS)].
MU. 382 B

Roxana
see above: Alessandro

Scipione
[Scipio. An opera]. [Words by P.A. Rolli after A. Zeno]. [Score]. pp.30. [Imperfect: wants title (supplied in MS)]. [*I: Walsh: London*, c.1745] fol. [Inscribed 'R. Fitzwilliam 1767'].
MU. 381 C

Serse
Xerxes, an opera. [Words altered by S. Stampiglia after N. Minati]. [Score]. pp.107. Plate no. 633. *I. Walsh: London*, [1738] fol. [Inscribed 'R. Fitzwilliam 1767'].
MU. 408

Siroe
[Siroe, an opera]. [Words altered from P. Metastasio by N.F. Haym]. [Score]. pp.46. [Imperfect: wants title (supplied in MS)]. [*I: Walsh: London*, c.1747] fol. [Inscribed 'R. Fitzwilliam 1767'].
MU. 381 D

[Another copy]. [Imperfect: wants title (supplied in MS)].
MU. 1185[1]

see above: [12 Arias] [selections and arrangements: songs, arias and cantatas]

Sosarme
Sosarmes, an opera. [Words by M. Noris. English words by S. Humphreys]. [Score]. pp.83. Plate no.457. *I. Walsh: London*, [c.1735] fol. [Inscribed 'R. Fitzwilliam 1767'].
MU. 390 C

Sosarme, opera in tre atti, rappresentata . . . nell'anno 1732. Nos.20–3 of Arnold's edition (see 1. above): [1788] fol.
MU. 470

Tamerlano
[Tamerlane, an opera]. [Words by A. Piovene, adapted by N.F. Haym]. [Score]. pp.31. [Imperfect: wants title (supplied in MS). Probably plate no. 633 or 619]. [*Walsh: London*, c.1750] fol. [Inscribed 'R. Fitzwilliam 1767'].
MU. 386 C

Teseo
Teseo, opera in cinque atti, rappresentata . . . nell'anno 1713. [Words by N.F. Haym, translated and altered from P. Quinault]. Nos 30–4 of Arnold's edition (see 1. above): [1788] fol.
MU. 468

see above: [12 Arias] [selections and arrangements: songs, arias and cantatas]

Tolomeo
Ptolomy, an opera. [Words by N.F. Haym]. [Score]. pp.65. Plate no. 633. *I. Walsh: London*, [c.1740–3] fol. [Inscribed 'R. Fitzwilliam 1767'].
MU. 383 B

Xerxes
see above: Serse

5. Oratorios, odes and other choral works

Acis and Galatea
Acis and Galatea. A mask, as it was originally compos'd, with the overture, recitativo's, songs, duets & choruses, for voices and instruments. [Words

attributed to J. Gay, drawing on J. Dryden, A. Pope and J. Hughes]. [Score]. pp.89. [Imperfect: wants pp.1–2]. *I. Walsh: London*, [1743 or later] fol.
MU. 1354

[Another issue]. pp.38: *pagination irregular. W. Randall: London*, [1769] fol. [Inscribed 'Fitzwilliam 1799'. With a frontispiece].
MU. 407

Acis and Galatea, a serenata, composed for the Duke of Chandois in the year 1720. Nos.28–30 of Arnold's edition (see 1. above): [1788] fol.
MU. 464²

The overture, songs, duett, and trio, in Acis & Galatea, a masque. [Score]. pp.43. Nos.88–9 of 'The Piano-Forte Magazine'. *Harrison, Cluse, & Co: London*, [1798] 8°.
MU. 501²

Alexander Balus
Alexander Balus. An oratorio. [Words by T. Morell]. [Score]. pp.94. *I. Walsh: London*, [1748] fol.
MU. 478

Alexander Balus, an oratorio, in score; composed in the year, 1747. Nos.160–4 of Arnold's edition (see 1. above): [c.1795] fol. [With a frontispiece].
MU. 471

Alexander's Feast
Alexander's Feast, or the Power of Musick. An ode wrote in honour of St. Cecilia by Mr: Dryden . . . With the recitativo's, songs, symphonys and chorus's for voices & instruments. [Words adapted from Dryden with additions by N. Hamilton]. [Score]. pp.158. Plate no.634. *I. Walsh: London*, [c.1750] fol.
MU. 1352

[Another issue]. pp.166. *William Randall: London*, [1769] fol. [Inscribed 'R. Fitzwilliam 1772'. With a frontispiece].
MU. 392

Alexanders Feast, an Ode on Saint Cecilia's Day, the words by Dryden, the musick composed in the year 1736. Nos.65–7 of Arnold's edition (see 1. above): [1790] fol.
MU. 464⁴

L'Allegro, il Penseroso, ed il Moderato
L'Allegro, il Penseroso, ed il Moderato. The words taken from Milton. [Words adapted from Milton with the addition of 'Il Moderato' by C. Jennens]. [Score]. pp.63. *I. Walsh: London*, [c.1741] fol.
MU. 1353²

L'Allegro, il Penseroso, ed il Moderato, the words taken from Milton . . . to which is added . . . additional songs. [Score]. pp.115, 19. *W^m: Randall: London,* [1770] fol. [Inscribed 'R. Fitzwilliam 1770'. With a frontispiece].
MU. 397

L'Allegro, il Pensieroso, ed il Moderato, the words taken from Milton; the musick composed in the year 1739. Nos.150–3 of Arnold's edition (see 1. above): [c.1795] fol.
MU. 459

L'Allegro, il Penseroso, ed il Moderato. For the voice, harpsichord and piano forte. Nos.212–14 of 'The Piano-Forte Magazine'. pp.58. *Harrison, Cluse & Co: London,* [1801] 8°.
MU. 501^4

Athalia
The most celebrated songs in the oratorio call'd Athalia. [Words adapted from J. Racine's 'Athalie' by S. Humphreys]. [Score]. Plate no.545. pp.29. *I. Walsh: London,* [c.1735] fol.
MU. 1350^2

Athalia, an oratorio or sacred drama in score. The music composed in the year 1733. Nos.1–4 of Arnold's edition (see 1. above): [1787] fol.
MU. 444

Belshazzar
Belshazzar. An oratorio. [Words by C. Jennens]. pp.86. *I. Walsh: London,* [1745] fol.
MU. 1351

Belshazzar. An oratorio in score. pp.232. *Wright & Co: London,* [c.1783] fol. [With a subscribers' list. Bookplate of John Randall, who first sang the title role in 'Esther'. Inscribed 'Fitzwilliam 1801'. With a frontispiece].
MU. 346

Belshazzar, a sacred oratorio, in score, composed in the year, 1743. Nos.68–72 of Arnold's edition (see 1. above): [1790] fol.
MU. 450

The Choice of Hercules
The complete score of the Choice of Hercules. [Text probably adapted by T. Morell from a poem attributed to R. Lowth]. pp.85. *Willm: Randall: London,* [1773] fol. [Inscribed 'Fitzwilliam 1799'. With a frontispiece].
MU. 400

The Choice of Hercules, in score; composed in the year, 1745. Nos.55–6 of Arnold's edition (see 1. above): [1789] fol.
MU. 466^1

[Another copy].
MU. 472²

Deborah
The most celebrated songs in the oratorio call'd Deborah. [Words by S. Humphreys. Only the first three of the seven numbers are in fact from 'Deborah'. Nos.4–5 are from 'Esther', nos.6–7 from 'Athalia']. [Score]. pp.21. Plate nos.544–5. *I. Walsh: London*, [c.1735] fol.
MU. 1350¹

Deborah. An oratorio in score. pp.209, 4. *Wright & Co: London*, [c.1784] fol. [With a subscribers' list. Bookplate of Charles Wesley the younger. Inscribed 'Fitzwilliam 1801'. With a frontispiece].
MU. 342

Esther
Esther. An oratorio. [Words probably adapted from J. Racine's 'Esther' by A. Pope and J. Arbuthnot, with additional words by S. Humphreys]. [Score]. pp.94: *pagination irregular*. *I. Walsh: London*, [c.1751 or later] fol.
MU. 1253

Esther. An oratorio in score. pp.148, 94. [Imperfect: wants the second pagination sequence]. *Wright & Co: London*, [c.1783] fol. [With a subscribers' list. Inscribed 'Fitzwilliam 1799'. With a frontispiece].
MU. 343

Esther, a sacred oratorio, in score, composed in the year, 1720. Nos.135–9 of Arnold's edition (see 1. above): [c.1794] fol.
MU. 443

Hercules
Hercules in score. [Words by T. Broughton]. pp.97. *I. Walsh: London*, [1745] fol.
MU. 474¹

Hercules. An oratorio, in score, composed in the year 1744. Nos.34–7 of Arnold's edition (see 1. above): [c.1788–9] fol.
MU. 472¹

Israel in Egypt
Israel in Egypt. An oratorio, in score, as it was originally composed. [Words selected from the Bible and B.C.P. Psalms, probably by the composer]. pp.281. *Willᵐ: Randall: London*, [1771] fol. [With a subscribers' list. Inscribed 'Fitzwilliam 1799'. With a frontispiece].
MU. 403

Israel in Egypt, a sacred oratorio, in score, composed in the year 1738. Nos.92–8 of Arnold's edition (see 1. above): [c.1791] fol.
MU. 446

Jephtha

Jephtha, an oratorio in score . . . with . . . additional quintetto. [Words by T. Morell]. pp.208. *Willm: Randall: London*, [1770] fol. [With a subscribers' list. Inscribed 'Fitzwilliam 1799'. With a frontispiece].
MU. 394

Jephtha, a sacred oratorio. In score, composed in the year, 1751. Nos.116–21 of Arnold's edition (see 1. above): [c.1792] fol.
MU. 456

Joseph

Joseph, an oratorio in score. [Words by J. Miller]. pp.215. *H. Wright: London*, [c.1785] fol. [With a subscribers' list. Inscribed 'Fitzwilliam 1801'. With a frontispiece].
MU. 344

Joseph, a sacred oratorio; in score, composed in the year, 1746. Nos.107–11 of Arnold's edition (see 1. above): [c.1792] fol.
MU. 449

Joshua

Joshua, an oratorio in score as it was originally composed. [Words by T. Morell]. pp.203. *W^m: Randall: London*, [1774] fol. [With a subscribers' list. Inscribed 'Fitzwilliam 1799'. With a frontispiece. Proposal for 'Esther' subscription inside back cover].
MU. 402

[Another issue]. *H: Wright: London*, [c.1785] fol. [With a subscribers' list. With a frontispiece].
MU. 1381

O had I Jubal's lyre . . . in Joshua. ff.[2]. [*London*, c.1770] fol.
MU. 1197^7

Judas Maccabaeus

Judas Macchabaeus. An oratorio. [Words by T. Morell]. [Score]. pp.73: *final page misnumbered 48. I. Walsh: London*, [c.1749] fol.
MU. 1349^1

Judas Macchabaeus. An oratorio, in score as it was originally perform'd . . . with additional alterations. pp.208. *William Randall: London*, [1769] fol. [Inscribed 'Fitzwilliam 1799'. With a subscribers' list. With a frontispiece].
MU. 405

Judas Macchabaeus, a sacred oratorio, in score, with all the additional alterations, composed in the year 1746. Nos.39–43 of Arnold's edition (see 1. above): [1789] fol.
MU. 452

Judas Maccabaeus, a sacred oratorio. For the voice, and piano-forte. Nos.165–8 of 'The Piano-Forte Magazine'. pp.83. *Harrison, Cluse & Co: London*, [c.1800] 8°.

MU. 501³

Wise men flattring may decieve you. *The additional favourite song in Judas Macchabaeus.* ff.[2]. [*London*, c.1760] fol.

MU. 1197⁵

Messiah

Songs in Messiah, an oratorio. [Words adapted from the Bible by C. Jennens]. [Score]. pp.70. *I. Walsh: London*, [c.1764] fol.

MU. 856

Messiah, an oratorio in score as it was originally perform'd . . . To which are added his original alterations. pp.188, 35. *Mess.ʳˢ Randall & Abell: London*, [c.1769] fol. [With a subscribers' list. Inscribed 'Fitzwilliam 1799'. With a frontispiece].

MU. 399

[Another issue]. *H. Wright: London*, [c.1785–1800] fol.

MU. 1382

Messiah, a sacred oratorio, in score, with all the additional alterations, composed in the year 1741. Nos. 9–13 of Arnold's edition (see 1. above): [1787–8] fol.

MU. 447

The overture, songs and recitatives in the Messiah: a sacred oratorio. [Score]. Nos.84–5 of 'The Piano-Forte Magazine'. pp.42. *Harrison & Co: London*, [c.1798] 8°.

MU. 501¹

The sublime oratorio of the Messiah . . . For the voice & piano forte, with the choruses in score. pp.138. *G. Walker: London*, [1810ᵂᴹ] fol.

MU. 1179

Occasional Oratorio

The Occasional Oratorio. [Words adapted from J. Milton, E. Spenser and others by T. Morell. The additional song following p.71 is 'Thou shalt bring them in' from 'Israel in Egypt']. [Score]. pp.71, [3]. *I. Walsh: London*, [c.1748] fol.

MU. 1349²

The Occasional Oratorio in score. pp.176. *Wright & Co: London*, [1784] fol. [With a subscribers' list. Inscribed 'Fitzwilliam 1801'. With a frontispiece].

MU. 347

The Occasional Oratorio, in score, composed in the year 1745. Nos.99–105 of Arnold's edition (see 1. above): [c.1791] fol.

MU. 451

Ode for St Cecilia's Day
The complete score of the Ode for St Cecilia's Day, the words by M^r. Dryden, pp.71. *William Randall: London*, [1771] fol. [Inscribed 'Fitzwilliam 1799'. With a frontispiece].
MU. 406

Ode on S^r. Cecilia's Day; the words by Dryden, set to musick in the year, 1736. Nos. 105–6 of Arnold's edition (see 1. above): [c.1792] fol.
MU. 464^3

Ode for the birthday of Queen Anne
An ode, or serenata, for the birth day of Queen Ann, composed in the year 1713. No.54 of Arnold's edition (see 1. above): [1789] fol.
MU. 464^1

La Resurrezione
La Resurrezione, oratorio sacro, in partizione. [Words by C.S. Capece]. Nos.169–71 of Arnold's edition (see 1. above): [c.1796] fol.
MU. 458

Samson
Samson. An oratorio. The words taken from Milton. [Words adapted, principally from 'Samson Agonistes', by N. Hamilton]. [Score]. pp.178. *I. Walsh: London*, [c.1763] fol.
MU. 1348

Samson, an oratorio, in score, as it was originally compos'd. pp.185, 30. *Willm: Randall: London*, [1769] fol. [Inscribed 'Fitzwilliam 1799'. With a frontispiece].
MU. 404

Samson, a sacred oratorio, in score; the words taken from Milton, the musick composed in the year 1742. Nos.49–54 of Arnold's edition (see 1. above): [1789] fol.
MU. 448

Saul
Saul, an oratorio in score as it was originally composed . . . with . . . additional alterations. [Words by C. Jennens]. pp.250, 15. *W^m: Randall: London*, [1773] fol. [With a subscribers' list. Inscribed 'Fitzwilliam 1799'. With a frontispiece].
MU. 401

Saul, a sacred oratorio, in score, composed in the year, 1740. Nos.111–16 of Arnold's edition (see 1. above): [c.1792] fol.
MU. 445

Semele
Semele. [Words altered from W. Congreve]. [Score]. pp.85. *I. Walsh: London*, [1744] fol.
MU. 474^2

Semele, a dramatic performance in score, the words altered from Congreve, the musick composed in the year 1743. Nos.24–8 of Arnold's edition (see 1. above): [1788] fol. [Inscribed 'Fitzwilliam 1801'].
MU. 345

[Another copy].
MU. 465²

Solomon

Solomon. An oratorio. [Words attributed to T. Morell]. [Score]. pp.80. *I. Walsh: London*, [1749] fol.
MU. 1346²

Solomon. An oratorio in score. pp.326. *H: Wright: London*, [c.1787] fol. [Inscribed 'Fitzwilliam 1799'. With a frontispiece].
MU. 348

Solomon, a sacred oratorio, in score, with all the additional alterations, composed in the year, 1749. Nos.85–92 of Arnold's edition (see 1. above): [c.1790] fol.
MU. 453

Susanna

Susanna. An oratorio. [Author of words unknown]. [Score]. pp.94. *I. Walsh: London*, [1749] fol.
MU. 1347

Susanna. An oratorio in score. pp.196, 3. *Wright & Co: London*, [1784] fol. [With a subscribers' list. Inscribed 'Fitzwilliam 1801'. With a frontispiece].
MU. 349

Susanna, a sacred oratorio. In score, composed in the year, 1743. Nos.131–5 of Arnold's edition (see 1. above): [c.1793] fol.
MU. 454

Theodora

Theodora. An oratorio. [Words by T. Morell]. [Score]. pp.93. *I. Walsh: London*, [1751] fol. [Inscribed 'W. Jackson', perhaps the composer and organist William Jackson of Exeter, or his namesake of Masham].
MU. 1346¹

Theodora, an oratorio in score. pp.200. *H: Wright: London*, [1787] fol. [With a subscribers' list. Inscribed 'Fitzwilliam 1801'. With a frontispiece].
MU. 350

Theodora, an oratorio, in score, composed in the year 1750. Nos.5–8 of Arnold's edition (see 1. above): [1787] fol.
MU. 455

Triumph of Time and Truth
The Triumph of Time and Truth, an oratorio. [Score]. pp.67. *I. Walsh: London,*
[1757] fol. [With label of the cellist Charles Jane Ashley].
MU. 473

The Triumph of Time and Truth, an oratorio, in score; composed in the year,
1751. Nos.165–9 of Arnold's edition (see 1. above): [c.1795] fol.
MU. 457

6. Instrumental works

Capricio pour le clavecin
Capricio pour le clavecin . . . Opera terza. No.5. *Imprimé aux dépens de Gerhard
Fredrik Witvogel: Amsterdam,* [c.1732] s.sh. fol. [The opus number is the
publisher's own].
MU. 433², bound with MU. MS 78

Concertante, in nine parts
see below: select harmony

Concerti grossi
[Op. 3]. Concerti grossi con due violini e violoncello di concertino obligati e due
altri violini, viola e basso di concerto grosso . . . Opera terza. [9 parts]. *I. Walsh:
London,* [c.1752] fol. [Inscribed 'Fitzwilliam 1799' in violin 2 only].
MU. 320 E¹, 320 F¹, 320 G³, 320 H³, 320 I³, 320 J³, 320 K³, 320 M³, 320 N³

[Op. 6]. Twelve grand concertos for violins &c. in seven parts . . . Opera sexta. 3d
edition. [7 parts]. *I. Walsh: London,* [1746] fol.
MU. 320 G², 320 H², 320 I², 320 J², 320 K², 320 M², 320 N²

[Op. 6]. Twelve grand concertos, in score; composed in the year, 1737. Nos. 60–4
of Arnold's edition (see 1. above): [1789] fol.
MU. 463

Concertos for organ or harpsichord
[Op. 4]. Six concertos for the harpsicord or organ. [Keyboard only]. pp.48.
Printed for & sold by I. Walsh: London, [1738] fol.
MU. 1353¹

[Another issue]. [c.1750–5] fol. [Inscribed 'R. Fitzwilliam 1768'. This is the first
item in a volume assembled by the Founder (see 'Numerical list')].
MU. 319¹

[Second set]. A second set of six concertos for the harpsicord or organ.
[Keyboard only]. pp.61. *Printed for I. Walsh: London,* [c.1740–60] fol.
MU. 319²

[Second set]. Two concertos for the organ and harpsicord with the instrumental parts for violins, hoboys, &c. in seven parts . . . 2^d. set. [Keyboard only]. pp.18. I. *Walsh: London*, [c.1761] fol.
MU. 319^4

[Third set. Op. 7]. A third set of six concertos for the harpsichord or organ. [Keyboard only]. pp.51. I. *Walsh: London*, [1761] fol.
MU. 319^3

Fantasias
Fantasie pour le clavecin . . . Opera quinta. No. 11. *Imprime aux depens de Gerhard Fredrik Witvogel: Amsterdam*, [1732] s.sh. fol. [The opus number is the publisher's own].
MU. 433^4, bound with MU. MS 78

Fantasia pour le clavecin . . . Opera V. pp.7–11. [*Benjamin Goodison's Purcell subscription: London*, c.1787] fol. [Also advertised under the title 'Lessons by Handel'. Includes a capriccio and minuet].
MU. 341 B^6

Fugues
Six fugues or voluntarys for the organ or harpsicord . . . Troisieme ovarage. pp.23. Plate no. 543. I. *Walsh: London*, [c.1735 or later] obl. fol.
MU. 316^3

Lessons by Handel
see above: Fantasia pour le clavecin . . . Opera V

Music for the royal fireworks
The Musick for the royal fireworks, performed in the year 1749. No. 24 of Arnold's edition (see 1. above): [1788] fol.
MU. 462^5

Preludio et allegro
Preludio et allegro pour le clavecin . . . Opera quarta. No.10. *Imprime aux depens de Gerhard Fredrik Witvogel: Amsterdam*, [1732] s.sh. fol. [The opus number is the publisher's own].
MU. 433^3, bound with MU. MS 78

Select harmony
[Select Harmony. Fourth Collection. No. 1]. Concertante, in nine parts, for two violins and a violoncello obligati, composed in the year 1738. [Score]. Nos.98–9 of Arnold's edition (see 1. above): [c.1791] fol.
MU. 462^3

Sonatas

[Op.1]. Solos for a German flute, a hoboy or violin with a thorough bass for the harpsicord or bass violin. pp.63. *Iohn Walsh: London*, [c.1732] fol.
MU. 1178

[Op. 2]. VI Sonatas à deux violons, deux haubois ou deux flutes traversieres & basse continue . . . Second ouvrage. [3 parts]. Plate no. 408. *John Walsh: London*, [c.1750] fol. [Inscribed 'Fitzwilliam 1799' in violin 1. This is the first item of a set of sonatas assembled by the Founder (see 'Numerical list')].
MU. 318 A^1, 318 B^1, 318 D^1

[Op. 2]. Six sonatas, for two violins, two hautboys, or two German flutes, & a violoncello, first published at Amsterdam 1731. [Score]. Nos.47–8 of Arnold's edition (see 1. above): [1789] fol.
MU. 462^1

[Op. 5]. Seven sonatas or trios for two violins or German flutes with a thorough bass for the harpsicord or violoncello . . . Opera quinta. [3 parts]. Plate no. 653. *I. Walsh: London*, [1739 or later] fol.
MU. 318 A^2, 318 B^2, 318 D^2

[Op. 5]. Seven sonatas or trios, for two violins or two German flutes and a violoncello, composed & published in the year 1739. [Score]. Nos.48–9 of Arnold's edition (see 1. above): [1789] fol.
MU. 462^2

Sonata pour le clavecin . . . Opera seconda. No.4. *Imprime aux dépens de Gerhard Fredrik Witvogel: Amsterdam*, [1732] s.sh. fol. [The opus number is the publisher's own].
MU. 433^1, bound with MU. MS 78

Suites

Suites de pieces pour le clavecin . . . Premier volume. pp.94. [Imperfect: wants pp.42–3 (supplied in MS)]. Plate no.112. *Printed for the Author . . . engraved and printed at Cluer's printing-office: London*, [c.1725–7] obl. fol. [Inscribed 'Fitzwilliam 1781'].
MU. 315

Suites de pieces pour le clavecin . . . Second volume. pp.83. Plate no.490. *John Walsh: London*, [c.1733] obl. fol.
MU. 316^2, bound with MU. MS 79

Suites de pieces pour le clavecin . . . [vol. 1]. pp.94. Plate no.490. *John Walsh: London*, [c.1736 or later] obl. fol. [Inscribed 'R. Fitzwilliam 1767'].
MU. 316^1, bound with MU. MS 79

Suites de pieces pour le clavecin . . . Premier livre. pp.75. *Chez Mr. Le clerc le cadet . . . Le Sr. Le clerc . . . Mme. Boivin: Paris*, [c.1740] fol. [Inscribed 'R. Fitzwilliam

1764'. This is the first item in a volume assembled by the Founder (see 'Numerical list')].
MU. 317¹

Suites de pieces pour le clavecin . . . Deuxieme livre. pp.47. *Chez Mr. Le clerc le cadet . . . Le Sr. Le clerc . . . Mme. Boivin: Paris*, [c.1740] fol.
MU. 317²

Water Music
The Famous Water Peice. pp.[2]. [1 part only]. [*Daniel Wright: London*, 1733] fol. [With typed notes by Otto Deutsch].
MU. 506

Handel's celebrated Water Musick compleat. Set for the harpsicord. To which is added, two favourite minuets, with variations for the harpsicord, by Geminiani. pp.27. [Imperfect: wants p.27]. *I. Walsh: London*, [1743] fol.
MU. 477 B

The Celebrated Water Musick, in score, composed in the year 1716. Nos.23–4 of Arnold's edition (see 1. above): [1788] fol.
MU. 462⁴

7. Appendix

see L'ALLEGRO

see APOLLO'S FEAST

see ARIANNA

see FLORIDANTE

see NON

see O, O my treasure

see OTTONE

see POCKET

see POW'RFUL

see PRATT (J.)

see TU

HAPPY

Happys the love that meets return. *Mary Scot*. [Song, the words by A. Ramsay]. [*London*, c.1725] s.sh. fol.
MU. 1190⁴⁷

HARGRAVE (H.) *see* CLARI (G.C.M.)

HARINGTON (H.) *see* AMUSEMENT; *see* TURN

HARK

Hark away tis yᵉ merry ton'd horn *see* CAREY (H.), [Cephalus and Procris]

Hark, hark o'er the plains. *A new song.* [*London*, c.1746] s.sh. fol.
MU. 1189²⁸

HARMONIC SOCIETY OF CAMBRIDGE

A collection of glees and rounds, for three, four and five voices. Composed by the members of the Harmonic Society of Cambridge, and publish'd by William Dixon. pp.73. *Engrav'd and printed by the Editor: Cambridge,* [1796] obl. fol. [With a subscribers' list].
MU. 1383

HARPSICHORD MASTER

The second book of the harpsichord master containing a choice collection of lessons for the harpsichord or spinnett . . . by Dʳ: Blow, Mʳ: Courtivall, Mʳ: Clark, Mʳ. Barrett & Mʳ Crofftts, to which is added plain & easy rules for learners. ff. 4, 25. *I. Walsh: London,* 1700 obl. 4°.
MU. 1469

HARRISON (SAMUEL)

Glee, 'Oh Nanny! wilt thou gang with me'. Harmonized for four voices by Mʳ. Harrison . . . Dedicated . . . to the Right Honourable the Directors of the Concert of Antient Music. pp.6. *Printed for S. Harrison, and published by R. Birchall: London,* [c.1795] obl. fol. [Inscribed 'Fitzᵐ. 1803. from the Author'].
MU. 438, bound as MU. MS 166 C

HART (PHILIP)

Fugues for the organ or harpsichord: with lessons for the harpsichord. pp.50. *Printed by Tho: Cross for the Author: London,* [1704] obl. fol. [Inscribed 'R. Fitzwilliam 1771'].
MU. 417

HART (WILLIAM)

My time, O ye muses. *A song, the words taken from the Spectator.* [*London*, c.1725] s.sh. fol.
MU. 1190¹³

HASSE (JOHANN ADOLPH)

A favourite concerto . . . set for the harpsicord. [Op.4. No.1]. pp.5. *Peter Thompson: London*, [c.1755] fol.
MU. 1326[2]

The famous Salve Regina. [Score]. pp.14. *I: Walsh: London*, [1740] fol. [Inscribed 'Jos: Corfe', a singer at the Handel Commemoration and organist of Salisbury Cathedral].
MU. 515[1]

see THE SUMMER'S TALE

HAWDOWN (MATTHIAS)

So brightly sweet fair Nanny's eyes. *A new song set to musick by M: Hawdon.* [*London*, c.1755] s.sh. fol.
MU. 1189[21]

HAWES (W.) *see* MORLEY (T.), Triumphs of Oriana; *see* WEBER (C.M. VON), Der Freischütz

HAWKINS (SAMUEL)

Whilst Strephon gaz'd on Cloe's eyes. [Song]. [*London*, c.1720] s.sh. fol.
MU. 1190[84]

HAYDEN (GEORGE)

As I saw fair Clora. *A two part song.* [*London*, c.1715] s.sh. fol.
MU. 1197[15]

Turn fair Clora. *Damon and Clora. A two part song.* As I saw fair Clora. *A two part song.* ff.[2]. [c.1790] fol.
MU. 1211[13–14]

see TURN

HAYDN (FRANZ JOSEPH)

[The Creation]. The marvellous work, With verdure clad. Two favourite airs . . . in Haydn's celebrated oratorio of the Creation. pp.20. Plate no.239 of 'The Piano-Forte Magazine'. *Harrison, Cluse & Co: London* [c.1802] 8°.
MU. 501[6]

[Six sonates. Pour le clavecin ou le piano forte . . . Œuvre XIV]. pp.32.

[Imperfect: wants all before p.5 and pp.17–20]. Plate no.390. *Chés Jean Julien Hummel: Berlin and Amsterdam*, [1778] fol.
MU. 1192³

see PRATT (J.)

see THOMSON(G.)

HE THAT LOVES *see* STEVENS (R.J.S.), Unfading Beauty

HEAR ME MOURNING PRINCESS *see* DIDO AND ENEAS

HELLENDAAL (PIETER)

Eight solos for the violoncello with a thorough bass . . . dedicated to Mʳ. John Anderson . . . Op. Vᵗᵃ. pp.48. *Printed and sold at the Author's house: Cambridge*, [c.1770] fol.
MU. 1246

Tweedledum and Tweedledee. A chearful glee for four voices. [Words attributed to J. Byrom]. pp.7. *Printed & sold by the Author & Son: Cambridge*, [c.1780] fol.
MU. 1199

HINE (WILLIAM)

[Harm]onia Sacra Glocestriensis. [Or] select anthems for 1, 2, & 3 voices, and a Te-Deum and Jubilate, together with a voluntary for the organ. pp.53. [Imperfect: title torn]. [*London*, 1731] fol. [Inscribed 'R. Fitzwilliam 1771'. With a subscribers' list].
MU. 380 A

HOOK (JAMES)

A favourite concerto for the harpsichord with twelve variations to Lovely Nancy. Humbly dedicated to the Right Honᵇˡᵉ. Lord Tyrawly. [Op.5]. pp.15. *Welcker: London*, [1769] obl. fol.
MU. 1404²

Hook's Original Christmas Box. Vol. III . . . for juvenile amusement . . . dedicated to Miss Columbine . . . Op.86. pp.14. *Bland & Wellers: London*, [1798] fol.
MU. 1211¹²

see HANDEL (G.F.), Six grand chorusses [selections and arrangements: chorusses]

HORNPIPE

Miss Dawson's hornpipe, with variations. [*London*, c.1770] s.sh. fol.
MU. 1197⁹

HORSLEY (W.) *see* CALLCOTT (J.W.), A collection of glees, canons, and catches

HOW

How blest has my time been. *Jessy, or the Happy Pair*. [*London*, c.1750] s.sh. fol.
MU. 1197⁶⁶

How can you lovely Nancy. *Lovely Nancy, with variations*. [Song]. [*London*, c.1760] s.sh. fol.
MU. 1197⁷⁹

How charming Celia lookt last night. *A Song by a gentleman*. [*London*, c.1730] s.sh. fol.
MU. 1190⁷⁰

How pleas'd within my native bow'rs *see* WOOD (D.)

How pleasing is beauty *see* BAILDON (J.), [The Laurel . . . Book I. No.3]

How sweet are the flowers *see* THE SACRIFICE OF IPHIGENIA

HOWARD (SAMUEL)

The Amorous Goddess . . . for the voice, harpsichord, and violin. pp.14. *Harrison and Co: London*, [c.1785] obl. fol.
MU. 1375

The Generous Confession. [Song, begins: 'Too plain dear youth these tell-tale eyes']. Plate XXXIX of 'The Agreeable Amusement'. [*London*, c.1750] s.sh. fol.
MU. 1189³⁰

The Lass of St. Osyth. [Song, begins: 'At St. Osyth by the mill'. Words by Sir Charles Hanbury Williams]. [Imperfect: leaf torn]. *London*, [c.1740] s.sh. fol.
MU. 1189⁵

The Lass of the Hill. [Song, begins: 'At the brow of a hill a fair shepherdess dwelt'. Words by Mary Jones]. Plate XXI of 'The Agreeable Amusement'. [*London*, c.1750] s.sh. fol.
MU. 1189¹⁶

Myra. [Song, begins: 'Say Myra, why is gentle love'. Words by Lord Lyttelton]. [*London*, c.1745] s.sh. fol.
MU. 1189³

Why heaves my fond bosom? [Song]. [*London*, c.1744] s.sh. fol.
MU. 1197^{51}

Ye chearful virgins. A glee . . . The air by D^r. Howard. Harmonized and made a
duetto by R.J.S. Stevens. pp.3. *London*, [c.1790] obl. fol.
MU. 1250^8

[Another issue]. [c.1800]
MU. 1230^{12}

see THE SUMMER'S TALE; *see* WHERE, Where shall Celia fly

HUDSON (JOHN)

The Impartial Lover. On a Lady at Bromley. The words by a gentleman. [Song,
begins: 'When first I saw fair Fanny's eyes']. [*London*, c.1750] s.sh. fol.
MU. 1189^{39}

HUMMEL (JOHANN NEPOMUK)

[Op.12. No.1]. Grand trio concertante, for piano forte, violin & violoncello.
[Piano only]. Plate no.1778. *Cramer, Beale and Co: London*, [c.1850] fol.
MU. 1380

[Op.83]. Grand trio, per il piano-forte, violino e violoncello, concertante . . .
dedicato all stimatissimo Sig^{re}. J.B. Cramer. [3 parts]. *Presso T. Boosey & Co. . . . e
. . . presso C.F. Peters: In Londra . . . e Lipsia*, [1817^{WM}] fol.
MU. 1379

HUMPHRIES (J.S.)

XII Sonatas, for two violins; with a through bass for the harpsichord . . . Opera
prima. [3 parts]. *I: Walsh: London*, [c.1736] fol.
MU. 1170

HYDASPES *see* IDASPE

I

I am confirm'd *see* WEBBER (J.), Inconstancy in woman

I come my fairest treasure *see* NON

I have a silent sorrow here *see* CAVENDISH (G.)

I have rambled I own it. Sung . . . at Vauxhall. [*London*, c.1750] s.sh. fol.
MU. 1197^{31}

I sigh and lament me in vain *see* GIORDANI (T.)

IDASPE

[Songs in the new opera, call'd Hydaspes, *etc*]. [Music by F. Mancini, words by G.P. Candi]. pp.72. [Imperfect: wants title]. [*I. Walsh . . . P. Randall . . . and I. Hare: London*, [1710] fol.
MU. 1281

The instrumental musick in the opera of Hydaspes, for two violins wth. a thorough bass. The song part fitted to a hoboy, German flute or violin. The hoboy performing the song part forms a compleat concert as if a voice accompany'd. [3 parts only]. *I: Walsh . . . and I: Hare: London*, [c.1717] fol.
MU. 1422 A

see BABELL (W.), The 3^d. [altered in MS to 4th] book of the ladys entertainment

IF

If I live to grow old. *The Old Man's Wish*. [Song, words by W. Pope]. [*London*, c.1725] s.sh. fol.
MU. 1197^45

If love's a sweet passion *see* BAILDON (J.), [The Laurel . . . Book I. No.2]

IN

In airy dreams soft fancy flies. *A favourite song, adapted for the harpsichord, Ger: flute, violin, & guitar*. pp.3. *J. Preston: London*, [c.1785] fol.
MU. 1211^30

In diesen heil'gen Hallen *see* MOZART (W.A.), Within these sacred bowers

In good King Charls' golden days. *The Vicar of Bray, set for German flute*. [*London*, c.1750] s.sh. fol. [Underlay altered in contemporary MS].
MU. 1197^82

In infancy our hopes & fears. *Sung . . . at Vauxhall*. [From T.A. Arne's 'Artaxerxes'. Words translated from Metastasio by the composer]. [*London*, c.1775] s.sh. fol.
MU. 1197^10

In London stands a famous pile. *The prophetick ballad . . . upon Exchange Alley bubbles. To the tune of London is a fine town*. [Words by E. Ward]. [*London*, 1720] s.sh. fol.
MU. 1190^16

In love shou'd there meet a fond pair *see* BARNARD

In peace love tunes the shepherd's reed *see* ATTWOOD (T.)

In summers solstace. *Collinda's Retreat*. [Song]. [*London*, c.1730] s.sh. fol.
MU. 1190^12

In the dead of the night *see* THE WEDDING DAY

In these groves *see* CAREY (H.)

In vain to keep *see* TENDUCCI (G.F.)

In vain you tell *see* GEMINIANI (F.), The Tender Lover

INKLE AND YARICO

Ah will no change of clime. *M^rs^. Billington's additional song, introduced in the opera of Inkle and Yarico, with the harp accompaniment by M^r^. Meyer Junr.* [An adaptation of 'Nel cor più non mi sento', from G. Paisiello's 'La Molinara']. pp.4. *Longman and Broderip: London,* [c.1795] fol. [Inscribed 'A.M. Jeffery': later Mrs R.J.S. Stevens].
MU. 1287[8]

INSPIR'D

Inspir'd with Venus sweet alarms. *The Amorous Youth. A New Song.* [*London,* c.1725] s.sh. fol.
MU. 1190[35]

IRISH

The Irish Musical Repository: a choice selection of esteemed Irish songs, adapted for the voice, violin and German flute. pp.288. *B. Crosby & Co: London,* [c.1810] 12°. [With a frontispiece].
MU. 1206

JACKSON (JOSEPH)

Sally of the dale. [Song, begins: 'Leave your Parnassus sacred nine']. [*London,* c.1740] s.sh. fol.
MU. 1189[22]

JACKSON (WILLIAM)

Elegies . . . Opera terza. pp.41. *Printed for the Author, Sold at M^rs^. Johnson's: London,* [c.1762] fol.
MU. 1213

Love in thine eyes. *A favorite canzonet.* [No. 7 of 'A second set of twelve canzonets . . . Opera XIII']. pp.4. *A. Bland & Weller's Music Warehouse: London,* [c.1800] fol.
MU. 1211[18]

Susannah. [Song, begins: 'Twas when the seas were roaring']. *J. Phillips:* [*London,* c.1760] s.sh. fol.
MU. 1197[13]

JACQUET DE LA GUERRE (ELISABETH CLAUDE)

Cephale et Procris. Tragedie. [Score]. pp.xxxii, 148, [3]. *Par Christophe Ballard: Paris*, 1694 fol. [Inscribed 'R. Fitzwilliam 1767'].
MU. 340

THE JEALOUS DON *see* STORACE (S.), The Pirates

JOHN COME KISS ME NOW *see* THE CARMAN'S WHISTLE

JONES (RICHARD)

Suits or setts of lessons for the harpsicord or spinnet. Consisting of great variety of movements, as preludes, aires, toccats, all'mands, jiggs, corrents, borre's, sarabands, gavots, minuets. pp.58. Plate no. 196. *I: Walsh, London*, [1732] fol. [Inscribed 'R. Fitzwilliam 1768'].
MU. 488⁵, bound with MU. MS 208

JONES (T.) *see* MUSIC

JUPITER AND EUROPA

[3 songs: 'Europa fair'; 'This great world is a trouble'; 'What scenes of approaching delight'. Words by R. Leveridge. Music of the opera by J.E. Galliard, R. Leveridge, and Cobston, to whom the music of the final piece is specifically attributed]. ff.5 *of a collection*. [*London*, c.1723] fol.
MU. 1190⁵²⁻⁴

Hah, hah. *Chorus.* ⟨This great world but a trouble. *A song in Jupiter & Europa*⟩. [*London*, c.1725] s.sh. fol.
MU. 1190⁵ᴬ

KEEBLE (JOHN)

Select pieces ⟨A second–fourth set of⟩ for the organ . . . Dedicated to the Right Honble. Lady Mary Duncan. pp.133: *4 vols., continuously paginated. Longman and Broderip: London*, [c.1778–80] obl. fol. [Inscribed 'Fitzwilliam 1788'].
MU. 415

KEEBLE (JOHN) and KIRKMAN (JACOB)

Forty interludes to be played between the verses of the Psalms . . . Inscrib'd . . . To the Noblemen, & Gentlemen of the Select Vestry [of St George's Church, Hanover Square]. pp.33. *Birchall & Andrews: London*, [c.1787] obl. 4°. [Inscribed 'Fitzwilliam 1793'].
MU. 421 C

KELLNER (JOHANN CHRISTOPH)

Six fugues for the organ or harpsicord. pp.13. *A. Hummel, London*, [c.1770] fol. [Inscribed 'R. Fitzwilliam 1774'].
MU. 488⁶, bound with MU. MS 208

KELLY (MICHAEL)

[The Africans]. The overture, songs, duetts, chorusses, &c. in the Africans . . . written by G. Coleman. pp.41. *Kelly's Opera Saloon, London*, [c.1808] fol.
MU. 1187¹

Cinderella, or the Little Glass Slipper, a grand allegorical pantomimic spectacle. pp.43. Plate no.67. *Christmas: London*, [1812^WM] fol.
MU. 1187²

[The Gay Deceivers]. The comic opera of the Gay Deceivers . . . written by G. Coleman. pp.33. *M. Kelly: London*, [1804^WM] fol.
MU. 1187³

[Love Laughs at Locksmiths]. The comic opera of Love Laughs at Locksmiths. pp.43. Plate no.10. *H. Falkner: London*, [1814^WM] fol.
MU. 1187⁴

[Of Age Tomorrow]. The overture and music in the musical entertainment Of Age Tomorrow. [Words by T. Dibdin and G.M. Lewis]. pp.47. *Printed for Michael Kelly by Corri, Dussek & Co: London*, [c.1800] fol.
MU. 1368

[Of Age Tomorrow]. The Wife's Farewell, or, No my love no, the favorite ballad . . . in of Age To-morrow, written by M.G. Lewis. [Song, begins: 'While I hang on your bosom']. pp.3. *Michael Kelly: London*, [c.1800] fol. [Inscribed 'A.M. Jeffery': later Mrs R.J.S. Stevens].
MU. 1287⁴

The Peasant Boy, an opera . . . written by Wᵐ Dimond. pp.126. *Falkner's Opera Saloon: London*, [1817^WM] fol.
MU. 1187⁵

[Pizzarro]. The music of Pizzarro, a play. [Words by R.B. Sheridan]. pp.30. *M. Kelly: London*, [c.1799] fol.
MU. 1187⁶

[The Royal Oak]. The songs, duetts, &c. in the play of the Royal Oak . . . written by Wᵐ. Dimond. pp.22. *Kelly's Opera Saloon: London*, [1812^WM] fol.
MU. 1187⁷

We Fly by Night, or Long Stories, a musical farce . . . written by Arthur Griffinhoof [i.e. George Colman]. pp.32. *Mˡ. Kelly: London*, [c.1806] fol.
MU. 1187⁸

[The Wood Daemon]. The songs, chorusses & music, in the grand dramatic romance, of the Wood Daemon, or the Clock has Struck . . . written by G.M. Lewis. pp.35. *M^l. Kelly: London*, [c.1807] fol.
MU. 1187^9

[The Young Hussar]. The overture & music, of the Young Hussar, or Love & Mercy . . . written by W^m. Dimond. pp.50. *M^l. Kelly: London*, [1817^WM] fol.
MU. 1187^10

KELWAY (JOSEPH)

Six sonatas for the harpsicord. pp.39. ⟨*Sold at Welcker's Musick Shop*⟩ [from label]: [*London*, 1764] obl. fol. [With a subscribers' list. Inscribed 'R. Fitzwilliam 1768'].
MU. 485^4

KENT (JAMES)

Twelve anthems. 2 vols. [Imperfect: wants vol. II]. *Preston and Son: London*, [c.1780] fol.
MU. 1202

Hear my prayer o God, a solemn anthem, sung in the oratorio's. [Score]. pp.5. *Sold by W. Sibley: London*, [1823^WM] fol.
MU. 1324^3

KILLICK (THOMAS)

Concerto, for the piano forte, with accompaniments for a full orchestra . . . dedicated to M^rs. Monty Wigram. [Piano only]. *Published for the Author, by Goulding, D'Almaine Potter & Co: London*, [1817^WM] fol.
MU. 1296

The morning & evening hymns, newly adapted for the organ or piano forte. pp.3. *Printed for the Author, by J. Balls: London*, [1821^WM] fol.
MU. 1288 B^26

KING (MATTHEW PETER)

Oh this love! or the Masqueraders. A comic opera in three acts . . . written by James Kenney. pp.79. *Phipps & Co: London*, [1808^WM] fol.
MU. 1186^1

Plots, or the North Tower, a melo dramatic opera in three acts . . . written by S.J. Arnold. pp.91. *J. Power* [the name W. Power deleted]: *London*, [c.1811] fol.
MU. 1186^2

Turn out, a musical farce in two acts . . . written by James Kenney. pp.43. *Wm Dale: London*, [1809^WM] fol.
MU. 1186³

Up All Night, or the Smugglers Cave, a comic opera in three acts . . . written by S.J. Arnold. pp.149. *Goulding, Phipps, D'Almaine & Co: London*, [1811^WM] fol.
MU. 1186⁴

KNYVETT (WILLIAM)

Jesse. A glee for four voices from Burn's poems. [Begins: 'True hearted was he the sad swain']. pp.5. *Printed for the Author, by R^t. Birchall: London*, [c.1800] fol.
MU. 1211²⁰

KOZELUCH (L.) *see* THOMSON (G.)

KREUTZER (RUDOLPH)

[Lodoiska]. The much admired romance in the opera of Lodoiska. [Song, begins: 'Adieu! my Fernando'. Original words, by M. de Jaure, begin: 'La douce clarté de l'aurore']. pp.3. *R^t. Birchall: London*, [1795] fol. [Inscribed 'A.M. Jeffery': later Mrs R.J.S. Stevens. The English words of this song, copied out on a slip bearing her name on the reverse, are pasted at the front of the volume].
MU. 1287⁷

LA GUERRE *see* JACQUET DE LA GUERRE

LALANDE (MICHEL RICHARD DE)

Motets de feu M^r. de la Lande . . . avec un discours sur la vie et les oeuvres de l'autheur. 21 vols, *bound in 7. Chez le S^r. Boivin: Paris*, 1729 fol. [With a frontispiece. Some contemporary MS corrections. Inscribed 'R. Fitzwilliam 1769'].
MU. 330–6

LAMPE (JOHANN FRIEDRICH)

The Parent Bird. [Song]. [*London*, c.1750] s.sh. fol.
MU. 1189²⁴

Pyramus and Thisbe: a mock-opera. The words taken from Shakespeare. [Score]. pp.39. *I. Walsh: London*, [1745] fol.
MU. 1183 A

see THE SUMMER'S TALE

LAMPUGNANI (G.B.) *see* THE SUMMER'S TALE

LANNEARE (N.) *see* PLAYFORD (J.), Select musicall ayres and dialogues; Select ayres and dialogues for one, two, and three voyces

LASS

The Lass of Patties Mill. [Song, words by A. Ramsay]. [*London*, c.1725] s.sh. fol.
MU. 1190⁴²

LATE

Late I came from roses on bushes. *Remarks on the town and South Sea cheat, a song. The words by Mʳ Durfey.* [*London*, c.1720] s.sh. fol.
MU. 1190³⁶

LAWES (H.) *see* PLAYFORD (J.), Select musicall ayres and dialogues; Select ayres and dialogues for one, two, and three voyces; Select ayres and dialogues to sing to the theorbo lute; *see* STEVENS (R.J.S.), Seven glees . . . Opera, 6

LAWES (W.) *see* PLAYFORD (J.), Select musicall ayres and dialogues

THE LAZY MORN *see* P. (S.)

LEAVE YOUR PARNASSUS *see* JACKSON (J.)

LEO (L.) *see* PRATT (J.)

LE ROUX (GASPARD)

Pieces de clavessin propres à jouer sur un & deux clavessins . . . avec la maniere de les joüer. [2 parts]. *Chez Estienne Roger: Amsterdam*, [c.1710] fol. [Not imperfect as sometimes stated. Only a few of the pieces have the optional second part. Inscribed 'R. Fitzwilliam 1769'].
MU. 360

LET

Let others sing *see* DEFESCH (W.), Polly of the Plain

Let youthful bards *see* WORGAN (J.), Miranda

LEVERIDGE (RICHARD)

The Wheel of Life. [Song, begins: 'The wheel of life is turning quickly round'. Also known as 'The Wheel of Fortune']. [*London*, c.1725] s.sh. fol.
MU. 1190[41]

see JUPITER AND EUROPA

LIFE'S LIKE A SHIP *see* CAREY (G.S.), The Sailor's Allegory

LINLEY (THOMAS, THE ELDER)

In my pleasant native plains, the favourite roundelay . . . in the Carnival of Venice. [Words by R. Tickell]. pp.[3]. *S. & P. Thompson: London*, [1781] fol. [Inscribed 'A.M. Jeffery': later Mrs R.J.S. Stevens].
MU. 1287[28]

see THE DUENNA

see THE GENTLE SHEPHERD

see THE ROYAL MERCHANT

LINLEY (T., THE YOUNGER) *see* THE DUENNA

LIONEL AND CLARISSA

Lionel & Clarissa, a comic opera . . . by the author of Love in a Village [i.e. I. Bickerstaff], the musick compos'd by several eminent masters [arranged by C. Dibdin]. pp.77. *Printed for the Author, & sold by J. Johnston: London*, [c.1770] obl. fol. [With a frontispiece].
MU. 1251[1]

LOCKE (MATTHEW)

Modern church-musick pre-accus'd, censur'd, and obstructed in its performance before His Majesty, Aprill 1. 1666. Vindicated by the author. [Comprises settings of the responses to the Ten Commandments and of the Nicene Creed]. pp. [4]. [1666] fol. [Inscribed 'Fitzwilliam 1803'. This item, bound with MSS of Blow and others, is included in the contemporary MS table of contents, and is therefore an integral part of the compilation, which has belonged both to Philip Hayes and to Samuel Arnold, whose inscriptions appear in vol. 1].
MU. 367, bound with MU. MS 117 B

[Psyche]. The English Opera; or the vocal musick in Psyche, with the instrumental therein intermix'd. To which is adjoyned the instrumental musick in the Tempest. pp.72. *Printed by T. Ratcliff, and N. Thompson for the Author: London*, [1675] 4°.
MU. 1247

The Tempest *see above*: Psyche

LONG (SAMUEL)

Of all my experience. [Song]. [*London*, c.1750] s.sh. fol.
MU. 1189[34]

LORDS

Lords and ladies, who deal in the sport. *The pleasures of Belsize.* [Song]. [*London*, c.1720] s.sh. fol.
MU. 1190[17]

LOVE

Love in thine eyes *see* JACKSON (W.)

Love like wind *see* M. (F.)

LOVE AND WINE

Love and wine by turns possess me. *A song set by an eminent master.* [*London*, c.1720] s.sh. fol.
MU. 1190[64]

[Love and Wine]. Wine's a mistress gay and easy. *Bass song . . . in the entertainment of Love and Wine.* [*London*, c.1725] s.sh. fol.
MU. 1190[29]

LULLI (GIOVANNI BATTISTA)

Acis et Galatée, pastorale heroïque. [Words by J.G. de Campistron]. [Score]. pp.li, 183. *Par Christophe Ballard: Paris,* 1686 fol. [Inscribed 'R. Fitzwilliam 1767'. Some contemporary MS alterations].
MU. 326

Atys. Tragedie . . . Seconde edition. [Words by P. Quinault]. [Score]. pp.225. *A l'Entrée de la Porte de l'Academie Royale de Musique: Paris,* 1709 fol.
MU. 1266

Bellerophon. Tragedie. [Words by T. Corneille, Fontenelle and Boileau]. [Score]. ff.154. *Par Christophe Ballard: Paris,* 1679 fol. [Inscribed 'R. Fitzwilliam 1767'].
MU. 321[1]

Persée. Tragedie. [Words by P. Quinault]. [Score]. pp.xlviii, 328. *Par Christophe Ballard: Paris,* 1682 fol. [Inscribed 'St Albans' and 'R. Fitzwilliam 1767'].
MU. 323

Phaëton. Tragedie. [Words by P. Quinault]. [Score]. pp.lxvi, 275. *Par Christophe Ballard: Paris,* 1683 fol.
MU. 321[2]

Proserpine. Tragedie. [Words by P. Quinault]. [Score]. pp.72, 355. *Par Christophe Ballard: Paris*, 1680 fol. [Inscribed 'R. Fitzwilliam 1767'].
MU. 322

Roland. Tragedie. [Words by P. Quinault]. [Score]. pp.lvi, 344. *Par Christophe Ballard: Paris*, 1685 fol. [With some contemporary alterations in MS. Inscribed 'R. Fitzwilliam 1767'].
MU. 324

[Le Temple de la paix]. Ballet du temple de la paix. [Words by P. Quinault]. [Score]. pp.216. *Par Christophe Ballard: Paris*, 1685 fol. [Inscribed 'R. Fitzwilliam 1767'].
MU. 325

see COLASSE (P.), Achille et Polixene

LULLY (LOUIS DE)

Orphée. Tragedie. [Words by Du Boullay]. [Score]. pp.255. *Par Christophe Ballard: Paris*, 1690 fol. [Inscribed 'R. Fitzwilliam 1767'].
MU. 327

LULMAN (CHARLES)

In vino veritas: or, the happy toper, by Mr. Cross-grove. [Song, begins: 'Will you credit a miser']. [*London*, c.1725] s.sh. fol.
MU. 1190[83]

M. (F.)

The Constant Tarr. [Song, begins: 'Love like wind is often changing']. [*London*, c.1720] s.sh. fol.
MU. 1190[31]

MANCINI (F.) *see* BABELL (W.), The 3ᵈ. [altered in MS to 4ᵗʰ] book of the ladys entertainment; *see* IDASPE; *see* OVERTURES

THE MANLY HEART *see* MOZART (W.A.)

MARCELLO (BENEDETTO)

Estro poetico-armonico. Parafrasi sopra li primi ⟨secondi⟩ venticinque salmi. Poesia di Girolamo Ascanio Giustiani . . . Tomo primo ⟨– ottavo⟩. [Score]. 8 vols. *Apresso Domenico Lovisa: Venice*, 1724–6 fol. [With a frontispiece to each vol. Inscribed 'Fitzwilliam 1778'].
MU. 409

MARCH

March of the thirty-fifth regiment. [Score]. [*London*, c.1780] s.sh. fol.
MU. 1197[16]

Bellisle March *see* ALL, All hail to the King

MARCHAND (LOUIS)

Pieces de clavecin . . . dediées au Roy. pp.12. *Chez Estienne Roger: Amsterdam*,
[c.1710] obl. fol. [Inscribed 'Fitzwilliam 1799'].
MU. 361 D

MARCHANT

On a lady of quality. [Song, begins: 'As Cupid one day roving saw']. [*London*,
c.1730] s.sh. fol.
MU. 1190[7]

MARIAGE

[Le Mariage Mexicain]. The favorite pas de trois in Le Mariage Mexicain . . . N°.
16 . . . N°. V. [Music by J. d'Egville. Arranged for flute/violin and keyboard].
pp.9–14 *of a collection. Theobald Monzani: London*, [c.1805–7] fol.
MU. 380 C

MARPURG (FRIEDRICH WILHELM)

Clavierstücke mit einem practischen Unterricht für Anfänger und Geübtere . . .
〈Zweite-Dritte Sammlung〉. 3 vols. *Bey Haude und Spener: Berlin*, 1762–3 obl.
fol. [Vol. 1 is prefaced by 16 plates].
MU. 1238[1–3]

MARTINI (GIOVANNI BATTISTA)

Duetti da camera, consagrati all'Altezza Reale Elettorale di Maria Antonia di
Baviera Principessa Elettorale di Sassonia. pp.46. 〈*Nella Stamperia di Lelio dalla
Volpe: Bologna*, 1763〉 obl. fol. [Inscribed 'Fitzwilliam 1793'].
MU. 480

Sonate per l'organo e il cembalo. pp.25. *Nella Stamp. di Lelio dalla Volpe: Bologna*,
[c.1745] fol.
MU. 1358

MARTYN (BENDALL)

Fourteen sonatas for two violins with a bass for the violoncello and a through bass for the harpsicord. [4 parts]. *I. Walsh: London*, [1763] fol.
MU. 318 A^{10}, 318 B^{10}, 318 C^5, 318 D^{10}

[Another copy]. [3 parts only].
MU. 1369

MASCITTI (MICHELE)

Solos for a violin with a thorough bass for the harpsicord or bass violin . . . Opera 2da. [Number supplied in MS]. pp.50. *I: Walsh . . . & I: Hare: London*, [c.1712] fol. [With contemporary alterations in MS. Several pp. inscribed 'Concerto La Motte'].
MU. 1192^2

MATTOX

Love's Victim. Y^e words by M^r: Monlass. [Song, begins: 'A slighted shepherd, in a vale']. [*London*, c.1720] s.sh. fol.
MU. 1189^{50}

MAZZAFERRATA (GIOVANNI BATTISTA)

Canzonette, e cantate a due voci . . . Opera terza. Dedicate al Molto Reverendo Padre D. Pietro Alberto Gratioli Veneziano. [Edited by Marino Silvani]. pp.112. *Per Giacomo Monti: Bologna*, 1680 obl. fol. [Inscribed 'R. Fitzwilliam 1767'].
MU. 481

MAZZINGHI (JOSEPH)

The Captive to his Bird. A favorite song, sung . . . by M^r. Incledon, in his new entertainment of Variety. [Begins: 'O! sing sweet bird']. pp.3. *Goulding Phipps D'Almane & Co: London*, [1807^{WM}] fol.
MU. 1287^{32}

The Wreath, a pastoral glee for three voices. [Begins: 'Ye shepherds tell me']. pp.7. *Goulding, Phipps & D'Almaine: London*, [1803^{WM}] fol.
MU. 1211^{23}

THE MERCHANT OF VENICE *see* ARNE (T.A.), The Blind Beggar of Bethnal Green [cantatas, operas, oratorios]

MEYER *see* INKLE AND YARICO

MIDAS

Midas. A comic opera . . . For the harpsichord, voice, German flute, violin, or guitar. [Words by K. O'Hara. Music from popular airs]. pp.67. *I. Walsh: London,* [1764] obl. fol.
MU. 1257²

MILLER (EDWARD)

Elements of thorough bass and composition . . . with proper lessons for practice . . . Dedicated to . . . Lord Viscount Gallway . . . Opera quinta. pp.88. *Printed & sold by Broderip & Wilkinson . . . and by the Author at Doncaster: London,* [c.1800] fol.
MU. 1325

The psalms of David, for the use of parish churches. The words selected from the version of Tate & Brady by the Rev^d. George Hay Drummond. The music selected, adapted and composed by Edward Miller. pp.xlvii, 142. *W. Miller: London,* [c.1790] 8°. [Inscribed 'RJS Stevens. Charterhouse 1796. Given me by Dr John Moore, Lord Archbishop of Canterbury'].
MU. 1297

MINUET

Lord How's new minuet. [Score]. [*London, c.1770*] s.sh. fol.
MU. 1197⁸¹

MIO CARO BEN *see* ASTARTO

MOORE (THOMAS)

Oh lady fair! *A ballad for three voices. Dedicated to the R^t. Honble. Lady Charlotte Rawdon . . . The music and words by Thos. Moore Esqr.* pp.7. *J. & T. Carpenter: London,* 1802 fol.
MU. 1211⁵

When time who steals our years away. A ballad, dedicated to M^rs. Henry Tighe, of Rosanna. The music and words by Thos. Moore. pp.4. *J. & T. Carpenter: London,* 1802 fol.
MU. 1287³⁰

MORGAN (J.) *see* BLEST

MORLEY (THOMAS)

Six canzonets for two voices . . . first publish'd . . . 1599. [Originally published as 'First book of canzonets to two voyces']. pp.17. *Welcker: London*, [c.1770] obl. fol. [Inscribed 'R. Fitzwilliam 1775'].
MU. 421 A

[Triumphs of Oriana]. Part 1 ⟨2⟩ of a collection of madrigals for five and six voices called the Triumphs of Oriana, now first published in score . . . dedicated . . . to Earl Fortescue. [Edited by William Hawes]. [*London*, 1814] fol. [The project is incomplete: part 2 breaks off after the first page of no.xv. This is one of the 25 large paper copies mentioned in the proposal which appears on titles. The name of the original subscriber has been deleted and 'Earl Fitzwilliam' substituted, probably the bookseller's mistake for the Founder, although neither part bears his usual inscription].
MU. 413 A–B

MORNING

The morning cloud was ting'd with gold. *Colin and Dolly*. [Song]. [*London*, c.1755] s.sh. fol.
MU. 1189[51]

The morning is charming. *A hunting song for two voices*. [*London*, c.1750] s.sh. fol.
MU. 1197[34]

MORNINGTON (G.C.) *see* AMUSEMENT

MOTEZUMA

Motezuma. Overture. [Music by A.M.G. Sacchini]. [Keyboard]. pp.5. [*London*, c.1775] fol.
MU. 1400[6]

MOULDS (JOHN)

Down in the valley where sweet violets grew, a celebrated song . . . written and composed by John Moulds. [Begins: 'Don't you remember a poor peasant's daughter']. ff.[2]. *R. Wornum: London*, [c.1800] fol.
MU. 1287[10]

MOZART (WOLFGANG AMADEUS)

Zwey Deutsche Arien zum singen beym clavier . . . II[ter] Theil. [Comprises 'Das Veilchen', 'Trennungslied']. pp.13. *Bey Ataria: Vienna*, [c.1789] obl. fol.
MU. 1169

The manly heart. A favorite duett . . . with an accompaniment for the pianoforte. ['Bei Männern, welche Liebe fühlen', from 'Die Zauberflöte'. Original words by E. Schikaneder]. pp.5. *Longman and Broderip: London,* [c.1795] fol.
MU. 1211[31]

Within these sacred bowers, a favorite ballad. ['In diesen heil'gen Hallen', from 'Die Zauberflöte'. Original words by E. Schikaneder]. ff.2–3. *H. Andrews:* [*London,* c.1810] fol.
MU. 1197[47]

see PRATT (J.)

MUCH

Much I love a charming creature. *The Bashful Maid. A new song.* [London, c.1725] s.sh. fol.
MU. 1190[78]

MUDGE (RICHARD)

Six concertos in seven parts, five for four violins, a tenor violin, and violoncello, with a thorough bass for the harpsicord. and one concerto for the organ or harpsicord, with instruments . . . To which is added, Non Nobis Domine, in 8 parts. [8 parts]. *I. Walsh: London,* [1749] fol.
MU. 320 G[16], 320 H[16], 320 I[16], 320 J[16], 320 K[16], 320 L[4], 320 M[16], 320 N[16]

MUFFAT (GOTTLIEB)

Componimenti musicali per il cembalo. ⟨All' augustissimo . . . Carlo VI⟩. pp.[107]. *Sculpit in rame et fatti stampare Da Giovanni Christiano Leopold: Augsburg,* [1727] obl. fol. [With a separate volume of modern MS notes].
MU. 1174[1–2]

[72 Versetl sammt 12 Toccaten besonders beim Kirchen-Dienst, bey Choral-Aembtern und Vesperen dienlich.] pp.88. [Imperfect: wants title and pp.87–8, the latter supplied in MS]. [*Vienna,* 1726] obl. fol.
MU. 1245

MUGNIÉ (JEAN)

L'Amour piqué par une abeille, imitation d'anacreon, pour le forte piano. pp.12. *Se vend chez l'auteur . . . Engraved & publish'd by J. Davies: London,* [1803] fol. [Inscribed 'Fitzwilliam 1805. De la part de l'auteur'].
MU. 380 E[4]

La Colombe reperdue, an air for the piano forte, with or without additional keys . . . dedicated to Miss H.C. pp.3. *J. Davies: London,* [1803] fol.
MU. 380 E[2]

A Grand military divertimento, in which is introduced a second pastorale & pollaca, for the piano forte with accompaniments for a flute & French horn . . . dedicated . . . to His Royal Highness the Duke of York. [3 parts]. *Lavenu & Mitchell: London*, [1803[WM]] fol. [Inscribed 'Fitzwilliam 1805. De la part de l'auteur'].
MU. 380 E[3]

Le Papillon, caprice pour le piano forte . . . dedié a Mademoiselle Young. pp.10. *J. Davies: London*, [1803] fol. [Inscribed 'Fitzwilliam 1805. De la part de l'auteur'].
MU. 380 E[1]

MUSIC

Music purposely composed for the harp . . . An hymn to the Deity, from the much admired sacred drama of David & Goliah, by M[rs]. Hannah More . . . To which are added a selection of vocal compositions in various styles, with an accompanyment for the same instrument. [By Thomas Jones]. [Score]. pp.47. *Broderip & Wilkinson: London*, 1800 fol. [Inscribed 'This Copy is most respectfully presented to Lord Viscount Fitzwilliam by the Author Thomas Jones, Wigmore Street, 30th March 1800'. Also inscribed 'Fitzwilliam 1800'].
MU. 434

MUSICAL

The Musical Miscellany; being a collection of choice songs, set to the violin and flute ⟨choice songs, and lyrick poems: with the basses to each tune, and transpos'd for the flute⟩. By the most eminent masters. Volume the first ⟨–sixth⟩. 6 vols. *John Watts: London*, 1729–31 8°. [With a frontispiece to each vol.].
MU. 1267–9

MY

My banks they are furnish'd with bees. [Music by T.A. Arne, words by W. Shenstone]. [Song]. [c.1780] s.sh. fol.
MU. 1197[28]

My dearest life were thou my wife. *The Chaise Marine*. [Song]. [*London*, c.1765] s.sh. fol.
MU. 1197[43]

My lodging is on the cold ground. *My Lodging. A favourite mad song*. [Words from 'The Rivals', an adaptation of 'Two Noble Kinsmen' attributed to Sir W. Davenant]. *F[m]*: [*London*, c.1780] s.sh. fol. [Inscribed 'A.M. Jeffery': later Mrs R.J.S. Stevens].
MU. 1287[20]

My mother wou'd fain have oblig'd me to wed. *The Girl of Spirit*. [Song]. [*London*, c.1776] s.sh. fol.
MU. 1197[20]

My soger laddie is over the seas. *The Soger Laddie*. [Words chiefly by A. Ramsay]. [Song]. [*London*, c.1750] s.sh. fol.
MU. 1189[12]

[Another edition]. [c.1760] s.sh. fol.
MU. 1197[44]

My time, O ye muses *see* HART (W.)

MYRTILLO

How happy are we. *A song in the mask of Martillo* [i.e. 'Myrtillo', music by J.C. Pepusch. Libretto by C. Cibber (1717) does not include this number]. [*London*, c.1716] s.sh. fol.
MU. 1190[6]

NAPIER (W.) *see* SCOTS

NARES (JAMES)

These lessons for the harpsicord, with a sonata in score for the harpsicord or organ are . . . dedicated to . . . the Countess of Carlisle . . . Opera II. pp.53. *Printed for the Author & sold at Johnson's Musick Shop: London*, [c.1759] obl. fol. [Inscribed 'R. Fitzwilliam 1768'].
MU. 485[5]

A morning and evening service . . . together with six anthems in score. pp.2, 62. *John Preston: London*, 1788 fol. [With a frontispiece. Inscribed 'Fitzwilliam 1792'].
MU. 365[1]

A treatise on singing. [Includes 2 sets of duets]. pp.40. *Welcker: London*, [c.1770] obl. fol. [Inscribed 'Fitzwilliam 1775'].
MU. 421 B

NEAR

Near the side of a pond. *The Miller's Song*. [*London*, c.1750] s.sh. fol.
MU. 1189[29]

NO

No Highland lad *see* DAVIES (R.), The Irish Lassie

No more Florilla *see* GRANO (G.B.)

No more my song shall be ye swains. *The Highland Queen*. [Song, words by Mac Vicar]. [*London*, c.1770] s.sh. fol.
MU. 1197[18]

No more silly pipe be thy sonnets addrest. *Molly. A new song*. [*London*, c.1750] s.sh. fol.
MU. 1189[41]

No nymph that trips the verdant plains. *A new song sung at the public gardens*. [*London*, c.1756] s.sh. fol.
MU. 1197[65]

NON

Non e si vago e bello / I come my fairest treasure. *A song in English and Italian. The English words by M*. *Leveridge*. [From G.F. Handel's 'Giulio Cesare'. Words by N.F. Haym]. ff.[2]. [*London*, c.1730] fol.
MU. 1190[30]

NORRIS (T.) *see* AMUSEMENT

NOVELLO (VINCENT)

The Fitzwilliam Music, being a collection of sacred pieces selected from manuscripts of Italian composers in the Fitzwilliam Museum. 5 vols. *Published for the Editor: London*, 1825 fol. [With a subscribers' list. Inscribed 'Presented to The Fitzwilliam Museum by V. Novello 1826'].
MU. 410

[Another copy]. [Inscribed 'R.R. Terry', first organist of Westminster Cathedral, and reviver of Tudor liturgical music].
MU. 1463–7

NOW I KNOW *see* WESLEY (C.)

NUSSEN (FREDERICK)

Musica di camera, or some old tunes new sett, and some new ones. Compos'd for the harpsichord, Opera 3[za]. For the practice and amusement of the R[t]. Hon[ble]. the Lady Frances Greville. pp.27. *I. Walsh: London*, [c.1762] obl. fol. [Inscribed 'Fitzwilliam 1799'].
MU. 484[2]

NYMPH

A nymph of the plain. *The jolly young swain. A new song.* [*London*, c.1710] s.sh. fol.
MU. 1190[11]

A nymph there lives. *Molly. A new song.* [*London*, c.1730] s.sh. fol.
MU. 1189[37]

O

O blest abode *see* GAMBALL (J.)

O give thanks *see* WHALLEY (M.)

O lady fair *see* MOORE (T.)

O lovely charmer *see* FLORIDANTE

O lovely maid how dear's thy power. *The Agreeable Amusement.* [Music probably by W. Defesch]. [Song]. [*London*, c.1745] s.sh. fol.
MU. 1189[6]

O mine awn Jenny *see* YOSLINGTON

O mistress mine *see* STEVENS (R.J.S.)

O my treasure, crown my pleasure. *The Impatient Lover. The words made to a favourite Italian air.* ['Vanne segui', from G.F. Handel's 'Floridante']. [*London*, c.1725] s.sh. fol.
MU. 1190[82]

O say bonny lass. A favorite new Scotch song and duett . . . for the harpsichord, violin, German flute & guitar. pp.2. [*London*, c.1785] fol. [Inscribed 'A.M. Jeffery': later Mrs R.J.S. Stevens].
MU. 1287[22]

O say bonny lass, a favorite song & duett. ff.[2]. [*London*, c.1790] fol.
MU. 1211[34]

O! sing sweet bird *see* MAZZINGHI (J.), The Captive to his Bird

O sleep *see* ECCLES (J.), [Semele]

O strike the harp *see* STEVENS (R.J.S.), Bragela

O tarry *see* WEBBE (S., THE ELDER), The Traveller

O thou wert born to please me *see* COMUS

O! Thou who thro' the silent air *see* ATTWOOD (T.)

OBSERVE, OBSERVE YOU TUNEFUL CHARMER
see ASTIANASSE

OF

Of all my experience *see* LONG (S.)

Of all the girls *see* W. (V.)

Of all the various states of life. *Wedlock.* [Song]. [*London*, c.1765] s.sh. fol.
MU. 1197[22]

Of Linster fam'd for maidens fair. *Lucy and Collin.* [Song, words by Tickell].
[*London*, c.1730] s.sh. fol.
MU. 1197[77]

OH NANNY WILT THOU FLY WITH ME *see* CARTER (C.T.); *see*
HARRISON (S.)

OLD

Old women will you go a sheering. *N°. 14. Juvenile Amusement.* [Song for 3 voices
and keyboard]. ff.[2]. [c.1800] fol.
MU. 1211[4]

ON

On that lone bank *see* DIGNUM (C.), Fair Rosale

On the tay's verdant banks. *Moggy's Complaint of Jockey.* [Song]. [*London*, c.1750]
s.sh. fol.
MU. 1189[19]

ONLY TELL HIM *see* FISIN (J.)

ORLANDINI (G.H.) *see* ARSACE

OSWALD (JAMES)

The Wheel-Barrow, a favorite cantata. ff.[2]. [*London*, c.1765] fol.
MU. 1197[73]

OTHO *see* OTTONE

OTTONE

[The quarterly collection of vocal music, containing the choicest songs for the last
three months . . . being the 'Additional Songs' in Otho]. [Music by G.F. Handel,

words by N.F. Haym, after S.B. Pallavicino]. ff.12. [Imperfect: wants title]. [*In°
Walsh . . . and Ios Hare: London*, 1726] fol.
MU. 1356³

OVER THE MOUNTAIN *see* PIERCY (H.)

OVERTURES

Six overtures, for violins in all their parts . . . in the operas of Astartus, Croesus,
Camilla, Hydaspes, Thomyris, Rinaldo. [Score and parts]. [Imperfect: comprises
score and 3 parts only (with a second copy of bass) of 'Camilla' (by G.B.
Bononcini); score and 4 parts only (with a second copy of bass) of 'Hydaspes' (F.
Mancini); 3 parts only (with a second copy of bass) of 'Thomyris' (pasticcio
arranged by J.C. Pepusch)]. *I: Walsh: London*, [c.1724] fol.
MU. 1421 B, 1422 B, 1423 B

P. (S.)

The Rising Beauty. [Song, begins: 'The lazy morn as yet undrest']. [*London*,
c.1740] s.sh. fol.
MU. 1189³⁶

PACINI (ANTONIO FRANCESCO GAETANO SAVERIO)

Imite le mon fils. La nouvelle Valentine à son fils. Stances composées par Mᶜ. de
P*** . . . avec accompagnement de piano ou harpe. [Song, begins: 'Vous n'avez
point trahi votre sainte promesse']. ff.4. Plate no. 786. *Au magasin de Musique de
Pacini: [Paris*, c.1820] fol.
MU. 1440³

PAER (FERDINANDO)

La nouvelle Valentine, stances élégiaques sur la mort de S.A.R. Monseigneur le
Duc de Berry. Paroles de Madame P— . . . Dediées à Madame la Duchesse de
Rozan, née Mademoiselle de Duras. [Song, begins: 'Sous le ciel doux et pur'].
pp.8. *Chez Janet et Cotelle: Paris*, [c.1820] fol.
MU. 1440¹

PAGE (J.) *see* HANDEL (G.F.), Eight anthems . . . dedicated to . . . the
Princess of Wales [selections and arrangements: anthems]

PAISIELLO (G.) *see* INKLE AND YARICO

PARADIES (DOMENICO)

A favorite concerto for the organ or harpsichord, with instrumental parts. [5 parts]. *Welcker: London,* [c.1768] fol. [Inscribed 'R. Fitzwilliam 1769'].
MU. 486[1]

[Another copy]. [4 parts only, with a second copy of violoncello].
MU. 1360[3]

A favourite minuet with variations. [Keyboard]. pp.5. *Welcker: London,* [c.1770] fol.
MU. 1360[2]

Sonate di gravicembalo, dedicate a sua Altezza Reale la Principessa Augusta. pp.47. *Printed for the Author by John Johnson: London,* [1754] fol. [Inscribed 'RICHARD FITZWILLIAM London 27[d] Dec[r]: 1770'].
MU. 428

[Another issue]. *Welcker: London,* [c.1770] fol.
MU. 1360[1]

THE PARENT BIRD *see* LAMPE (J.F.)

PARKE (WILLIAM THOMAS)

Overture to Netley Abbey. [Keyboard]. [Pasticcio, words by W. Pearce, compiled by W. Shield]. pp.10. [c.1795] obl. fol.
MU. 1399

PARRY (JOHN)

British Harmony, being a collection of antient Welsh airs . . . now first published with some additional variations. pp.38. *John Parry . . . & P. Hodgson: Ruabon, Denbighshire, and London,* 1781 fol. [With a subscribers' list. Inscribed 'Fitzwilliam 1790'].
MU. 380 B

PAXTON (S.) *see* WEBBE (S., THE ELDER), A collection of masses; *see* AMUSEMENT

PEEP

Peep behind the Curtain. Overture. [Music by F.H. Barthelemon. Part of 'Orpheus', words by D. Garrick]. [Keyboard]. ff.5. [c.1800] obl. fol.
MU. 1429[2]

PEGGE (S.) *see* SIR

PEPUSCH (JOHANN CHRISTOPH)

The Beggars Opera . . . For the voice, harpsichord, and violin. [Words by J. Gay]. [Score]. pp.26. Plate nos. 17–18 of 'The New Musical Magazine'. *Harrison & Co: London*, [1784] obl. fol.
MU. 1248¹

Six English cantatas humbly inscrib'd to the most noble the Marchioness of Kent ⟨second book [indicated in MS]⟩. [Words by J. Hughes and others]. 2 vols, *comprising 12 cantatas in all. J: Walsh: London*, [1730–1] fol. [Each vol. inscribed 'Fitzwilliam 1799'].
MU. 366⁴⁻⁵

The God of love had lost his bow. *Cantata.* pp.3. [*London*, c.1720] fol.
MU. 1190⁶⁵

XXIV Solos for a violin with a through bass for the harpsicord or bass violin ⟨Parti secunda⟩. 2 vols., *continuously paginated. I.Walsh [& I. Hare]: London*, [1707–8] obl. fol. [Inscribed in a child's hand, 'Willa: Bertie', presumably the patron and composer Willoughby Bertie, fourth Earl of Abingdon. Also inscribed 'R. Fitzwilliam 1772'].
MU. 313

see CORELLI, The score of the four setts of sonatas [collected works]

see CORELLI, The score of the four operas [collected works]

see DIDO AND ENEAS

see MYRTILLO

see OVERTURES

see POLLY

see THOMYRIS

PEREZ (DAVIDDE)

Mattinuto de' Morti. [Score]. pp.156. *Presso Roberto Bremner: London*, [1774] fol. [With a frontispiece and subscribers' list. Inside front and back covers is a translation of the text in contemporary MS. Inscribed 'Fitzwilliam 1799'].
MU. 309

PERGOLESI (GIOVANNI BATTISTA)

Missa. [In D for 5 voices and instruments]. pp.36. [*Benjamin Goodison's Purcell subscription: London*, 1787] fol. [The project is incomplete: the mass breaks off at the 'Qui tollis' of the 'Gloria'. Inscribed 'Fitzwilliam 1799'].
MU. 341 B⁹

Mottetto: Domine ad adjuvandum me festina. pp.12. [*Benjamin Goodison's Purcell subscription: London*, c.1790] fol.
MU. 341 B[8]

Stabat mater. [Score]. pp.29. *Chez M[r]. Bayard . . ., M[r]. le Clerc . . ., M[lle]. Castagneri . . . M[r]. Desbreton: Paris*, [c.1760] fol.
MU. 528

PERIODICAL

Periodical overture for the harpsicord, piano-forte &. No 1 ⟨–12⟩. To be continued monthly. pp.49, *continuously paginated. Longman, Lukey & Co: London*, [c.1775] obl. fol. [With attributions in modern MS].
MU. 1425

PHILIDOR (F.A.D.) *see* ROUSSEAU (J.J.)

PHOEBUS

Phoebus meaner themes disdaining. *The British Fair. Sung . . . at Vauxhall.* [*London*, c.1765] s.sh. fol.
MU. 1197[38]

PICCINI (NICOLÒ)

La Buona Figliuola. [Overture]. [Keyboard]. pp.5. [*R. Bremner: London*, 1767] fol.
MU. 1400[2]

La Buona Figliuola Maritata. [Overture]. [Keyboard]. pp.5. [*R. Bremner: London*, 1767] fol.
MU. 1400[3]

Roland. Opera en trois actes . . . dédié a la reine. [Words by J.F. Marmontel]. [Score]. pp.466. *Ches l'Auteur . . ., M. De la Chevardiere . . ., M. d'Enouville: Paris*, [c.1778] fol.
MU. 1226

La Schiava. [Overture]. [Keyboard]. pp.5. [*London*, c. 1775] fol.
MU. 1400[4]

PIERCY (H.)

The Beggar Girl, a favorite ballad for the piano forte or harp, also, as a duett. [Begins: 'Over the mountain and over the moor']. pp.4. *Printed for and sold by the Author: London*, [c.1800] fol. [Inscribed 'A.M. Jeffery': later Mrs R.J.S. Stevens].
MU. 1287[5]

PIRRO E DEMETRIO

Songs in the new opera of Pyrrhus and Demetrius. With the Italian words grav'd under the English to such as are sung in Italian. [Music by A. Scarlatti with additions by N.F. Haym. Words by A. Morselli, translated by O. MacSwiney]. ff.3, 54. *John Cullen: London,* [1709] fol.
MU. 1280

see BABELL (W.), The 3ᵈ. book of the ladys entertainment

PLAYFORD (HENRY)

Harmonia sacra . . . The first book. The 2ᵈ edition. pp.130. [Imperfect: wants pp.1–2]. *Printed by William Pearson, for Henry Playford: London,* 1703 fol. [With a frontispiece. Some markings in text and drawings suggesting use by a child. Inscribed 'R. Fitzwilliam 1768'].
MU. 372¹

[Another copy]. [Imperfect: wants pp.1–2. Inscribed 'Fitzwilliam 1808'].
MU. 373¹

Harmonia sacra . . . The second book. ff.8, pp.9–74. *Printed by Edward Jones, for Henry Playford: London,* 1693 fol. [With sketch of an angel on title].
MU. 372²

[Another copy].
MU. 373²

Harmonia sacra . . . The first book. The 3ᵈ. edition. ⟨Book II⟩. 2 vols. *Printed by William Pearson, for S.H.: London,* 1714 fol. [With a frontispiece].
MU. 374¹⁻²

Two divine hymns: being a suppliment to the second book of Harmonia Sacra. pp.8. *Printed by W. Pearson . . . for Henry Playford: London,* [c.1700] fol.
MU. 372³

[Another copy].
MU. 373³

PLAYFORD (JOHN)

Select musicall ayres and dialogues, in three bookes . . . composed by . . . Dr. John Wilson, Dr. Charles Colman, Mr. Henry Lawes, Mr. William Lawes, Mr. William Webbe, Mr. Nicholas Lanneare, Mr. William Smegergill alias Caesar, Mr. Edward Colman, Mr. Jeremy Savile. 3 vols, *of which 2 and 3 are continuously paginated. Printed by T. H[arper] for John Playford: London,* 1653 fol.
MU. 1327

Select ayres and dialogues for one, two, and three voyces; to the theorbo-lute or basse-viol. Composed by John Wilson, Charles Colman . . ., Henry Lawes,

Nicholas Laneare, William Webbe . . . and other excellent masters of musick. 3 vols, *continuously paginated. Printed by W. Godbid for John Playford: London,* 1659 fol. [With a frontispiece, on which are four lines of verse in MS, signed 'NH St Alban's 26th July 1732'].
MU. 1328

Select ayres and dialogues to sing to the theorbo-lute or basse-viol. Composed by M^r. Henry Lawes . . . and other excellent masters. The second book. [A selection from Lawes's first and second books of 'Ayres and dialogues' (1653, 1655). Also issued under his name as the second book of 'The Treasury of Musick']. pp.120. [Imperfect: wants pp.97–104]. *Printed by William Godbid for John Playford: London,* 1669 fol. [Inscribed 'R. Fitzwilliam 1768'].
MU. 377¹, bound with MU. MS 118

[Another copy]. [Imperfect: wants pp.57–8, 89–96, 105–20].
MU. 771 A

Choice ayres, songs, & dialogues to sing to the theorbo-lute, or bass-viol. Being most of the newest ayres, and songs . . . The second edition corrected and enlarged. pp.87. *Printed by W. Godbid, and are to be sold by John Playford: London,* 1675 fol.
MU. 377², bound with MU. MS 118

Choice ayres & songs to sing to the theorbo-lute or bass-viol, being most of the newest ayres and songs . . . The second book. pp.67. *Printed by Anne Godbid, and are sold by John Playford: London,* 1679 fol.
MU. 377³, bound with MU. MS 118

Musick's Delight on the cithren, restored and refined to a more easie and pleasant manner of playing . . . with lessons al a mode, being the choicest of our late new ayres, corants, sarabands, tunes, and jiggs. To which is added several new songs. *Unpaginated* [pieces numbered to 111, a misprint for 101]. *Printed by W.G. and are sold by J. Playford: London,* 1666 obl. 8°. [Blank staves have been used to add extra tunes in contemporary MS. Numerous names, handwriting exercises, etc., suggest that this was a child's book. Names and dialect suggest a Scottish provenance: the town of Leith is mentioned].
MU. 1317

PLEYEL (IGNAZ JOSEPH)

Henry's Cottage Maid. A favorite song. [Begins: 'Ah! where can fly my soul's true love?']. [Score]. pp.4. *Longman and Broderip: London,* [c.1795] fol. [Inscribed 'A.M. Jeffery': later Mrs R.J.S. Stevens].
MU. 1287²³

see THOMSON (G.)

A PLIGHTED FAITH *see* STORACE (S.), The Siege of Belgrade

POCKET

A pocket companion for gentlemen and ladies, being a collection of favourite songs, out of the most celebrated opera's, compos'd by M[r]. Handel, Bononcini, Attilio, &c. in English and Italian, to which is added several choice songs of M[r]. Handel's, never before printed. Vol. II. Carefully corrected and figur'd for the harpsicord. The whole transpos'd for the flute in the most proper keys. [Imperfect: vol. II only]. *Engrav'd & printed at Cluer's Printing Office . . . and sold there, and by B. Creake: London*, [c.1725] 8°. [With a frontispiece and subscribers' list].
MU. 1274

POLLAROLI (C.F.) *see* ZIANI (P.A.)

POLLY

Polly; an opera. Being the second part of the Beggar's Opera. For the voice, harpsichord, and violin. [Music arranged by J.C. Pepusch. Words by John Gay]. [Score]. pp.24. Plate nos. 18–19 of 'The New Musical Magazine'. *Harrison & Co: London*, [1784] obl. fol.
MU. 1248[2]

POPELEY (WILLIAM)

Come Delia come, let's shun ye heat. The words by M[r]. Dart. [Song]. *R. Meares: [London*, c.1720] s.sh. fol.
MU. 1190[20]

PORPORA (NICCOLÒ ANTONIO)

All' Altezza Reale di Frederico Prencipe Reale di Vallia . . . Queste nuovamente composte opre di musica vocale . . . dedica . . . Nicolò Porpora. [Comprises 12 cantatas and duets]. pp.82. [*London*], 1735 obl. fol. [Inscribed 'Fitzwilliam 1799'].
MU. 493

PORTA (GIOVANNI)

Strazo sempia furia. *A song.* ff.[2]. [*London*, c.1730] fol.
MU. 1190[8]

PORTER (SAMUEL)

Cathedral music in score . . . To the Reverend the Dean & Chapter of . . . Canterbury . . . the following . . . are dedicated. pp.98. *W.J. Porter:* [c.1815] fol. [Inscribed 'Fitzwilliam 1815'. W.J. Porter, son of the composer, was Fitzwilliam's chaplain].
MU. 370

POW'RFUL

[Pow'rful Guardians. Aria from G.F. Handel's 'Alexander Balus']. ff.[2]. [Imperfect: wants f.1]. [c.1790] fol.
MU. 1197^{83a}

A POX ON REPINING *see* TURNER (W.), A catch (a 4 voc.) in praise of claret

PRATT (JOHN)

A collection of anthems in score, selected from the works of Handel, Haydn, Mozart, Clari, Leo and Carissimi. With a separate arrangement for the organ or piano forte . . . dedicated . . . to Rev^d. the Provost & Fellows of Kings College. pp.120. *Published for the Editor, by Preston: London*, [c.1825] fol. [With a subscribers' list. Inscribed 'Presented to The Fitzwilliam Museum by J. Pratt, 1828'].
MU. 492

PRELUDES

Select preludes [& vollentarys] for the violin . . . by [all the greatest masters in Europe]. [Melody]. ff.35. [Imperfect: title and contents torn]. *I. [Walsh] and I. Hare: London*, [1705]. Single sheets, originally stab-stitched.
MU. 1334^3

PRITHEE BILLY *see* VANBRUGHE (G.), Advice to a friend

PSALMS

Psalms, hymns and anthems; for the use of the children of the hospital for . . . exposed and deserted young children. pp.48. [*London*, c.1790] 8°.
MU. 1272

PUNTO (G.) *see* THE ROYAL MERCHANT

PURCELL (DANIEL)

The Iudgment of Paris. A pastoral composed for the Music = Prize. [Words by W. Congreve]. [Score]. pp.82. *J. Walsh: London*, [c.1702] fol. [Part of p.6 not printed but supplied in MS].
MU. 378^2

see ECCLES (J.) and PURCELL (D.)

PURCELL (HENRY)

Arrangement: 1. Goodison's edition
               2. Vocal music
                    a. Sacred music
                    b. Odes
                    c. Dramatic music
                    d. Songs
               3. Instrumental music
               4. Appendix

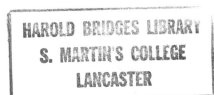

1. Goodison's edition

[The works of Henry Purcell, in five classes, edited by Benjamin Goodison]. [*London*, c.1788–90] fol. [Only 5 parts published. Includes works by other composers. This is a complete set, bound out of sequence. See also separate entries. With proposal and subscribers' lists. Inscribed 'Fitzwilliam 1799'].
MU. 341 A$^{1-4}$, 341 B$^{1-9}$

2. Vocal music

a. Sacred music

Anthems and other sacred pieces. [*Benjamin Goodison's Purcell subscription*]. [The last of the six anthems is incomplete: no more published].
MU. 341 A^4

Harmonia sacra, or select anthems in score, for one two, and three voices. pp.34. *I. Walsh: London*, [c.1730 or later] fol. [Inscribed 'R. Fitzwilliam 1771'].
MU. 366^2

Te Deum et Jubilate, for voices and instruments, perform'd . . . on the thanksgiving-day, for the glorious successes of Her Majesty's army . . . The second edition. pp.48. [*J. Walsh . . ., J. Hare . . . and P. Randall*] [covered by a pasted slip reading 'Sold by Mickepher Rawlins']: *London*, [1707] fol. [With a long note in an eighteenth-century hand concerning an earlier edition of this work. This copy belonged to the double bass player Domenico Dragonetti, who left it to Vincent Novello. A long note in Novello's hand concerns its provenance and his decision to give it to the Fitzwilliam Museum, where he had spent 'so many happy hours' studying 'the sterling works of the delightful composers of the *good* old school'].
MU. 491^1

[Another issue]. Te Deum et Jubilate, for voices and instruments. Perform'd before the sons of the clergy. [Imperfect: wants pp.19–48]. *Iohn Walsh: London*, [c.1731 or later] fol. [Inscribed 'R. Fitzwilliam 1771'].
MU. 366^3

b. Odes

Odes and choral songs. [Comprises: 1. The song performed at the Yorkshire feast 1689; 2. Commemoration Ode; 3. Ode on the Queen's birthday. [*Benjamin Goodison's Purcell subscription*]. Inscribed 'Fitzwilliam 1799'].
MU. 341 A^2, 341 B^1

c. Dramatic music

Amphitryon; or, The Two Sofia's. A comedy . . . Written by Mr. Dryden. To which is added, the musick of the songs. pp.57, 13. *Printed for J. Tonson . . . and M. Tonson: London*, 1691 4°. [With a separate title page to the songs: 'The songs in Amphitryon with the musick. *J. Heptinstall for Jacob Tonson: London*, 1690'].
MU. 1315

[Dioclesian]. The vocal and instrumental musick of the Prophetess, or the History of Dioclesian. [Score]. pp.173. *Printed by J. Heptinstall, for the Author: London*, 1691 fol. [Inscribed 'R. Fitzwilliam 1774'].
MU. 379

The Indian Queen *see below*: The Tempest

King Arthur *see below*: Oedipus

[Oedipus]. The music of the masque in Oedipus. King Arthur. [*Benjamin Goodison's Purcell subscription*].
MU. 341 B^2

The Tempest. The Indian Queen. [*Benjamin Goodison's Purcell subscription*].
MU. 341 A^1

[The Tempest]. Come unto these yellow sands. A favorite song in the Tempest. ff.[2]. *Robt. Birchall: London*, [c.1795] fol.
MU. 1211^{35}

[The Tempest]. Full fathom five thy father lies. A favorite song in the Tempest. pp.3. *Robert Birchall: London*, [c.1790] fol.
MU. 1211^{37}

d. Songs

Bess of Bedlam. [Song, begins: 'From silent shad's and the Elizium groves']. ff.63–4 *of a collection. [London*, c.1720] fol.
MU. 1197^3

Orpheus Britannicus. A collection of all the choicest songs for one, two, and three voices. ⟨The second book, which renders the first compleat⟩. 2 vols. *Printed by J. Heptinstall ⟨William Pearson⟩, for Henry Playford: London*, 1698–1702 fol. [With a frontispiece to each volume. Both volumes inscribed 'R. Fitzwilliam 1766'].
MU. 375^1, 376

[Another edition]. Orpheus Britannicus . . . ⟨The second book, which renders the first compleat⟩. The second edition with large additions. 2 vols. *Printed by William Pearson, and sold by John Young: London*, 1706–12 fol. [With a frontispiece. Inscribed 'R.M. Bacon', presumably Richard Mackenzie Bacon, editor of 'The Quarterly Musical Magazine and Review', 1818–30].
MU. 1306.

3. Instrumental music

A collection of ayres, compos'd for the theatre, and upon other occasions. [4 parts]. *Printed by J. Heptinstall, for Frances Purcell . . . sold by B. Aylmer: London*, 1697. fol.
MU. 1307–10

A choice collection of lessons for the harpsichord or spinnet . . . The third edition with additions & instructions for beginers. pp.63. *Printed on copper plates for Mrs. Frances Purcell . . . and are to be sold at her house: London*, [c.1700] 8°. [Inscribed 'R. Fitzwilliam 1766'].
MU. 419

Sonnata's of III parts: two viollins and basse: to the organ or harpsecord. [4 parts]. *Printed for the Author: and sold by I. Playford and I. Carr: London*, 1683 4°.
MU. 1311–14

Ten sonatas in four parts. [4 parts]. *Printed by J. Heptinstall: London*, 1697 fol. [Inscribed 'J. Talbot. 1697', presumably James Talbot, Regius Professor of Hebrew at Cambridge and writer on musical instruments. His ode on Purcell's death appears in 'Orpheus Britannicus'].
MU. 507–10

Voluntary. Said to be Purcell's. [*Benjamin Goodison's Purcell subscription*].
MU. 341 A^3

4. Appendix

see ANTHEMS

see CATCH CLUB

PYRRHUS *see* PIRRO E DEMETRIO

QUARLES (CHARLES)

Lesson. pp.[2]. [*Benjamin Goodison's Purcell subscription: London*, c.1790] fol.
MU. 341 B^3

QUEEN

Queen of citty's raise thy head. *The Silver Thames or Queen of Citty's*. [*London*, c.1720] s.sh. fol.
MU. 1190[62]

RAIL NO MORE *see* BOYCE (W.)

RAMEAU (JEAN PHILIPPE)

Five concertos for the harpsicord . . . accompanied with a violin or German flute or two violins or viola. With some select pieces for the harpsicord alone. [Score, with separate optional violin 2. Imperfect: wants optional violin 2]. *I. Walsh: London*, [1750] fol. [Inscribed 'R. Fitzwilliam 1771'].
MU. 486[2]

Les Festes de l'Hymen et de l'Amour, ou les Dieux d'Egypte, ballet heroïque. [Words by L. de Cahusac]. [Score]. pp.144. *Chez l'Auteur . . . La Veuve Boivin . . . M. Leclair: Paris*, [c.1749] obl. fol. [Inscribed 'Fitzwilliam 1782'].
MU. 490[1]

Les Fêtes de Polymnie. Balles héroique. [Words by L. de Cahusac]. [Score]. pp.151. *Chez Madame Boivin . . . le S[r]. le Clerc . . . l'Auteur: Paris*, [c.1753] obl. fol. [Inscribed 'Fitzwilliam 1782'].
MU. 490[2]

A collection of lessons for the harpsicord . . . Opera seconda. pp.29. *I. Walsh: London*, [1760] obl. fol. [Inscribed 'R. Fitzwilliam 1770'].
MU. 484[3]

A 2[d] collection of lessons for the harpsicord . . . Opera 3[za]. [Figures in MS]. pp.27. *I. Walsh: London*, [1764] obl. fol. [Inscribed 'R. Fitzwilliam 1771'].
MU. 484[4]

Pieces de clavecin en concerts. [Score]. pp.40. *Chez L'Auteur . . . La Veuve Boivin . . . M. Le Clair: Paris*, 1741 fol. [Inscribed 'R. Fitzwilliam 1769'].
MU. 427

Pigmalion, acte de ballet. [Words by La Motte, arranged by B. de Savot]. [Score]. pp.43. *Chez l'Auteur . . . La Veuve Boivin . . . M. Leclair: Paris*, [c.1750] obl. fol. [Inscribed 'Fitzwilliam 1765'].
MU. 359

[Another copy]. [Imperfect: wants title. Inscribed 'Fitzwilliam 1782'].
MU. 358

Les Surprises de l'Amour. Ballet composé de III actes séparés . . . Les paroles sont de Mr Bernard. [The acts are entitled: 'L'Enlevement d'Adonis', 'La Lyre Enchantée', 'Anacreon'. They are followed by 'Les Sibarites. Ballet en un acte

ajouté aux Surprises de l'Amour']. [Score]. pp.57, 55, 65, 56. *Chez M. Leclerc . . . M. Bayard . . . Mlle. Castagnery . . . M. D'aumont: Paris,* [1757] fol. [Inscribed 'Fitzwilliam 1782', and on a preliminary blank, apparently in the same hand, '6.2 Livres Paris 20 Jul 1781'. With a few corrections in contemporary MS].
MU. 303

RAVENSCROFT (JOHN)

Foolish woman fly mens charms. *A song.* [*London,* c.1725] s.sh. fol.
MU. 1190^{15}

RAYMOND

Damon's Request. [Song, begins: 'Ye gentle gales that fan the air']. [*London,* c.1750] s.sh. fol.
MU. 1197^{8}

REEVE (WILLIAM), DAVY (JOHN) and BRAHAM (JOHN)

Thirty Thousand, or Who's the Richest? A comic opera . . . the words by T. Dibdin. pp.73. *Joseph Dale & Son: London,* [c.1805] fol.
MU. 1186^{6}

REST LADY FAIR *see* WINTER (J.D.)

RESTLESS

Restless to pass the tedious day. *Henry to Emma. A song. The words by a gentl^n. Set by a person of quality.* [*London,* c.1720] s.sh. fol.
MU. 1190^{72}

RICCI (F.P.) *see* WEBBE (S., THE ELDER), A collection of masses

RICCIOTTI (CARLO BACCICCIA)

VI. Concerti armonici a quattro violini obligati, alto viola, violoncello obligato e basso continuo. [7 parts]. *J. Walsh: London,* [1775] fol. [The attribution to Ricciotti is disputed].
MU. 320 G^{15}, 320 H^{15}, 320 I^{15}, 320 J^{15}, 320 K^{15}, 320 M^{15}, 320 N^{15}

RICH GRIPE *see* TURNER (W.), An Epigram

RICHARDSON (WILLIAM)

Lessons for the harpsichord or spinet; containing an overture, a ground, and a chacoon, with several almands and airs. ff.[14]. *Printed for yᵉ Author: London*, 1708 [altered in MS to 1704] obl. fol.
MU. 361 B

RICHTER (F.X.) *see* THE SUMMER'S TALE

RILEY (WILLIAM)

Roger of the Dale. [Song, begins: 'Ye gentle winds that fan the sea']. [*London*, c.1750] s.sh. fol.
MU. 1197[78]

ROBERTS (H.) *see* CALLIOPE

ROGER (ESTIENNE)

VI Suittes, divers airs avec leurs variations & fugues, pour le clavessin, de divers excellents maîtres. pp.57. *Chez Estienne Roger: Amsterdam*, [c.1710] fol. [Inscribed 'R. Fitzwilliam 1765'].
MU. 436

ROSEINGRAVE (THOMAS)

Voluntarys and fugues made on purpose for the organ or harpsicord. pp. 29. Plate no. 193. *I: Walsh: London*, [c.1730] fol. [Inscribed 'R. Fitzwilliam 1768'].
MU. 486[3]

ROSEINGRAVE (T.) *see* SCARLATTI (D.), Forty two suits of lessons

ROSEINGRAVE (THOMAS) and SCARLATTI (DOMENICO)

Six double fugues for the organ or harpsicord . . . To which is added, Sigʳ. Dominico Scarlatti's celebrated lesson for the harpsichord, with several additions by Mʳ. Roseingrave. pp.25. *I. Walsh: London*, [1750] obl. fol. [Inscribed 'R. Fitzwilliam 1772'].
MU. 484[5]

ROSS (JOHN)

A first set of ten songs, in score, dedicated . . . to Sir Willᵐ. Forbes, Barᵗ. of Craigevar . . . Op. 2. pp.43. *Printed for the Author, & sold by Preston & Son: London*, [c.1790] fol.
MU. 1200

ROUSSEAU (JEAN JACQUES)

Le Devin du Village. Intermède ... avec l'ariette ajoutée par M^r. Philidor. [Score]. pp.101. *Chez Le Clerc.: Paris,* [c.1765] fol.
MU. 1214

THE ROYAL MERCHANT

Royal Merchant. Overture. [By Thomas Linley the elder]. [Keyboard]. ff.5. [*London*, c.1768] obl. fol. [This is the first item of a pair containing on blanks violin 2 of quartet Op.2 by Giovanni Punto (Johann Wenzel Stich), in MS signed 'Jean Challon'].
MU. 1429^1

THE ROYAL REVENGE

Oh, thou connubial god. Epithalamium in an invocation of Hymen. Sung in the play call'd the Royal Revenge. [*London*, c.1720] s.sh. fol.
MU. 1190^{86}

ROZELLI

Cupid's Defeat. [Song, begins: 'Since Caelia's unkind']. [*London*, c.1745] s.sh. fol.
MU. 1189^{42}

RUSSEL (D.) *see* THE SUMMER'S TALE

SACCHINI (ANTONIO MARIA GASPARO)

Il Cid. Overture. [Keyboard]. pp.5. [*London*, c.1775] fol.
MU. 1400^5

see MOTEZUMA

see TAMERLANO

THE SACRIFICE OF IPHIGENIA

How sweet are the flowers. *A favourite song in the Sacrifice of Iphigenia.* [By T.A. Arne]. [*London*, c.1765] s.sh. fol.
MU. 1197^{12}

SAD AND FEARFUL IS THE STORY *see* BARTHELEMON (F.H.)

SAINT GERMAIN (DE) *see* THE SUMMER'S TALE

SAMMARTINI (G.) *see* SAN MARTINI (G.)

SAN MARTINI (GIUSEPPE)

Giuseppe S^t. Martini's concertos for the harpsicord or organ with the instrumental parts for violins &c. Opera nona. [Keyboard only]. *I. Walsh: London,* [1754] fol. [Inscribed 'R. Fitzwilliam 1770'].
MU. 486^4

Eight overtures in eight parts, for violins, hoboys, French horns, &c. with a through bass for the harpsicord or violoncello. And six grand concertos for violins &c. [12 parts, with a second copy of violoncello/cembalo]. *I. Walsh: London,* [1752] fol.
MU. 320 B^1, 320 C^1, 320 D, 320 E^2, 320 F^2, 320 G^{12}, 320 H^{12}, 320 I^{12}, 320 J^{12}, 320 K^{12}, 320 L^2, 320 M^{12}, 320 N^{12}

XII Sonate a due violini, e violoncello, e cembalo, se piace, Opera terza, dedicata all' Altezza Reale di Augusta Principessa di Vallia. [3 parts]. *I. Walsh: London,* [1747] fol.
MU. 318 A^9, 318 B^9, 318 D^9

SARTI (GIUSEPPE)

Ah! proteggete o Dei. *Duetto.* pp.3. [*Benjamin Goodison's Purcell subscription: London,* c.1790] fol.
MU. 341 B^5

SAVILE (J.) *see* PLAYFORD (J.), Select musicall ayres and dialogues

SAY MYRA *see* HOWARD (S.), Myra

SCARLAIT (A.) *see* THOMYRIS

SCARLATTI (A.) *see* BABELL (W.), The 3^d. book of the ladys entertainment; *see* PIRRO E DEMETRIO; *see* THOMYRIS

SCARLATTI (DOMENICO)

Essercizi per gravicembalo. pp.110. [*London,* 1739] obl. fol. [Inscribed 'R. Fitzwilliam 1769'].
MU. 422

Forty two suits of lessons for the harpsicord . . . revised [by] T. Roseingrave. 2 vols. [Imperfect: wants vol.II]. *John Johnson: London,* [c.1748] obl. fol. [Inscribed 'Fitzwilliam 1799'].
MU. 362 C

Libro de XII sonatas modernas para clavicordio. [Edited by J. Worgan]. pp.41. *Printed for the Editor & sold by J. Johnson: London*, [1752] fol. [Inscribed 'R. Fitzwilliam 1771'].
MU. 486⁵

Six sonatas for the harpsichord . . . Vol. III. pp.25. *John Johnson: London*, [1757] obl. fol. [Vols.I and II are comprised by 'Forty two suits of lessons for the harpsicord . . . revised [by] T. Roseingrave'].
MU. 362 D

Thirty sonatas, for the harpsichord or piano-forte; publish'd (by permission) from manuscripts in the possession of Lord Viscount Fitzwilliam. [i.e. MU. MS 147]. pp.63. *Rᵗ. Birchall: London*, [1800] fol. [Inscribed 'Fitzwilliam 1800'].
MU. 423

see ROSEINGRAVE (T.) and SCARLATTI (D.)

SCHENCK (JEAN)

Select lessons for the bass viol of two parts . . . the first collection. [1 part only]. *I. Walsh and I. Hare: London*, [c. 1730] obl. fol.
MU.882

SCHMIDLIN (JOHANNES)

Singendes und Spielendes Vergnügen reiner Andacht, oder Geistreiche Gesänge, nach der Wahl des Besten gesammlet . . . mit Musicalischen Compositionen begleitet . . . Zweyte, vermehrt- und privilegirte Auflage. pp.941, [2]. *Getruckt in Bürgklischer Truckerey: Zurich*, 1758 8°. [With a frontispiece. Contemporary MS leaves (one containing instructions for the cittern) bound at front and back].
MU. 1275

SCOTS

A selection of the most favourite Scots-songs, chiefly pastoral, adapted for the harpsichord, with an accompaniment for a violin, by eminent masters . . . inscribed to . . . the Duchess of Gordon. [Edited by William Napier]. pp.iv, 16, 77, ii. *Willᵐ. Napier: London*, [1790] fol. [With a subscribers' list. Inscribed 'R.J.S. Stevens, Charter house, 1822'].
MU. 1298

SEE

See after the toils *see* ECCLES (J.), [Semele]

See that nymph *see* VANBRUGHE (G.), The Lovely Mourner

See that rill *see* TURNER (W.), On decanting a flask of Florence

See the purple morn *see* TENDUCCI (G.F.), Tenducci's new rondeau

SEXTON (W.) *see* HANDEL (G.F.), Eight anthems . . . dedicated to . . .
the Princess of Wales [selections and arrangements: anthems]

SHAPE

A shape alone let others prize. [Song]. [*London*, c.1750] s.sh. fol.
MU. 1189[18]

SHAW *see* CAVENDISH (G.)

SHEPHERD WHEN THOU SEE'ST ME FLY *see* YOUNG (A.)

SHIELD (WILLIAM)

The Billet Doux. A favourite ballad . . . Written by J. O'Keefe. pp.3. *Harrison &
Co: London*, [1798] fol.
MU. 1287[16]

[The Farmer]. The Plough Boy, sung . . . in the Farmer. Written by J. O'Keefe.
[Begins: 'A flaxen headed cow boy']. pp.4. *Longman and Broderip: London*,
[c.1790] fol.
MU. 1287[9]

From night till morn I take my glass. A favorite duett . . . the accompanyments
by M[r]. Shield. pp.4. *Longman and Broderip: London*, [c.1790] fol.
MU. 1211[3]

The Poor Soldier, a comic opera . . . selected and compos'd by William Shield.
[Words by J. O'Keefe]. pp.30. *J: Bland: London*, [1782] obl. fol.
MU. 1254[2]

Rosina, a comic opera. [Words by F. Brooke]. pp.38. *Willm. Napier: London*,
[1783] obl. fol. [With figured bass in MS].
MU. 1258[1]

[Rosina]. When the rosy morn appearing . . . in the opera of Rosina. pp.6–8 *of a
collection. Goulding D'Almaine Potter & Co: London*, [1820[WM]] fol.
MU. 592

[The Siege of Belgrade]. Tho you think by this to vex me. A favorite song . . . in
the Siege of Belgrade, composed by W. Shield. [Opera actually by S. Storace,
using material from Martin y Soler's 'Una Cosa Rara']. pp.4. *G. Walker: London*,
[c.1800] fol.
MU. 1211[24]

[The Wandering Melodist]. Sally Roy, a Scottish ballad . . . in . . . the
Wandering Melodist. The words by M[r]. Rannie. [Begins: 'Fair Sally once the
village pride']. pp.3. *Goulding, Phipps & D'Almaine: London*, [c.1800] fol. [Ini-
tialled 'A.M.J.', i.e. A.M. Jeffery: later Mrs R.J.S. Stevens].
MU. 1287[6]

[The Woodman]. The streamlet that flow'd round her cot. A favorite song . . . in the Woodman. [Words by B. Dudley]. pp.4. *Longman and Broderip: London,* [1791] fol. [Inscribed 'A.M. Jeffery': later Mrs R.J.S. Stevens].
MU. 1287[27]

see PARKE (W.T.)

SIGH NO MORE *see* STEVENS (R.J.S.)

SILVANI (M.) *see* MAZZAFERRATA (G.B.)

SILVIA

Silvia bright nymph who long had found. *A new song.* [London, c.1750] s.sh. fol.
MU. 1189[25]

SIME (DAVID)

The Edinburgh Musical Miscellany: a collection of the most approved Scotch, English and Irish songs. [Melody]. 2 vols. *W. Gordon ⟨John Turner⟩: Edinburgh,* 1792–3 8°. [With a frontispiece to vol. I].
MU. 1208 A–B

SIMPSON (CHRISTOPHER)

Chelys, minuritionum artificio exornata: sive, minuritiones ad basin, etiam ex-tempore modulandi ratio . . . The division-viol: or, the art of playing ex-tempore upon a ground . . . Editio tertia: prioribus longe auctior. pp.67, 13. *Printed by William Pearson, for Richard Mears . . . and Allexander Livingston: London,* 1712 fol. [With contemporary record of domestic accounts in MS on blanks].
MU. 1320

SINCE

Since Caelia's unkind *see* ROZELLI

Since first I saw your face, a favorite glee for four voices. [By T. Ford]. ff.[2]. *J. Dale: London,* [c.1800] fol.
MU. 1211[15]

SING

Sing ye muses praises sounding. *The Happy Pair. Set by an eminent master.* [Song]. [London, c.1725] s.sh. fol.
MU. 1190[32]

SINGING CHARMS THE BLESS'D ABOVE *see* TURNER (W.),
A song (On Mira's singing and beauty)

SIR

Sir, what's o'clock? *The Stutterers. A glee, for three voices.* [MS attribution to
Samuel Pegge]. pp.4. [c.1810] obl. fol.
MU. 1288 A^9

SLEEP

Sleep poor babe. *For the Harpsicord.* [Song]. *p.3 of a collection.* [c.1790] fol.
MU. 1287^{33}

A SLIGHTED SHEPHERD *see* MATTOX

SMEGERGILL (W.) *see* PLAYFORD (J.), Select musicall ayres and
dialogues

SMILING

The smiling morn, the breathing spring. *The Birks of Endermay.* [Words by D.
Mallet]. [Song]. [*London*, c.1750] s.sh. fol.
MU. 1189^{4a}

SMITH (CLEMENT)

Old England for ever & God save the King, in commemoration of His Majesty's
entering the fiftieth year of his reign, written by the Rev^d. D.G. Delafosse.
[Score]. pp.3. *L. Lavenu: London*, [1810] fol.
MU. 380 D^2

SMITH (JOHN CHRISTOPHER)

The Fairies, an opera. The words taken from Shakespear, &c. [Words adapted by
D. Garrick]. [Score]. pp.92. *I. Walsh: London*, [1755] fol. [With some perform-
ance markings].
MU. 1183 B

A collection of lessons for the harpsicord . . . Opera III ⟨IV⟩. 2 vols, *continuously
paginated. I. Walsh: London*, [c.1757] obl. fol.
MU. 483$^{2-3}$

Suites de pieces pour le clavecin. [Second book]. pp.82. Plate no. 490. *John
Walsh: London*, [c.1737] obl. fol. [Inscribed 'Fitzwilliam 1782'].
MU. 483^1

XII Sonatas for the harpsicord. Opera quinta. Most humbly inscrib'd to Her Royal Highness the Princess Dowager of Wales. pp.75. *I. Walsh: London*, [1765] obl. fol.
MU. 483⁴

The Tempest, an opera. The words taken from Shakespear &c.. [Words adapted by D. Garrick]. [Score]. pp.110. *I. Walsh: London*, [1756] fol.
MU. 1183 C

SMITH (JOHN STAFFORD)

A collection of English songs, in score for three and four voices, composed about the year 1500, taken from M.S.S. of the same age. pp.12, 65. *J. Bland: London*, 1779 [date in MS] fol. [Inscribed 'Fitzwilliam 1793'. With a subscribers' list].
MU. 494²

see AMUSEMENT

SMITH (THEODORE)

Three favourite duets, for two performers on one harpsichord or piano forte, dedicated to the Right Honorable Lady Ann and Lady Sarah Windsor. [The same work as 'Trois sonates en duo' published in Berlin as Op.1]. pp.15. *Rᵗ. Birchall: London*, [c.1790] fol. [Inscribed 'A.M. Jeffery': later Mrs R.J.S. Stevens].
MU. 1288 C

Six sonatas for the harpsichord or piano forte, with an accompanyment for a violin. Dedicated to Miss Quin . . . Opera VIII. pp.35. *Welcker: London*, [c.1790] obl. fol.
MU. 1244¹

SNOW (JOHN)

The Bird. A favourite song. [Begins: 'The bird that hears her nestlings cry']. [*London*, c.1760] s.sh. fol.
MU. 1197⁷²

SO BRIGHTLY SWEET *see* HAWDOWN (M.)

SOBER LAY *see* STEVENS (R.J.S.)

SOFT, SENSIBLE AND TRUE *see* SUETT (R.)

SOLER (ANTONIO)

XXVII Sonatas para clave. pp.91. *Que ha impresso Roberto Birchall: London,* [c.1795] obl. fol. [Inscribed 'Fitzwilliam 1796'. Facing the title the Founder has written, 'The originals of these harpsichord lessons were given to me by Father Soler, at the Escurial, the 14th. February, 1772. Father Soler had been instructed by Scarlatti'. There is no record of such MSS in the Museum].
MU. 418

SOLER (M. y) *see* COMUS; *see* SHIELD (W.), The Siege of Belgrade; *see* STORACE (S.), The Siege of Belgrade

SOME

Some kind angel, gently flying. *The Separation.* [Song]. [*London*, c.1760] s.sh. fol.
MU. 1197[69]

Some of my heroes *see* STEVENS (R.J.S.)

SONGS

[French songs]. pp.12, 2–16. [Imperfect: wants title and various pages. A collection of songs, the underlay in handwritten style, with piano or harp accompaniment. The songs are 'Romance', 'La Séparation', 'Eléonore', 'Clément Marot et Marguerite de Valois', 'Le Troubadour', 'Arthur et Emma', 'La Chapelle de Seugy', an incomplete piece concerning lovers meeting in a ruined church, 'Le Guerrier', 'Clara', 'Les Regrets', 'L'Amant inconsolable', 'Refrain d'Alain Chartier', 'Le Chevalier', 'Rosamonde'. Performance markings have been added in MS]. [c.1820] fol.
MU. 1440[5]

SOUS LE CIEL DOUX ET PUR *see* GUIGOU; *see* PAER (F.); *see* SPONTINI (G.)

SPOIL'D CHILD

Since, then I'm doom'd. I am a brisk and sprightly lad. *Sung ... in the Spoil'd Child.* [Words probably by I. Bickerstaff]. pp.3. [c.1790] fol. [Inscribed 'A.M. Jeffery': later Mrs R.J.S. Stevens].
MU. 1287[18]

SPONTINI (GASPARE)

La nouvelle Valentine, stances élégiaques sur la mort de S.A.R. Monseigneur le Duc de Berry, paroles de madame P⎯ ... Dédiées à son Excellence Monsieur

le Comte de Pradel. [Begins: 'Sous le ciel doux et pur']. ff.6. *Chez M^{elles}. Erard: Paris*, [c.1820] fol. [Inscribed 'Hommage de l'auteur des paroles'].
MU. 1440^4

STAND BY! *see* CAREY (H.), The Provoked Husband

STANLEY (JOHN)

Twelve [corrected in MS to '4'] cantatas for the voice, harpsichord, and violin. pp.16. Plate no. 80 of 'The New Musical Magazine'. *Harrison & Co: London*, [c.1785] obl. fol.
MU. 1227

Six concertos set for the harpsicord or organ . . . N.B. The 1st. & 2^d. repienos, tenor, & basso repieno of his violin concertos, are the instrumental parts to the above. pp.32. *I. Walsh: London*, [c.1754] fol. [Inscribed 'R. Fitzwilliam 1775'].
MU. 486^6

Six concertos in seven parts for four violins, a tenor, with a bass for the harpsicord and violoncello. [7 parts]. *I. Walsh: London*, [c.1750] fol.
MU. 320 G^{13}, 320 H^{13}, 320 I^{13}, 320 J^{13}, 320 K^{13}, 320 M^{13}, 320 N^{13}

Eight solo's for a German flute, violin or harpsicord . . . Opera prima. pp.33. *J. Johnson: London*, [1740] obl. fol.
MU. 1229

Ten voluntarys for the organ or harpsicord . . . Opera 5th: [figure in MS]. pp.38. *John Johnson: London*, [c.1750] obl. fol. [Inscribed 'R. Fitzwilliam 1775'].
MU. 484^6

Ten voluntarys for the organ or harpsicord . . . Opera sesta. pp.32. *John Johnson: London*, [1752] obl. fol.
MU. 484^7

Ten voluntaries for the organ or harpsichord . . . Opera settima. pp.33. *John Johnson: London*, [1754] obl. fol.
MU. 484^8

see THE SUMMER'S TALE

STARTER (JAN JANSZOON)

Friesche Lust-Hof, beplant met verscheyde stichtelyke Minne-Liedekens, Gedichten, ende Boertige Kluchten. Den tweeden druck op nieuws vermeerdert ende verbetert. 2 vols, *the second unpaginated. Voor de Weduwe van Dirck Pietersz: Voscuyl: Amsterdam*, [c.1622–5] obl. 4°. [With a frontispiece and illustrations].
MU. 1336

STEFFANI (AGOSTINO)

Duetti. pp.16. [*Benjamin Goodison's Purcell subscription: London*, 1787] fol. [The final piece is incomplete: no more published].
MU. 341 B⁴

STEINER (JOHANN LUDWIG)

[Neues Gesang-Buch auserlesener, geistreicher Liedern, zum Lob und Preis Gottes . . . Mit neuen . . . zu drey und vier Stimmen gesetzten Melodeyen, und einem . . . General-Bass versehen. pp.792. [Imperfect: wants title]. [*Bey Heidegger und Rahn: Zürich*, 1723] 8°.
MU. 1454

STEPHENSON (JOSEPH)

Church harmony sacred to devotion, being a choice set of new anthem & psalm tunes . . . The 3ᵈ: edition. pp.51. *Printed for J. Rivington & J. Fletcher . . . James Fletcher . . . the Author: London*, [1760] fol.
MU. 476²

STEVENS (RICHARD JOHN SAMUEL)

All in the downs. A favorite song by Mʳ. Gay. pp.4. *S.A. & P. Thompson: London*, [c.1785] fol. [6 copies].
MU. 1288 B¹⁵⁻²⁰

Blow blow thou winter wind. *Glee, for four voices. The poetry from Shakespeare's, As you like it.* pp.5. *Printed for the Author: London*, [c.1800] obl. fol. [Inscribed by Stevens 'First publication, separate'].
MU. 1250³

Bragela. The poetry from Ossian. Trio for two soprano's and a bass, with an accompaniment for two performers on one piano forte. [Words by J. Macpherson. Begins: 'O strike the harp']. pp.12. *Printed & sold for the Author, by Preston: London*, [1821ᵂᴹ] fol.
MU. 1288 B⁹

The collect for the first Sunday in Advent, for four voices. [Begins: 'Almighty God, give us grace']. pp.4. *Preston: London*, [c.1810] fol. [5 copies, one corrected by Stevens].
MU. 1384

Crabbed age and youth. *Chearful glee for four voices. The poetry from Shakespear.* pp.4. *Printed for the Author: London*, [c.1798] obl. fol.
MU. 1230¹⁵

[Another copy].
MU. 1250^{13}

Doubt thou the stars are fire. *Glee, for four voices. Poetry from Shakespeare's Hamlet. Harmoniz'd from a song of the author's.* pp.8–9 *of a collection. Printed for the Author: London*, [c.1790] obl. fol. [2 copies].
MU. 1288 A$^{3-4}$

Floreat Aeternum, &c. An ancient Charterhouse sentiment, set to music for Founders Day, 1811. pp.3. *Preston: London*, [c.1811] fol. [With a second copy of p.3].
MU. 1288 B^{13}

From Oberon in fairy land. *Fairy glee for four voices . . . The poetry attributed to Ben Johnson.* pp.7. [*London*, c.1796] obl. fol.
MU. 1230^{11}

[Another copy].
MU. 1250^{10}

Eight glees for four and five voices . . . inscribed to His Grace the duke of Hamilton and Brandon . . . Opera 3. pp.43. *Broderip & Wilkinson: London*, [c.1800] obl. fol. [Stevens gave this copy to a Mrs Brown in 1807. He has noted that nos.2 and 4 were composed for a Miss Thurlow].
MU. 1250^{1}

[Another copy].
MU. 1230^{4}

Eight glees. Expressly composed for ladies . . . inscribed to Miss Maria & Miss Frances Simpson . . . Op.IV. pp.30. *Printed for the Author:* [*London*, c.1795] obl. fol.
MU. 1250^{2}

[Another issue]. [c.1800]. [With Stevens's MS note of the dedicatees' married names].
MU. 1230^{5}

[Another copy of one of the two above]. [Imperfect: wants title and pp.1–2, 6–9, 22–6].
MU. 1289 B–F

Seven glees, with a witches song & chorus, and two glees from melodies, by Henry Lawes . . . Opera, 6. pp.59. *Printed for the Author, Charterhouse, by Preston: London*, [c.1800] obl. fol. [This is the first item in a compilation of Stevens's works which the composer has revised and annotated throughout].
MU. 1230^{1}

Ten glees for three, four, five & six voices . . . Op.V. pp.59. *Printed for the Author: London*, [c.1789] obl. fol.
MU. 1230^{6}

[Another copy].
MU. 1250⁴

He may come if he dare, or, The Corsican Tyrant. The poetry by Edward Coxe. [Begins: 'To subdue the Armadas', [c.1805] fol. [This is the first item in a volume originally labelled 'A.M. Jeffery': later Mrs R.J.S. Stevens].
MU. 1287¹

[Another 7 copies].
MU. 1288 B¹⁻⁷

✠ O mistress mine. *Glee, for five voices.* [Words from Shakespeare's 'Twelfth Night']. pp.5. *Printed by Longman and Broderip (for the Author): London,* [c.1790] obl. fol. [Most of the items in 1288, all unbound, are associated with Anna Jeffery, who married Stevens in 1810. Several have been inscribed to her by the composer].
MU. 1288 A¹

[Another issue]. *Printed for the Author, by Longman, Clementi & Co: London,* [c.1800].
MU. 1230⁸

[Another copy].
MU. 1250⁶

Our tars so fam'd in story. [Song, begins: 'Ye British youths who danger brave']. pp.3. *Printed for the Author:* [*London,* c.1795] fol.
MU. 1287²

[Another copy].
MU. 1288 B²³

Sacred music, for one, two, three, & four voices. From the works of the most esteemed composers, Italian & English . . . Vol.I ⟨–III⟩. 3 vols. *Printed for the Editor: London,* [c.1802] fol. [Inscribed 'R.J.S. Stevens, Charterhouse, 1802', with notes of sources in his hand].
MU. 1290 A–C

✠ Sigh no more ladies. *Glee.* [Words from Shakespeare's 'Much Ado about Nothing']. pp.20–3 *of a collection. Longman and Broderip: London,* [c.1790] obl. fol.
MU. 1230⁷

[Another issue]. pp.310–11 *of a collection. F. Linley: London,* [c.1798] fol.
MU. 1211²²

[Another issue]. pp.19–23 *of a collection. Longman, Clementi, & Co: London,* [c.1800] obl. fol.
MU. 1250⁵

[Another copy].
MU. 1288 A^2

✻ Sober lay and mirthful glee. To the Society of Harmonist's . . . (The poetry by Samuel Birch). pp.5. *Printed for the Author*: [*London*, c.1800] fol. [3 copies. 1288 B^{12} is inscribed by Stevens, 'Miss Jeffery with the authors most respectful compliments'].
MU. 1288 B$^{10-12}$

✻ Some of my heroes are low. *Glee for 5 voices. The poetry from Ossian . . . dedicated to . . . Thomas Carter.* [Words by J. Macpherson]. pp.9. *Printed for the Author: London*, [c.1790] obl. fol.
MU. 1288 A^7

[Another issue]. [c.1790].
MU. 1288 A^8

[Another copy].
MU. 1230^{13}

[Another copy].
MU. 1250^{11}

Three sonatas for the harpsichord or piano-forte, with an accompaniment for a violin . . . inscribed to Miss Thurlow . . . Opera prima. [2 parts]. *Printed for the Author by S.A. & P. Thompson: London*, [c.1786] fol.
MU. 1292

Ten songs with an accompaniment for two violins . . . inscribed to the Right Honorable Lady Anna Maria Bowes . . . Opera II. pp.26. *Printed for the Author by A. & P. Thompson: London*, [c.1788] fol.
MU. 1291

To banish life's troubles. An Anacreontic song . . . the words by M^r. Oakman. pp.4. *Printed for S.A. & P. Thompson: London*, [c.1790] fol.
MU. 1289 I

To what age must we live without love? A trio, for two soprano's & a bass; with an accompaniment for two performers on the piano forte . . . The poetry by Richard Cumberland. pp.7. *Printed & sold for the Author, by Preston: London*, [c.1803] fol. [Inscribed 'Miss Jeffery. From the Author'].
MU. 1288 B^8

[Another copy].
MU. 1211^{27}

Unfading Beauty. A sonnet. The words by Thomas Carew. [Begins: 'He that loves a rosy cheek']. [*London*, c.1790] s.sh. fol. [2 copies].
MU. 1288 B$^{21-2}$

✻ What shall he have who merits most? *Archer's glee. The words by a lady* [i.e. Lady

de Crespigny], *upon the Duke of Clarence's giving a buglehorn to be shot for by the Royal Surry Bowmen, to whom this glee is respectfully inscribed.* pp.6. [c.1795] obl. fol.
MU. 1250⁹

[Another copy].
MU. 1289 A

[Another issue]. *Printed for the Author*: [c.1800].
MU. 1230¹⁰

✴ When the toil of day is o'er, a favorite glee for 4 voices . . . The poetry by Mʳ Merry. pp.5. *Printed for the Author*: [c.1800] obl. fol.
MU. 1230¹⁴

[Another copy].
MU. 1250¹²

Who is it that this dark night. *Dialogue and duetto, the poetry by Sir Philip Sidney . . . dedicated to Mʳˢ. Hughes.* pp.5. *Printed for the Author*: [c.1795] fol.
MU. 1293

✴Who is Sylvia? A new glee for five voices . . . in the comedy, of the Two Gentlemen of Verona . . . the words by Shakespeare. pp.7. *Printed & sold by Preston: London*, [c.1807ᵂᴹ] fol. [Inscribed 'Miss Jeffery from the Author. May. 1808'].
MU. 1288 B¹⁴

✴ Ye spotted snakes! Glee for four voices. Words from Shakespeare. pp.6. *Printed by Longman, Clementi & Co: London*, [c.1800] obl. fol.
MU. 1230⁹

[Another copy]. [Inscribed by Stevens, 'The Burthen added for Miss Marlow to sing at Lord Exeters'].
MU. 1250⁷

see AMUSEMENT

see CHARMING

see FORD (T.)

see GLEES

see HOWARD (S.), Ye chearful virgins

see TATTERSALL (W.D.)

see WHEN, When Chloris, like an angel, walks

STEVENSON (SIR JOHN ANDREW)

Tell me where is fancy bred, a duett . . . with an accompaniment for the piano forte or harp, the words from Shakespeare . . . Dedicated to . . . Mʳ. J. Spray.

pp.6. *Printed (by permission of the Proprietor) by H. Hime . . . & sold by Clementi & Co: Liverpool*, [c.1806] fol. [Stamped 'G. Walker, London'].
MU. 1211[28]

STICH (J.W.) *see* THE ROYAL MERCHANT

STORACE (STEPHEN)

[Mahmoud]. Toll toll the knell. A favorite song . . . in Mahmoud. pp.3. *J. Dale: London*, [1797] fol.
MU. 1287[26]

[The Pirates]. The jealous Don, a favorite Duett . . . in the Pirates. [Begins: 'The jealous Don won't you assume']. pp.3. *G. Walker: London*, [1807[WM]] fol.
MU. 1211[2]

[The Prize]. Ah tell me softly, a favorite duett . . . in the Prize, or, 2, 5, 3, 8. pp.3. *J. Dale: London*, [c.1798] fol.
MU. 1211[25]

[The Siege of Belgrade]. A Plighted Faith. *A favorite duett . . . in the Siege of Belgrade*. [Incorporates material from Martin y Soler's 'Una Cosa Rara']. pp.4. *J. Dale: London*, [1791] fol.
MU. 1211[32]

see SHIELD (W.), The Siege of Belgrade

STRAZO SEMPIA FURIA *see* PORTA (G.)

THE STREAMLET THAT FLOW'D *see* SHIELD (W.), The Woodman

STRECH'D

Strech'd on the ground beneath an aged oake. *The Forsaken Shepherd*. [Song]. [*London*, c.1730] s.sh. fol.
MU. 1190[66]

SUETT (RICHARD)

Soft, sensible and true, a favorite duet. pp.3. *Thomas Preston: London*, [c.1800] fol.
MU. 1211[16]

THE SUMMER'S TALE

The Summer's Tale. A musical comedy . . . The music by Abel, Arne, Arnold, Boyce, Bach, Cocchi, Ciampi, C. S[t]. Germain, Giardini, Hasse, Howard, Lampe,

Lampugnani, Richter, Russel, Stanley. [Words by R. Cumberland]. pp.79. *I. Walsh: London*, [1766] obl. fol.
MU. 1257[1]

[Another copy]. [Inscribed 'R.J.S. Stevens, Charter house, 1817'].
MU. 1177[1]

SUPINE

Supine in Silvia's snowy arms he lies. *A song by an Italian author.* [*London*, c.1730] s.sh. fol.
MU. 1190[69]

SWEET THRUSH *see* ARNE (M.), The Thrush

SYMONDS (HENRY)

Six sets of lessons for the harpsicord. Dedicated to the right Honourable the countess of Sunderland. pp.53. *Printed by William Smith . . . and sold by the Author: London*, [c.1734] obl. fol. [Inscribed 'R. Fitzwilliam 1768'].
MU. 362 B

TALESTRI

Talestri, regina delle Amazzoni. Dramma per musica. [Music and words by Maria Antonia Walpurgis of Bavaria]. [Score]. 3 vols, *continuously paginated.* ⟨*Nello Stamparia di Bernado Cristoforo Breitkopf e figlio: Leipzig*, 1765⟩ obl. fol.
MU. 1259

TAMERLANO

Tamerlano. Overture. [Opera, music by A.M.G. Sacchini]. pp.5. [*London*, c.1775] fol. [One bar added in contemporary MS].
MU. 1400[7]

TARTINI (GIUSEPPE)

Tartini's celebrated Art of Bowing for the violin . . . with an accompaniment for a bass. pp.13. *A. Hamilton: London*, [1801^WM] fol.
MU. 311[2]

II Concerti . . . accommodati per il cembalo, da L: Frischmuth. 2 vols, *continuously paginated, comprises 4 pieces in all. Apresso Arnoldo Olofsen: Amsterdam*, [c.1755] obl. fol. [Each vol. inscribed 'R. Fitzwilliam 1771'].
MU. 361 A[1-2]

XII Solos for a violin with a thorough bass for the harpsicord or violoncello. pp.57. *I. Walsh: London*, [1742] fol. [Inscribed 'Fitzwilliam 1799'].
MU. 310

[Another copy].
MU. 311³

Six solos for a violin with a thorough bass for the harpsicord or violoncello . . . Opera seconda. [A different work from that published under the same opus number in Rome]. pp.35. *I. Walsh: London*, [1746] fol.
MU. 488⁷, bound with MU. MS 208

The celebrated sonata del diavolo or devil's solo, for the violin, with an accompaniment for a violoncello . . . never before published in this country. pp.9. *A. Hamilton: London*, [1801ᵂᴹ] fol.
MU. 311¹

TATTERSALL (WILLIAM DECHAIR)

Improved Psalmody. Vol.I. The psalms of David, from a poetical version . . . by James Merrick . . . with new music collected from the most eminent composers . . . Dedicated to the King. pp.44, [1], 329, 20. *T. Skillern: London*, 1794 obl. 4°. [Inscribed 'The Gift of William Dechair Tattersall M.A. to R.J.S. Stevens. July 1798 – Charterhouse'. The unnumbered page is apparently a proof sheet of p.I of the text of Merrick's translation (MU. 1300, not included in this catalogue). On the equivalent page in MU.1300 Stevens has noted that he set Psalm I at Tattersall's request. With a subscribers' list].
MU. 1299

TELL

Tell me, lovely shepherd *see* BOYCE (W.)

Tell me, tell me, charming creature *see* WEBBER (J.)

Tell me where *see* STEVENSON (SIR J.A.)

TENDUCCI (GIUSTO FERDINANDO)

In vain to keep my heart you strive. *Sung . . . at Ranelagh*. [*London*, c.1763] s.sh. fol.
MU. 1197⁶²

[The Revenge of Athridates]. The overture to the Revenge of Athridates. [Keyboard]. pp.4. [c.1770] fol.
MU. 1411

Tenducci's new rondeau . . . Adapted for the harpsichord with English words.

[Song, begins: 'See the purple morn arise']. pp.4. *To be had of M*^{r}. *Tenducci* . . . *at M*^{r}. *Babbs Music Shop* . . . *at M*^{r}. *Portals: London*, 1779 obl. fol.
MU. 1401

TENDUCI (G.F.) *see* TENDUCCI (G.F.)

THAT

That Jenny's my friend. [Song]. [*London*, c.1750] s.sh. fol.
MU. 1189[31]

THEN COME KISS ME NOW *see* THE CARMAN'S WHISTLE

THERE

There is a lady *see* FORD (T.)

There's auld Rob Moris. *A Scotch dialogue between mither & doughter*. [*London*, c.1725] s.sh. fol.
MU. 1190[45]

THO YOU THINK *see* SHIELD (W.), The Siege of Belgrade

THOMAS AND SALLY

When I was a young one. *A favourite song* . . . *in the new entertainment of Thomas and Sally*. [Music by T.A. Arne]. [*London*, c.1760] s.sh. fol.
MU. 1197[70]

THOMIRIS *see* THOMYRIS

THOMSON (GEORGE)

The select melodies of Scotland . . . Ireland and Wales, united to the songs of Robt. Burns, Sir Walter Scott Bar^t. and other distinguished poets: with symphonies & accompaniments for the piano forte by Pleyel, Kozeluch, Haydn & Beethoven . . . in five [actually 6] volumes . . . Vol.1 ⟨–6⟩. *Preston* ⟨*John Moir for the Proprietor, G. Thomson*⟩: *London & Edinburgh*, 1822–4 8°. [With numerous illustrations].
MU. 502–4

THOMYRIS

Songs in the new opera of Thomiris, Queen of Scythia. Collected out of the works of the most celebrated Italian authors, viz. Scarlait, Bononchini, Albinoni

. . . more correct then the former edition. [Music arranged by J.C. Pepusch. Words by P.A. Motteux]. pp.51. [Imperfect: wants p.37, supplied in photocopy from Royal Academy of Music]. *John Cullen: London*, [1707] fol.
MU. 1282

The symphonys or instrumental parts in the opera call'd Thomyris. [3 parts, of different issues]. *I. Walsh . . . P. Randall . . . I. Hare ⟨I Walsh . . . I. Hare . . . P. Randall⟩: London* [1707–9] fol.
MU. 1423 A

THOU

Thou rising sun whose gladsome ray. *Jessy. Or the rising sun.* [Song]. Plate no. XXVI of 'The Agreeable Amusement'. [*London*, c.1750] s.sh. fol.
MU. 1189²⁰

THRO' THE WOOD LASSIE *see* ARNE (M.)

THY

Thy father, away *see* ARTAXERXES

Thy vain pursuit fond youth give o'er. *The Generous Repulse.* [Song]. *D. Wright Junʳ:* [*London*, c.1730] s.sh. fol.
MU. 1189⁴⁹

THYRSIS WHEN HE LEFT ME *see* CALLCOTT (J.W.), Thyrsis

TIS HE'S AN HONEST FELLOW *see* GRAVES (J.)

TO

To an arbour of woodbine. *Sung by Mʳ. Beard.* [From 'Robin Hood'. Music by C. Burney. Words by M. Mendez]. [*London*, 1751] s.sh. fol.
MU. 1189⁵²

[Another copy].
MU. 1197¹¹

To banish life's troubles *see* STEVENS (R.J.S.)

To Caelia thus fond Damon said. *Damon to Caelia.* [*London*, c.1750] s.sh. fol.
MU. 1197⁶⁸

To Fanny fair I would impart. *Fanny.* [Song]. [*London*, c.1750] s.sh. fol.
MU. 1189⁵³

To make me feel a virgins charms *see* DEFESCH (W.)

To proclaim King George the second *see* GRAVES (J.), A song on His Majesty

To subdue the Armadas *see* STEVENS (R.J.S.), He may come if he dare

To what age *see* STEVENS (R.J.S.)

To woo me and win me. *Colin's Success.* [By W. Defesch]. [*London*, c.1755] s.sh. fol.
MU. 1189³²

TOAST

Toast about, to the church. *The Coronation. A catch for four voices.* [*London*, c.1728] s.sh. fol.
MU. 1190⁶⁸

TOLL TOLL THE KNELL *see* STORACE (S.), Mahmoud

TOO PLAIN DEAR YOUTH *see* HOWARD (S.), The Generous Confession

TRAETTA (TOMMASO)

Antigono. Overture. [Keyboard]. pp.5. [*Bremner: London*, 1776] fol.
MU. 1400⁹

TRAJETTA (T.) *see* TRAETTA (T.)

TRAVERS (JOHN)

Eighteen canzonets, for two, and three voices; (the words chiefly by Matthew Prior Esqʳ.). pp.64. *Printed for the Author by John Simpson: London*, [c.1745] fol. [With a subscribers' list].
MU. 1361

[Another copy].
MU. 515³

The whole book of Psalms . . . Number V ⟨–VIII⟩. [Numbers in MS]. 2 vols. [Imperfect: wants vol. I, comprising nos.1–4]. *John Johnson: London*, [c.1750] fol.
MU. 1362

TRIAL (J.C.) *see* BERTON (P.M.) and TRIAL (J.C.)

TRUE HEARTED WAS HE *see* KNYVETT (W.)

TU

Tu mia speranza tu mio conforto / My hopes my pleasure. *A song in imitation of the bagpipes in English and Italian.* [Apparently part of 'The Monthly Mask of Vocal Music'. From G.F. Handel's 'Amadigi'. Words attributed to J.J. Heidegger]. ff.[2]. [*London*, c.1720] fol.
MU. 1190^{60}

TURN

Turn fair Clora. *Damon and Clora. A two part song.* [Music by H. Harington]. As I saw fair Clora. *A two part song . . . set by M^r* [George] *Hayden.* ff.[2]. *A. Bland's Music Warehouse: London*, [c.1790] fol.
MU. 1211$^{13-14}$

see HAYDEN (G.)

TURNER (WILLIAM)

 A catch (a 4 voc.) in praise of claret. [Begins: 'A pox on repining']. p.4 *of a collection.* [*London*, c.1720] fol.
MU. 1190^{38}

An Epigram. Gripe and Shifter. [Song, begins: 'Rich Gripe does all his thoughts and cunning bend']. p.3 *of a collection.* [*London*, c.1720] fol.
MU. 1190^{39}

On decanting a flask of Florence. A song. [Begins: 'See that rill, rowl down hill']. p.6 *of a collection.* [*London*, c.1720] fol.
MU. 1190^{37}

A song (On Mira's singing and beauty). [Begins: 'Singing charms the bless'd above']. p.6 *of a collection.* [*London*, c.1720] fol.
MU. 1190^{24}

'TWAS WHEN THE SEAS WERE ROARING *see* JACKSON (W.), Susannah

UNIVERSAL HARMONY

Universal Harmony, or the Gentleman & Ladie's Social Companion: consisting of . . . English & Scots songs. pp.129. [Imperfect: wants title and pp.1–6, 12, 15–16, 18–25, 27–9, 31–3, 35–6, 38–57, 59–77, 80, 86–100, 113, 116, 118, 127. There are 2 copies of p.106]. [*J. Newbery: London*, c.1745] 4°.
MU. 1330

[Another issue]. *Printed for the Proprietors, & sold by J. Newbery: London*, [c.1746].
[With a frontispiece].
MU. 1331

VAIN IS BEAUTY'S GAUDY FLOW'R *see* ARNE (T.A.), Judith
[cantatas, operas, oratorios]

VAINLY NOW YE STRIVE *see* ARNE (T.A.), Lotharia [single songs]

VALENTINE (ROBERT)

Six setts of aires and a chacoon for two flutes & a bass. [3 parts]. *I. Walsh . . . and
I: Hare: London*, [1718] fol.
MU. 511–13

VANBRUGHE (GEORGE)

Advice to a friend in love. The words by M^r. Carey. [Song, begins: 'Prithee Billy,
be'n't so silly']. [*London*, c.1715] s.sh. fol.
MU. 1190^{75}

Lesbia's reproach and denial. The words by M^r. Carey. [Song, begins: 'The
groves, the plains']. [*London*, c.1730] s.sh. fol.
MU. 1190^{77}

The Lovely Mourner. A new song. [Begins: 'See that nymph in mourning'].
[*London*, c.1720] s.sh. fol.
MU. 1190^{81}

VANNE SEGUI *see* O, O my treasure

VENERE BELLA *see* HANDEL (G.F.) [operas and other stage works:
Giulio Cesare]

VERACINI (FRANCESCO MARIA)

Sonate accademiche a violino e basso, dedicate alla Sacra Real Maesta di Augusto
III Re di Pollonia . . . Opera seconda. pp.91. *A Londra, e a Firenze per l'Autore*:
[1744] obl. fol. [With a frontispiece. Inscribed 'R. Fitzwilliam 1771'].
MU. 312

VIVALDI (ANTONIO)

La Cetra. Concerti consacrati all . . . Real Maesta di Carlo VI . . . Opera nona.
Libro primo ⟨secondo⟩. [1 part only]. Plate nos. 533–4. *Spesa di Michele Carlo le
Cene: Amsterdam*, [c.1722] fol.
MU. 1418

Il Cimento dell' Armonia e dell' Inventione. Concerti a 4 e 5. Consacrati all' Illustrissimo Signore il Signor Venceslao Conte di Marzin ... Opera ottava. Libro primo ⟨secondo⟩. [Imperfect: vol. I has 5 parts of which violin 2 lacks all after p.16; vol. II has 3 parts only]. Plate nos. 520–1. *Spesa di Michele Carlo le Cene: Amsterdam*, [c.1722] fol.
MU. 1420

Vivaldi's most celebrated concertos, in all their parts ... Opera terza. [L'Estro Armonico, nos. 1–7]. [5 parts only]. *I: Walsh ... and I: Hare: London*, [1715] fol.
MU. 1412 A

The second part of Vivaldi's most celebrated concerto's in all their parts ... parti 2ᵈ. [L'Estro Armonico, nos. 8–12]. [4 parts only]. *I: Walsh ... and I: Hare: London*, [1717] fol.
MU. 1412 B

VI Concerti a flauto traverso, violino primo e secondo, alto viola, organo e violoncello ... Opera decima. [5 parts]. Plate no. 544. *A Spesa di Michele Carlo le Cene: Amsterdam*, [c.1730] fol.
MU. 1415

Sei concerti a violino principale, violino primo e secondo, alto viola, organo e violoncello ... Opera undecima. [5 parts]. Plate no. 545. *A Spesa di Michele Carlo le Cene: Amsterdam*, [c.1730] fol.
MU. 1416

Sei concerti a violino principale, violino primo e secondo, alto viola, organo e violoncello ... Opera duodecima. [5 parts]. Plate no. 546. *A Spesa di Michele Carlo le Cene: Amsterdam*, [c.1730] fol.
MU. 1417

Two celebrated concertos, the one commonly call'd the Cuckow, and the other Extravaganza. [4 parts only]. *I: Walsh ... and I: Hare: London*, [1720] fol.
MU. 1419

Select Harmony; being XII concertos in six parts ... collected from the works of Antonio Vivaldi, viz. his 6ᵗʰ. 7ᵗʰ. 8ᵗʰ. and 9ᵗʰ operas ... The whole carefully corected. [4 parts only, with a second copy of organo e violoncello]. *I: Walsh ... and Ioseph Hare: London*, [1730] fol.
MU. 1413

La Stravaganza. Concerti da D. Antonio Vivaldi. Opera quarta. Vivaldis Extravaganzas in six parts ... Opera 4ᵗᵃ. [4 parts only, with a second copy of organo e violoncello]. *I: Walsh ... and Ioseph Hare: London*, [1728] fol.
MU. 1414

V O I A M A N T E *see* G I A R D I N I (F.)

VOUS N'AVEZ POINT TRAHI *see* PACINI (A.F.G.S.)

W. (V.)

Nancy gay. [Song, begins: 'Of all the girls I ever saw']. [*London*, c.1767] s.sh. fol.
MU. 1197[53]

WAGENSEIL (GEORG CHRISTOPH)

Six concertos for the harpsicord or organ with accompanyments for two violins
and a bass. [Keyboard only]. *I. Walsh: London*, [1761] fol. [Inscribed 'R.
Fitzwilliam 1767'].
MU. 486[8]

A lesson for the harpsichord or piano forte . . . To which is added a favorite Irish
Air Gramachee Molly with variations. pp.8. *C. and S. Thompson: London*, [c.1775]
obl. fol.
MU. 1404[3]

Six sonatas for the harpsicord. With accompaniment for a violin . . . Opera
prima. [Keyboard only]. *A: Hummel: London*, [c.1760] obl. fol. [Inscribed 'R.
Fitzwilliam 1767'].
MU. 485[6]

Six sonatas for the harpsichord, with accompaniment for a violin . . . Opera 2[da].
[Keyboard only]. *A: Hummel: London*, [1761] fol. [Inscribed 'R. Fitzwilliam
1767'].
MU. 486[9]

Six sonatas for the harpsicord . . . Opera III. pp.25. *A: Hummel: London*, [c.1760]
obl. fol. [Inscribed 'R. Fitzwilliam 1767'].
MU. 485[7]

WALPURGIS (M.A.) *see* TALESTRI

WANHAL (JAN BAPTIST)

Two favorite lessons for the harpsicord or piano forte. pp.8. *G. Gardom: London*,
[1774] obl. fol.
MU. 1397

Six trios a serenade pour un violin, alto & basse. Deux cors de chasse, ad libitum
. . . Œvre premiere. [5 parts]. Plate no. 317. *Chez J.J. Hummel: Amsterdam*,
[c.1770] fol.
MU. 1376

WARREN (THOMAS)

A collection of catches, canons and glees . . . never before published. pp.31, 31. *Welcker: London*, [c.1765–95] obl. fol. [Inscribed 'Fitzwilliam 1799'].
MU. 357 A

A second ⟨–fourth⟩ collection of catches, canons and glees . . . inscrib'd to . . . the Catch-Club. *Peter Welcker: London*, [c.1765–95] obl. fol. [Each inscribed 'Fitzwilliam 1799'].
MU. 357 B$^{1-3}$

A [fifth] ⟨–tenth⟩ collection of catches, canons and glees . . . inscribed to . . . the Catch Club. *Welcker: London*, [c.1765–95] obl. fol. [With a label stating that these volumes belonged to Thomas Love Peacock].
MU. 1231$^{1-6}$

An eleventh collection of catches, canons and glees . . . inscribed to . . . the Catch Club. *Welcker: London*, [c.1765–95] obl. fol.
MU. 1264

An eighteenth collection of catches, canons and glees . . . inscribed to . . . the Catch Club. [Imperfect: wants pp.11–14, 19–30, 37–46, 55 onwards]. *Longman and Broderip: London*, [c.1765–95] obl. fol.
MU. 1263

A nineteenth collection of catches, canons and glees . . . inscribed to . . . the Catch Club. [Imperfect: wants p.40 onwards]. *Printed for the Editor by Longman and Broderip: London*, [c.1765–95] obl. fol.
MU. 1249

A twenty sixth collection of catches, canons and glees . . . inscribed to . . . the Catch Club. *Printed for the Editor by Longman and Broderip: London*, [c.1765–95] obl. fol. [Inscribed 'Fitzwilliam 1791'].
MU. 357 C

Index to a collection of vocal harmony consisting of canons, catches, glees, &c. . . . selected by T. Warren . . . Arranged by G. Gwilt. pp.6. *Printed for G. Gwilt . . . by Nichols, Son, and Bentley: London*, 1813 4°.
MU. 1457^{1}

A general index to Warren's collection of catches, canons, and glees. Published in thirty-two numbers. Arranged by . . . G. Gwilt. pp.23. *Printed for G. Gwilt: [London, c.1810]* 4°.
MU. 1457^{2}

THE WAY TO KEEP HIM

Attend all ye fair. *Sung . . . in the Way to Keep Him. [London, c.1760]* s.sh. fol.
MU. 1197^{61}

WEBBE (SAMUEL, THE ELDER)

[A second book of catches,] canons [and glees]. pp.32. [Imperfect: title damaged]. *Welcker: London*, [c.1770] obl. fol.
MU. 1406

A second book of catches, canons and glees. pp.32. *Longman and Broderip: London*, [c.1780–90] obl. fol.
MU. 1377^2

A third book of catches canons and glees. pp.41. *Welcker: London*, [c.1775] obl. fol.
MU. 1377^3

A fourth book of catches, canons and glees . . . with canzonettes for two voices. pp.47. *S.A. and P. Thompson: London*, [c.1780] obl. fol.
MU. 1377^4

A Vth. book of catches, canons & glees. pp.35. *J. Bland: London*, [c.1790] obl. fol.
MU. 1377^5

[Another issue]. A V book of catches, canons & glees. pp.35. *A. Hamilton: London*, [c.1800] obl. fol.
MU. 1405^1

A VIth. book of catches, canons & glees. pp.32. *J. Bland: London*, [c.1790] obl. fol.
MU. 1377^6

[Another issue]. A VI book of catches, canons & glees. pp.32. *A. Hamilton: London*, [c.1800] obl. fol.
MU. 1405^2

A seventh book of catches, canons & glees. pp.54. *J. Bland: London*, [c.1790] obl. fol.
MU. 1377^7

 The Ladies' Catch Book . . . the words of which will not offend the nicest delicacy. pp.30. *S and A Thompson: London*, [1778] obl. fol.
MU. 1377^1

[Another copy]. [Imperfect: wants title].
MU. 1407

An eighth book of glees, canons, and catches . . . Dedicated to the Rev^d. M^r. Beecher. pp.59. *Printed for the Author . . . and to be had at Blands Music Warehouse: London*, [c.1795] obl. fol.
MU. 1377^8

[Another copy].
MU. 1409

A selection of glees, duetts, canzonets &c. . . . Vol:I ⟨–III⟩. [Numbers altered in MS]. *Printed for the Author, by R^t. Birchall: London*, [1812^{WM}] fol.
MU. 1218

A collection of masses . . . by S. Webbe . . . with others . . . by Ricci & Paxton. pp.iv, 380. *Printed for the Proprietors & sold by J. Bland: London*, ⟨1792⟩ obl. 8°. [With a subscribers' list].
MU. 1301

The Traveller, a favorite ballad. [Begins: 'O tarry gentle traveller']. pp.3. *L. Lavenu: London*, [1801^WM] fol. [Initialled 'A.M.J.', i.e. A.M. Jeffery: later Mrs R.J.S. Stevens].
MU. 1287^15

see AMUSEMENT

WEBBE (SAMUEL, THE ELDER) and WEBBE (SAMUEL, THE YOUNGER)

Ninth book. A collection of vocal music . . . dedicated to Sir Henry C: Englefield. pp.58. *Printed for the Authors, and sold by Longman & Broderip: London*, [c.1795] obl. fol.
MU. 1377^9

[Another issue]. [Imperfect: one song only]. ⟨*Broderip & Wilkinson: London*⟩, [c.1793] obl. fol.
MU. 1408

WEBBE (SAMUEL, THE YOUNGER)

Convito armonico. A collection of madrigals, elegies, glees, canons, catches and duets, selected from the works of the most eminent composers . . . Vol:1 ⟨–2⟩. [Figure in MS]. 4 vols. [Imperfect: wants vols. III–IV]. *Printed for the publishers, by Hime & Son: Liverpool*, [1808–23] fol. [Vols. III–IV bear the imprint of Chappell & Co. With a subscribers' list in vol. II].
MU. 497–8

see WEBBE (SAMUEL, THE ELDER) and WEBBE (SAMUEL, THE YOUNGER)

WEBBE (W.) *see* PLAYFORD (J.), Select musicall ayres and dialogues; Select ayres and dialogues for one, two, and three voyces

WEBBER (JOHN)

Inconstancy in woman. A song. [Begins: 'I am confirm'd a woman can']. p.7 *of a collection*. [*London*, c.1720] fol.
MU. 1190^23

Tell me, tell me, charming creature. *A song.* [*London*, c.1730] s.sh. fol.
MU. 1190^27

WEBER (CARL MARIA VON)

[Der Freischütz]. The whole of the music . . . in the celebrated melodrame called Der Freischütz; or, The Seventh Bullet . . . arranged for the English stage by W^m. Hawes; the poetry translated from the German by W. M^c. Gregor Logan. [Original words by F. Kind, after J.A. Apel and F. Laun]. pp.182. Plate nos. 1308, 1373–4, 1828, 1606, 1333–4, 1376, 1427, 1613, 1812, 1330, 1575, 1606, 1572, 1665, 1606–7, 1664, 1328, 1824, 1608, 1612, 1654, 1836. *Published for the Royal Harmonic Institution* ⟨*Welsh & Hawes . . . at the Royal Harmonic Institution*⟩: London, [c.1827] fol. [Inscribed 'R.J.S. Stevens, Charterhouse', and marked by him with bass figuration and performance notes].
MU. 1302.

Oberon, or the Elf King's Oath, the popular romantic and fairy opera . . . the poetry by J.R. Planché [after C.M. Wieland] . . . with an accompaniment for the piano forte . . . Part. [*sic*: vol. no. not filled in]. pp.197. *Published at the Royal Harmonic Institution . . . by Welsh & Hawes: London*, [c.1826] fol. [Inscribed 'R.J.S. Stevens, Charterhouse', and marked by him with bass figuration and performance notes].
MU. 1303

THE WEDDING DAY

In the dead of the night. As sung . . . in the Wedding Day. [2 versions. Words by E. Inchbald]. pp.4. *R^t. Birchall: London*, [1794^WM] fol. [Inscribed 'A.M. Jeffery': later Mrs R.J.S. Stevens].
MU. 1287^19

WEIDEMAN (CHARLES FREDERICK)

When first by fond Damon. *Sung at Vaux-Hall-Gardens*. [*London*, c.1750] s.sh. fol.
MU. 1189^14

[Another copy].
MU. 1197^59

WELLESLEY (G.C.), Earl of Mornington, *see* AMUSEMENT

WERT THOU FAIRER *see* DEFESCH (W.), Mutual Love

WESLEY (CHARLES)

Now I know what it is to have strove, a pastoral glee, for three voices, the words from Shenstone. pp.3. *R^t. Birchall: London*, [1806^WM] fol. [Inscribed, apparently in Lord Fitzwilliam's hand, 'From the author. 1807'].
MU. 380 D^1

WESLEY (S.) *see* HANDEL (G.F.) [selections and arrangements: Fitzwilliam music]

WHALLEY (M.)

O give thanks. *A favorite anthem, in score.* pp.7. *Printed for the Author by Longman Clementi and Comp*: London, [c.1798] fol.
MU. 1324²

WHAT

What beauties does Flora disclose? *Charming Moggy.* [*London*, c.1725] s.sh. fol.
MU. 1190⁴⁸

What Cato advises. *Cato's Advice.* [By Henry Carey]. p.48 *of a collection.* [c.1740] fol.
MU. 1189⁴

What means that tender sigh *see* ARNE (T.A.), Excuse for a love slip [single songs]

What shall he have *see* STEVENS (R.J.S.)

What's this dull town to me. *Robin Adair . . . with an accompaniment for the piano forte.* ff.[2]. *Major's Cheap Music Shop: London*, [c.1810] fol.
MU. 1288 B²⁴

WHEELER (R.)

Six glees for three and four voices. pp.38. *Printed for the Proprietor: London*, [c.1805] obl. fol.
MU. 1262

WHEN

When Britain first *see* ARNE (T.A.), Judgment of Paris [cantatas, operas, oratorios]; Rule Britannia [single songs]

When Chloris, like an angel, walks. [Song. Words attributed in MS of R.J.S. Stevens to R.H. Lord Marlow]. pp.5. *Preston: London*, [c.1780] fol. [Inscribed 'R.J.S. Stevens, Never published'].
MU. 1289 H

When-e're I meet my Celia's eyes. *A favourite medley.* [Song]. pp.4. [*London*, c.1760] fol.
MU. 1197³⁰

When first a babe *see* ARNOLD (S.), Little Bess the ballad singer

When first by fond Damon *see* WEIDEMAN (C.F.)

When first I saw *see* HUDSON (J.)

When first you courted me *see* CORRI (D.), Donald

When I survey Clarinda's charms *see* HANDEL (G.F.) [selections and arrangements: minuets]

When I was a young one *see* THOMAS AND SALLY

When late I wander'd *see* ARNE (T.A.), Thomas & Sally [single songs]

When the hills and lofty mountains. *Charming Billy. A new song.* [*London*, c.1725] s.sh. fol.
MU. 1190⁵⁸

When the rosy morn *see* SHIELD (W.), [Rosina]

When the toil *see* STEVENS (R.J.S.)

When time who steals *see* MOORE (T.)

WHERE

Where ah where shall I my shepherd find. *O my poor heart, heigh ho, a favorite duett with an accompaniment for the piano forte or harp.* [With MS attribution to Lord Barrymore]. pp.3. *L. Lavenu: London*, [c.1800] fol.
MU. 1211⁷

Where shall Celia fly for shelter. Sung . . . at Vauxhall. [By S. Howard]. [*London*, c.1765] s.sh. fol.
MU. 1197³⁶

Where the jessamine sweetens the bow'r. *Colin and Phoebe, a new pastoral ballad.* [*London*, c.1750] s.sh. fol.
MU. 1189³⁵

WHILE

While I hang on your bosom *see* KELLY (M.), [Of Age Tomorrow]

While some for pleasure waste their health. *My Nanny O.* [Song, words by A. Ramsay]. [*London*, c.1720] s.sh. fol.
MU. 1190⁴⁶

WHILST

Whilst Strephon gaz'd *see* HAWKINS (S.)

Whilst you to lovely Arabel *see* GRIFFES (E.)

WHO

Who is it *see* STEVENS (R.J.S.)

Who is Sylvia? *see* STEVENS (R.J.S.)

WHY

Why fair maid *see* ABRAMS (H.), Crazy Jane

Why heaves my fond bosom? *see* HOWARD (S.)

Why shine those charming eyes *see* DEFESCH (W.), To Lysander

WILL YOU CREDIT A MISER *see* LULMAN (C.)

WILLIAMS (WILLIAM)

Six sonata's in three parts. Three for two violins and three for two flutes. With a part for the base-violin or viol, and a figur'd base for the organ, harpsicord or arch-lute. [4 parts]. *John Hare . . . and John Walsh: London,* 1703 fol.
MU. 524–7

WILSON (J.) *see* PLAYFORD (J.), Select musicall ayres and dialogues; Select ayres and dialogues for one, two, and three voyces

WINE'S A MISTRESS *see* LOVE AND WINE

WINTER (J.D.)

Rest lady fair, a ballad for three voices . . . dedicated to T. Moore Esqr. as an answer to Oh lady fair. pp.7. *J. Davies: London,* [c.1799] fol.
MU. 1211^6

WISE MEN FLATTRING *see* HANDEL (G.F.) [oratorios, odes and other choral works: Judas Maccabaeus]

WITH

With horns and with hounds *see* BOYCE (W.), [The Secular Masque]

With woman and wine *see* BAILDON (J.), The Union of love and wine

WITHIN THESE SACRED BOWERS *see* MOZART (W.A.)

WOOD (D.)

The Landskip. [Song, begins: 'How pleas'd within my native bow'rs']. [*London*, c.1765] s.sh. fol.
MU. 1197¹²ᴬ

WOODWARD (RICHARD)

Cathedral music. Consisting of one complete service, seven anthems and Veni Creator Spiritus in score, for one, two, three, four five and six voices . . . Opera terza. pp.140. *Printed for the Author by Welcker: London*, [1771] fol. [Inscribed 'Fitzwilliam 1799'].
MU. 365²

WORGAN (JOHN)

Miranda. [Song, begins: 'Let youthful bards in wanton verse']. [*London*, c.1753] s.sh. fol.
MU. 1189³³

The Thief. Sung . . . at Vauxhall. [Begins: 'Before the urchin well cou'd go'. Words attributed to the Earl of Egremont]. [*London*, c.1750] s.sh. fol.
MU. 1197⁴²

see DID

see SCARLATTI (D.), Libro de XII sonatas modernas

THE WORLD, MY DEAR MYRA *see* GERARD (J.)

WOU'D

Wou'd you taste yᵉ noontide air. [Song, from T.A. Arne's 'Comus']. [*London*, c.1740] s.sh. fol. [This is the first item in a compilation of single songs with contemporary MS index].
MU. 1189¹

[Another issue].
MU. 1197¹

YE

Ye belles, and ye flirts. *A song for Ranelagh*. [Words by W. Whitehead]. [*London*, c.1750] s.sh. fol.
MU. 1189⁴⁴

Ye British youths *see* STEVENS (R.J.S.), Our tars so fam'd in story

Ye chearful virgins *see* HOWARD (S.)

Ye circum and uncircumcis'd. *The hubble bubbles. A ballad by M^r D'urfey, to the tune of O'er the hills and far away.* [*London*, c.1720] s.sh. fol. MU. 1190[14]

Ye fair marri'd dames *see* ARNE (T.A.), [The Way to Keep Him] [cantatas, operas, oratorios]

Ye gentle gales *see* RAYMOND

Ye gentle winds *see* RILEY (W.)

Ye ruling pow'rs attentive be. *The Lover's Wish.* [Song]. [*London*, c.1765] s.sh. fol. MU. 1197[39]

Ye shepherds tell me *see* MAZZINGHI (J.), The Wreath

Ye spotted snakes! *see* STEVENS (R.J.S.)

YOSLINGTON

O mine awn Jenny. *A new Scotch song. R. Mears: London*, [c.1720] s.sh. fol. MU. 1190[18]

YOU

You tell me I'm handsome. *The Judicious Fair.* [Song]. [*London*, c.1750] s.sh. fol. MU. 1189[23]

YOUNG (ANTONY)

The Shy Shepherdess. [Song, begins: 'Shepherd when thou see'st me fly']. [*London*, c.1720] s.sh. fol. MU. 1190[9]

YOUNG

Young Arabella Mamma's care. *Arabella or the Sisters. Sung . . . at Vauxhall.* [*London*, c.1770] s.sh. fol. MU. 1197[75]

Young Hobbinol *see* DAVIES (R.), Hobbinol

Young Molly *see* ARNE (M.), The Lass with the delicate air

Young Strephon once the blithest swain. *Strephon and Cloe. A pastoral sung . . . at Finch's Grotto Gardens.* [*London*, c.1764] s.sh. fol. MU. 1197[54]

ZIANI (PIETRO ANDREA)

XVII Sonates da organo o cimbalo del Sig Ziani Pollaroli Bassani e altri famosi autory. pp.38. *Chez Estienne Roger: Amsterdam*, [c.1705] obl. fol. [Inscribed 'R. Fitzwilliam 1771'].
MU. 362 A

ZIPOLI (DOMENICO)

A third collection of toccates, vollentarys and fuges for the organ or harpsicord, with particular great pieces for the church. pp.31. *I. Walsh: London*, [c.1730] fol. [Inscribed 'Fitzwilliam 1782'].
MU. 486[7]

1   George Bickham, *The musical entertainer*, 1, London, [1737], p. 49

2 Henry Carey, *A choice selection of six favourite songs*, [London, 1742], p. 18

Within the engraving:

W: Sykes Iunior Inventor.　　　　　　　　　H: Hulsbergh Fecit.

SONGS
in the New OPERA *Called*
ROSAMOND
Compos'd by
Mr. Tho: Clayton

London Printed for I Walsh Servt. to Her Maty. at ye Harp and Hoboy in Katherine Street near Somerset House
in ye Strand – and P. Randall at ye Violin and Lute by Paulsgrave head Court without Temple Barr.

3　Thomas Clayton, *Songs in the new opera call'd Rosamond*, London, [1707], frontispiece

MEDÉE,

TRAGEDIE

MISE

EN MUSIQUE

Par Monsieur CHARPENTIER.

A PARIS,
Par Christophe Ballard, seul Imprimeur du Roy pour la Musique,
ruë S. Jean de Beauvais, au Mont-Parnasse.

M. DC. XCXIIII.

4   Marc Antoine Charpentier, *Medée. Tragedie*, Paris, [1694], title-page

all, armies royall, prayſe him with glee. prayſe him with glee. prayſe him with glee.

Heere endeth all the tunes for the *Pſalmes*, the higheſt part ſinging the common Church tune.

The X Commaundements.

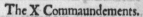

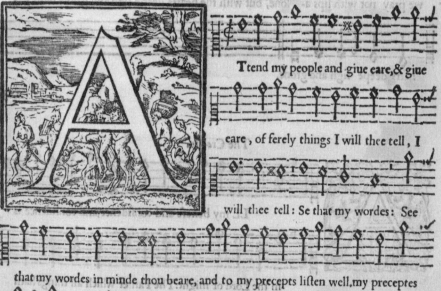

Ttend my people and giue eare, & giue

eare, of ferely things I will thee tell, I

will thee tell: Se that my wordes: See

that my wordes in minde thou beare, and to my precepts liſten well, my preceptes

liſten well. liſten well.

G.I.

5 William Damon, *The second booke of the musicke* [altus], [London], 1591, p. 41

FRONIMO

DIALOGO

DI VINCENTIO GALILEI
NOBILE FIORENTINO,

SOPRA L'ARTE DEL BENE INTAVOLARE,
ET RETTAMENTE SONARE LA MVSICA
Negli strumenti artificiali si di corde come di fia-
to, & in particulare nel Liuto.

*Nuouamente ristampato, & dall'Autore istesso arrichito,
& ornato di nouità di concetti, & d'essempi.*

IN VINEGGIA,
Appresso l'Herede di Girolamo Scotto,
M. D. LXXXIIII.

6   Vincentio Galilei, *Fronimo*, Venice, 1584, title-page

THE HYMN
OF
ADAM and EVE,
Out of the Fifth Book of
MILTON'S Paradise-Lost;
Set to Musick by
M.ᴿ GALLIARD.
1728.

7   Johann Ernst Galliard, *Hymn of Adam and Eve*, [London], 1728, title-page

8   Georg Frederic Handel, *Julius Caesar*, London, [1724], frontispiece

9 John Playford, *Select ayres and dialogues*, London, 1659, frontispiece

10 *A pocket companion for gentlemen and ladies*, II, London, [*c.* 1725], frontispiece

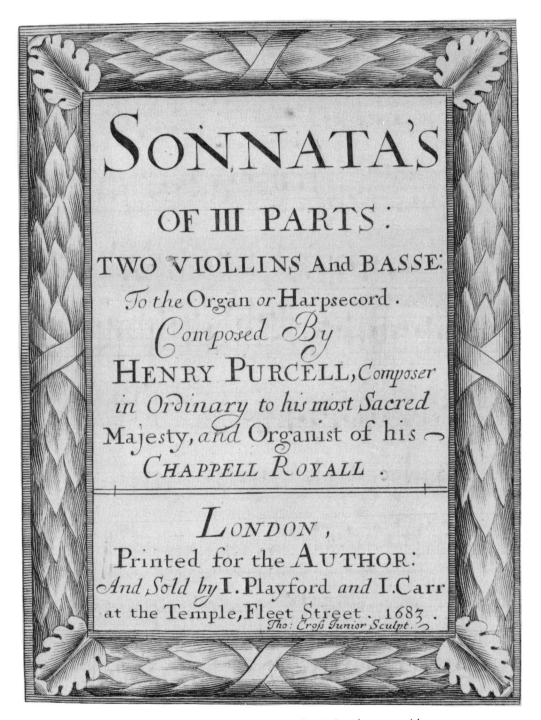

11   Henry Purcell, *Sonnata's of III parts* [bass], London, 1683, title-page

NUMERICAL LIST

THIS IS A summary list of all the items of early printed music contained in the present catalogue. Numbers in square brackets indicate items in the sequence which fall outside the scope of this catalogue, principally manuscripts and more recent printed music.

In essence, the numerical sequence now in use for manuscript and printed music in the Museum is the same as that set out in J.H. Fuller-Maitland and A.H. Mann, *Catalogue of the Music in the Fitzwilliam Museum, Cambridge* (1893). Apart from a few minor alterations to their numbering of printed music, the main change has been in the large number of new accessions which have for the most part been placed in sequence from the point at which the Fuller-Maitland and Mann catalogue ceased.

In general, each number (with or without a letter suffix) denotes a volume, while the presence of superscript numbers signifies that several items are bound into one volume. General information about such composite volumes (e.g. annotations, associations with individuals) is usually placed in the main entry for the first item in the volume; but in the case of volumes and groupings associated with the Founder the 'Chronological list' should also be consulted, by using his accession date as given in the main entry. In general, however, the gathering of items into volumes does not necessarily predate their acquisition by the Museum. Where, on the other hand, a number is subdivided by letter, this generally reflects a previous association between its component parts. Titles of works (in italics, without distinction between titles as such and first lines) are given in this list in severely abbreviated form, preceded where necessary by an indication in square brackets of the heading under which they are placed in the main catalogue. Where the instrumental parts of a publication are placed under separate numbers the different parts are briefly indicated.

[1–301]		304^3	*Pieces de clavecin*
302	BONONCINI (G.B.), *[Cantate et duetti]*	304^4	*Second collection of pieces for the harpsichord*
303	RAMEAU, *Les Surprises de l'Amour*	305–6	CORELLI, *The ... four operas, containing 48 sonatas ⟨twelve concertos⟩ ... Vol. I ⟨II⟩*
304^1	GEMINIANI, *[Sonatas Op. 1]. Le prime sonate*		
304^2	*Sonate ... Opera IV*	307	*XII Solos for a violin ... Opera quinta*

308	DUPORT, *Six sonatas*	318 B⁵	*XII Sonatas . . . ⟨Opera terza⟩* [violin 2]
309	PEREZ, *Mattinuto de' Morti*		
310	TARTINI, *XII Solos for a violin*	318 B⁶	*XII Sonatas . . . ⟨Opera quarta⟩* [violin 2]
311¹	*Sonata del diavolo*		
311²	*Art of Bowing*	318 B⁷	GEMINIANI, *[Sonatas Op. 1]. Sonatas . . . Made from the solos* [violin 2]
311³	*XII Solos for a violin*		
311⁴	GEMINIANI, *[Sonatas Op. 1]. XII Solo's*	318 B⁸	BOYCE, *Twelve sonatas* [violin 2]
311⁵	*Art of playing on the violin . . . Opera IX*	318 B⁹	SAN MARTINI, *XII Sonate . . . Opera terza* [violin 2]
312	VERACINI, *Sonate accademiche . . . Opera seconda*	318 B¹⁰	MARTYN, *Fourteen sonatas* [violin 2]
313	PEPUSCH, *XXIV Solos*	318 C¹	CORELLI, *XII Sonatas . . . ⟨Opera prima⟩* [bass]
[314]			
315	HANDEL, *Suites de pieces . . . Premier volume*	318 C²	*XII Sonatas . . . ⟨Opera secunda⟩* [bass]
316¹	*Suites de pieces . . . [Vol. I]* (bound with MU. MS 79)	318 C³	*XII Sonatas . . . ⟨Opera terza⟩* [bass]
316²	*Suites de pieces . . . Second volume* (bound with MU. MS 79)	318 C⁴	*XII Sonatas . . . ⟨Opera quarta⟩* [bass]
316³	*Six fugues . . . Troisieme ovarage* (bound with MU. MS 79)	318 C⁵	MARTYN, *Fourteen sonatas* [violoncello]
317¹	*Suites de pieces . . . Premier livre*	318 D¹	HANDEL, *VI Sonates . . . Second ouvrage* [bass]
317²	*Suites de pieces . . . Deuxieme livre*	318 D²	*Seven sonatas . . . Opera quinta* [bass]
318 A¹	*VI Sonates . . . Second ouvrage* [violin 1]	318 D³	CORELLI, *XII Sonatas . . . ⟨Opera prima⟩* [organ]
318 A²	*Seven sonatas . . . Opera quinta* [violin 1]	318 D⁴	*XII Sonatas . . . ⟨Opera secunda⟩* [second copy of bass]
318 A³	CORELLI, *XII Sonatas . . . ⟨Opera prima⟩* [violin 1]	318 D⁵	*XII Sonatas . . . ⟨Opera terza⟩* [organ]
318 A⁴	*XII Sonatas . . . ⟨Opera secunda⟩* [violin 1]	318 D⁶	*XII Sonatas . . . ⟨Opera quarta⟩* [second copy of bass]
318 A⁵	*XII Sonatas . . . ⟨Opera terza⟩* [violin 1]	318 D⁷	GEMINIANI, *[Sonatas Op. 1]. Sonatas . . . Made from the solos* [bass]
318 A⁶	*XII Sonatas . . . ⟨Opera quarta⟩* [violin 1]	318 D⁸	BOYCE, *Twelve sonatas* [bass]
318 A⁷	GEMINIANI, *[Sonatas Op. 1]. Sonatas . . . Made from the solos* [violin 1]	318 D⁹	SAN MARTINI, *XII Sonate . . . Opera terza* [bass]
318 A⁸	BOYCE, *Twelve sonatas* [violin 1]	318 D¹⁰	MARTYN, *Fourteen sonatas* [organ]
318 A⁹	SAN MARTINI, *XII Sonate . . . Opera terza* [violin 1]	319¹	HANDEL, *[Op.4]. Six concertos for the harpsicord*
318 A¹⁰	MARTYN, *Fourteen sonatas* [violin 1]	319²	*Second set of six concertos for the harpsicord*
318 B¹	HANDEL, *VI Sonates . . . Second ouvrage* [violin 2]	319³	*[Op.7]. Third set of six concertos for the harpsicord*
318 B²	*Seven sonatas . . . Opera quinta* [violin 2]	319⁴	*[Second set]. Two concertos for the organ*
318 B³	CORELLI, *XII Sonatas . . . ⟨Opera prima⟩* [violin 2]	320 A¹	GEMINIANI, *Concerti grossi . . . composti dalle sonate . . . dell opera IV* [viola 2]
318 B⁴	*XII Sonatas . . . ⟨Opera secunda⟩* [violin 2]	320 A²	*Concerti grossi . . . Op.ᵃ VII* [viola, ripieno]

320 B[1]	SAN MARTINI, *Eight overtures . . . And six grand concertos* [horn 2]	320 G[13]	STANLEY, *Six concertos* [violin 1, concertino]
320 C[1]	*Eight overtures . . . And six grand concertos* [tympani]	320 G[14]	BOYCE, *Eight symphonys . . . Opera seconda* [violin 1]
320 C[2]	BOYCE, *Eight symphonys . . . Opera seconda* [tympani/horn]	320 G[15]	RICCIOTTI, *VI. Concerti armonici* [violin 1]
320 D	SAN MARTINI, *Eight overtures . . . And six grand concertos* [trumpet 2]	320 G[16]	MUDGE, *Six concertos* [violin 1, concertino]
		320 H[1]	*Handel's overtures* [violin 2]
320 E[1]	HANDEL, *Concerti grossi . . . Opera terza* [flute/violin 2, ripieno]	320 H[2]	HANDEL, *Twelve grand concertos . . . Opera sexta* [violin 2, concertino]
320 E[2]	SAN MARTINI, *Eight overtures . . . And six grand concertos* [trumpet 1]	320 H[3]	*Concerti grossi . . . Opera terza* [violin/oboe 2, concertino]
320 F[1]	HANDEL, *Concerti grossi . . . Opera terza* [flute/violin 1, ripieno]	320 H[4]	GEMINIANI, *Concerti grossi . . . composti dalle sonate . . . dell opera IV* [violin 2, concertino]
320 F[2]	SAN MARTINI, *Eight overtures . . . And six grand concertos* [oboe and violin]	320 H[5]	*Concerti grossi . . . Opera seconda* [violin 2, concertino]
320 G[1]	*Handel's overtures* [violin 1]	320 H[6]	*Concerti grossi . . . Opera terza* [violin 2, concertino]
320 G[2]	HANDEL, *Twelve grand concertos . . . Opera sexta* [violin 1, concertino]	320 H[7]	*Concerti grossi . . . Op.ª VII* [violin 2, concertino]
320 G[3]	*Concerti grossi . . . Opera terza* [violin/oboe 1, concertino]	320 H[8]	CORELLI, *Concerti grossi . . . Opera sesta* [violin 2, concertino]
320 G[4]	GEMINIANI, *Concerti grossi . . . composti dalle sonate . . . dell opera IV* [violin 1, concertino]	320 H[9]	*Concerti grossi . . . da Francesco Geminiani composti delli sei soli della prima parte dell'opera quinta d'Arcangelo Corelli* [violin 2, concertino]
320 G[5]	*Concerti grossi . . . Opera seconda* [violin 1, concertino]		
320 G[6]	*Concerti grossi . . . Opera terza* [violin 1, concertino]	320 H[10]	*Concerti grossi . . . da Francesco Geminiani composti delli sei soli della seconda parte dell'opera quinta d'Arcangelo Corelli* [violin 2, concertino]
320 G[7]	*Concerti grossi . . . Op.ª VII* [violin 1, concertino]		
320 G[8]	CORELLI, *Concerti grossi . . . Opera sesta* [violin 1, concertino]	320 H[11]	*Concerti grossi . . . Composti delli sei sonate del'opera terza d'Arcangelo Corelli per Francesco Geminiani* [violin 2]
320 G[9]	*Concerti grossi . . . da Francesco Geminiani composti delli sei soli della prima parte dell'opera quinta d'Arcangelo Corelli* [violin 1, concertino]		
		320 H[12]	SAN MARTINI, *Eight overtures . . . And six grand concertos* [violin 2]
320 G[10]	*Concerti grossi . . . da Francesco Geminiani composti delli sei soli della seconda parte dell'opera quinta d'Arcangelo Corelli* [violin 1, concertino]	320 H[13]	STANLEY, *Six concertos* [violin 2, concertino]
		320 H[14]	BOYCE, *Eight symphonys . . . Opera seconda* [violin 2]
320 G[11]	*Concerti grossi . . . Composti delli sei sonate del'opera terza d'Arcangelo Corelli per Francesco Geminiani* [violin 1]	320 H[15]	RICCIOTTI, *VI. Concerti armonici* [violin 2]
		320 H[16]	MUDGE, *Six concertos* [violin 2, concertino]
320 G[12]	SAN MARTINI, *Eight overtures . . . And six grand concertos* [violin 1]	320 I[1]	*Handel's overtures* [oboe 1]
		320 I[2]	HANDEL, *Twelve grand concertos . . . Opera sexta* [violin 1, ripieno]

320 I³   *Concerti grossi ... Opera terza* [oboe/flute/violin 1]

320 I⁴   GEMINIANI, *Concerti grossi ... composti dalle sonate ... dell opera IV* [violin 1, ripieno]

320 I⁵   *Concerti grossi ... Opera seconda* [violin 1, ripieno]

320 I⁶   *Concerti grossi ... Opera terza* [violin 1, ripieno]

320 I⁷   *Concerti grossi ... Op.ᵃ VII* [violin 1, ripieno]

320 I⁸   CORELLI, *Concerti grossi ... Opera sesta* [violin 1, ripieno]

320 I⁹   *Concerti grossi ... da Francesco Geminiani composti delli sei soli della prima parte dell'opera quinta d'Arcangelo Corelli* [violin 1, ripieno]

320 I¹⁰   *Concerti grossi ... da Francesco Geminiani composti delli sei soli della seconda parte dell'opera quinta d'Arcangelo Corelli* [violin 1, ripieno]

320 I¹¹   *Concerti grossi ... Composti delli sei sonate del'opera terza d'Arcangelo Corelli per Francesco Geminiani* [violin 1, ripieno]

320 I¹²   SAN MARTINI, *Eight overtures ... And six grand concertos* [oboe/violin 1, ripieno]

320 I¹³   STANLEY, *Six concertos* [violin 1, ripieno]

320 I¹⁴   BOYCE, *Eight symphonys ... Opera seconda* [oboe 1]

320 I¹⁵   RICCIOTTI, *VI. Concerti armonici* [violin 3]

320 I¹⁶   MUDGE, *Six concertos* [violin 1, ripieno]

320 J¹   *Handel's overtures* [oboe 2]

320 J²   HANDEL, *Twelve grand concertos ... Opera sexta* [violin 2, ripieno]

320 J³   *Concerti grossi ... Opera terza* [oboe/violin 2, ripieno]

320 J⁴   GEMINIANI, *Concerti grossi ... composti dalle sonate ... dell opera IV* [violin 2, ripieno]

320 J⁵   *Concerti grossi ... Opera seconda* [violin 2, ripieno]

320 J⁶   *Concerti grossi ... Opera terza* [violin 2, ripieno]

320 J⁷   *Concerti grossi ... Op.ᵃ VII* [violin 2, ripieno]

320 J⁸   CORELLI, *Concerti grossi ... Opera sesta* [violin 2, ripieno]

320 J⁹   *Concerti grossi ... da Francesco Geminiani composti delli sei soli della prima parte dell'opera quinta d'Arcangelo Corelli* [violin 2, ripieno]

320 J¹⁰   *Concerti grossi ... da Francesco Geminiani composti delli sei soli della seconda parte dell'opera quinta d'Arcangelo Corelli* [violin 2, ripieno]

320 J¹¹   *Concerti grossi ... Composti delli sei sonate del'opera terza d'Arcangelo Corelli per Francesco Geminiani* [violin 2, ripieno]

320 J¹²   SAN MARTINI, *Eight overtures ... And six grand concertos* [oboe/violin 2, ripieno]

320 J¹³   STANLEY, *Six concertos* [violin 2, ripieno]

320 J¹⁴   BOYCE, *Eight symphonys ... Opera seconda* [oboe 2]

320 J¹⁵   RICCIOTTI, *VI. Concerti armonici* [violin 4]

320 J¹⁶   MUDGE, *Six concertos* [violin 2, ripieno]

320 K¹   *Handel's overtures* [tenor/viola]

320 K²   HANDEL, *Twelve grand concertos ... Opera sexta* [viola]

320 K³   *Concerti grossi ... Opera terza* [tenor/viola]

320 K⁴   GEMINIANI, *Concerti grossi ... composti dalle sonate ... dell opera IV* [viola 1]

320 K⁵   *Concerti grossi ... Opera seconda* [viola 1/2]

320 K⁶   *Concerti grossi ... Opera terza* [viola]

320 K⁷   *Concerti grossi ... Op.ᵃ VII* [viola, concertino]

320 K⁸   CORELLI, *Concerti grossi ... Opera sesta* [viola]

320 K⁹   *Concerti grossi ... da Francesco Geminiani composti delli sei soli della prima parte dell'opera quinta d'Arcangelo Corelli* [viola]

320 K¹⁰   *Concerti grossi ... da Francesco Geminiani composti delli sei soli della seconda parte dell'opera quinta d'Arcangelo Corelli* [viola]

320 K¹¹   *Concerti grossi . . . Composti delli sei sonate del'opera terza d'Arcangelo Corelli per Francesco Geminiani* [viola]

320 K¹²   SAN MARTINI, *Eight overtures . . . And six grand concertos* [viola]

320 K¹³   STANLEY, *Six concertos* [viola]

320 K¹⁴   BOYCE, *Eight symphonys . . . Opera seconda* [viola]

320 K¹⁵   RICCIOTTI, *VI. Concerti armonici* [viola]

320 K¹⁶   MUDGE, *Six concertos* [viola]

320 L¹   *Handel's overtures* [violin 3/horns/trumpets/drums]

320 L²   SAN MARTINI, *Eight overtures . . . And six grand concertos* [horn 1]

320 L³   BOYCE, *Eight symphonys . . . Opera seconda* [trumpets 1 and 2]

320 L⁴   MUDGE, *Six concertos* [trumpet]

320 M¹   *Handel's overtures* [violoncello/bassoon]

320 M²   HANDEL, *Twelve grand concertos . . . Opera sexta* [violoncello]

320 M³   *Concerti grossi . . . Opera terza* [bassoons 1 and 2/violoncellos 1 and 2]

320 M⁴   GEMINIANI, *Concerti grossi . . . composti dalle sonate . . . dell opera IV* [violoncello]

320 M⁵   *Concerti grossi . . . Opera seconda* [violoncello]

320 M⁶   *Concerti grossi . . . Opera terza* [violoncello, concertino]

320 M⁷   *Concerti grossi . . . Op.ᵃ VII* [violoncello, concertino]

320 M⁸   CORELLI, *Concerti grossi . . . Opera sesta* [violoncello, concertino]

320 M⁹   *Concerti grossi . . . da Francesco Geminiani composti delli sei soli della prima parte dell'opera quinta d'Arcangelo Corelli* [violoncello]

320 M¹⁰   *Concerti grossi . . . da Francesco Geminiani composti delli sei soli della seconda parte dell'opera quinta d'Arcangelo Corelli* [violoncello, concertino]

320 M¹¹   *Concerti grossi . . . Composti delli sei sonate del'opera terza d'Arcangelo Corelli per Francesco Geminiani* [violoncello]

320 M¹²   SAN MARTINI, *Eight overtures . . . And six grand concertos* [violoncello/cembalo]

320 M¹³   STANLEY, *Six concertos* [violoncello]

320 M¹⁴   BOYCE, *Eight symphonys . . . Opera seconda* [bass]

320 M¹⁵   RICCIOTTI, *VI. Concerti armonici* [violoncello obligato]

320 M¹⁶   MUDGE, *Six concertos* [violoncello]

320 N¹   *Handel's overtures* [basso continuo]

320 N²   HANDEL, *Twelve grand concertos . . . Opera sexta* [basso continuo]

320 N³   *Concerti grossi . . . Opera terza* [basso continuo]

320 N⁴   GEMINIANI, *Concerti grossi . . . composti dalle sonate . . . dell opera IV* [bass, ripieno]

320 N⁵   *Concerti grossi . . . Opera seconda* [bass, ripieno]

320 N⁶   *Concerti grossi . . . Opera terza* [bass, ripieno]

320 N⁷   *Concerti grossi . . . Op.ᵃ VII* [bass, ripieno]

320 N⁸   CORELLI, *Concerti grossi . . . Opera sesta* [bass, ripieno]

320 N⁹   *Concerti grossi . . . da Francesco Geminiani composti delli sei soli della prima parte dell'opera quinta d'Arcangelo Corelli* [bass, ripieno]

320 N¹⁰   *Concerti grossi . . . da Francesco Geminiani composti delli sei soli della seconda parte dell'opera quinta d'Arcangelo Corelli* [bass, ripieno]

320 N¹¹   *Concerti grossi . . . Composti delli sei sonate del'opera terza d'Arcangelo Corelli per Francesco Geminiani* [contra bass/organ]

320 N¹²   SAN MARTINI, *Eight overtures . . . And six grand concertos* [violoncello/cembalo]

320 N¹³   STANLEY, *Six concertos* [bass, ripieno]

320 N¹⁴   BOYCE, *Eight symphonys . . . Opera seconda* [bass]

320 N¹⁵   RICCIOTTI, *VI. Concerti armonici* [basso continuo]

320 N¹⁶   MUDGE, *Six concertos* [basso grosso e continuo]

321¹   LULLI (G.B.), *Bellerophon*

321²   *Phaëton*

322   *Proserpine*

323   *Persée*

324   *Roland*

325	*Temple de la paix*	357 B$^{1-3}$	*Second <–fourth> collection of catches*
326	*Acis et Galatée*	357 C	*A twenty sixth collection of catches*
327	LULLY (L. DE), *Orphée*	357 D	*Catch Club . . . Book I*
328	COLASSE, *Achille et Polixene*	358	RAMEAU, *Pigmalion*
329	DESMARETS, *Circé*	359	*[Another copy]*
330–6	LALANDE, *Motets*	360	LE ROUX, *Pieces de clavessin*
337	COLASSE, *Thetis et Pelée*	361 A$^{1-2}$	TARTINI, *II Concerti . . . accommodati per il cembalo*
338	*Enée et Lavinie*		
339	CHARPENTIER, *Medée*	361 B	RICHARDSON, *Lessons for the harpsichord*
340	JACQUET DE LA GUERRE, *Cephale et Procris*		
		361 C	ECCLES AND PURCELL (D.), *Collection of lessons and aires*
341 A^1	PURCELL (H.), *The Tempest, The Indian Queen* [Goodison]		
		361 D	MARCHAND, *Pieces de clavecin*
341 A^2	*Odes and choral songs* (completed by MU. 341 B^1) [Goodison]	361 E	FROBERGER, *10. Suittes de clavessin*
		361 F	BONONCINI (G.B.) *Divertimenti da camera*
341 A^3	*Voluntary* [Goodison]		
341 A^4	*Anthems* [Goodison]	362 A	ZIANI, *XVII Sonates da organo*
341 B^1	*Odes and choral songs* (completed by MU. 341 A^2) [Goodison]	362 B	SYMONDS, *Six sets of lessons for the harpsicord*
341 B^2	*Oedipus. King Arthur* [Goodison]	362 C	SCARLATTI (D.), *Forty two suits of lessons for the harpsicord* [Vol. I]
341 B^3	QUARLES, *Lesson* [Goodison]		
341 B^4	STEFFANI, *Duetti* [Goodison]	362 D	*Six sonatas for the harpsichord . . . Vol. III*
341 B^5	SARTI, *Ah! proteggete o Dei. Duetto* [Goodison]		
		362 E	BACH (J.C.), *Six sonatas for the piano forte . . . Opera 5*
341 B^6	HANDEL, *Fantasia* [Goodison]		
341 B^7	*Aria . . . Duetto, nel Muzio Scaevola* [Goodison]	363 A	BOYCE, *Ode [for the] installation of . . . [the] Chancellor of the University*
341 B^8	PERGOLESI, *Mottetto: Domine ad adjuvandum* [Goodison]		
		363 B	*Solomon*
341 B^9	*Missa* [in D] [Goodison]	364	*Fifteen anthems . . . Te Deum, and Jubilate*
342	HANDEL, *Deborah*		
343	*Esther*	365^1	NARES, *Morning and evening service . . . with six anthems*
344	*Joseph*		
345	*Semele* [Arnold]	365^2	WOODWARD, *Cathedral music . . . Opera terza*
346	*Belshazzar*		
347	*Occasional Oratorio*	366^1	BURNEY, *La musica . . . della settimana santa*
348	*Solomon*		
349	*Susanna*	366^2	PURCELL (H.), *Harmonia sacra*
350	*Theodora*	366^3	*Te Deum et Jubilate*
351 A–C	*Anthems . . . for . . . James Duke of Chandos . . . Vol. I<–III>*	366$^{4-5}$	PEPUSCH, *Six English cantatas* [2 vols.]
352	*Anthem. For the wedding of Frederick Prince of Wales* [Arnold]	367	LOCKE, *Modern church-musick preaccus'd* (bound with MU. MS 177 B)
353	*Dettingen Te Deum*		
354 A$^{1-3}$	*Six grand chorusses*	368	GREENE, *Forty select anthems*
354 B	*Twelve duets . . . trio in . . . Alcina*	369	AYRTON, *Anthem [written for] the degree of Doctor in Music*
355^1	*Handel's overtures*		
355^2	*Overtures to . . . anthems . . . for James Duke of Chandos*	370	PORTER, *Cathedral music*
		[371 A–B]	
[356]		372^1	PLAYFORD (H.), *Harmonia sacra . . . first book*
357 A	WARREN, *Collection of catches*		

372²	*Harmonia sacra . . . second book*	386 B	*[Alessandro]. Roxana, or Alexander*
372³	*Two divine hymns*	386 C	*[Tamerlano]. Tamerlane*
373¹	*Harmonia sacra . . . first book*	387 A	*[Poro]. Porus*
373²	*Harmonia sacra . . . second book*	387 B	*[Giustino]. Justin*
373³	*Two divine hymns*	388 A	*[Floridante]. Floridant*
374¹	*Harmonia sacra . . . first book*	388 B	*Radamisto*
374²	*Harmonia sacra . . . Book II*	388 C	*Rinaldo*
375¹	PURCELL (H.), *Orpheus Britannicus [Vol. I]*	389 A	*Orlando*
		389 B	*[Partenope]. Parthenope*
375²	BLOW, *Ode on the death of Mr. Henry Purcell*	390 A	*[Ezio]. Aetius*
		390 B	*[Flavio]. Flavius*
376	PURCELL (H.), *Orpheus Britannicus . . . second book*	390 C	*[Sosarme]. Sosarmes*
		391 A	*Alcina*
377¹	PLAYFORD (J.), *Select ayres and dialogues to sing to the theorbo-lute* (bound with MU. MS 118)	391 B	*Berenice*
		392	*Alexander's Feast*
		393	*Anthem . . . perform'd . . . at the funeral of Queen Caroline . . . Vol. II*
377²	*Choice ayres, songs, & dialogues* (bound with MU. MS 118)		
377³	*Choice ayres & songs . . . second book* (bound with MU. MS 118)	394	*Jephtha*
		395	*Thirteen celebrated Italian duets*
378¹	ECCLES, *Judgment of Paris*	396	*Handel's celebrated Coronation Anthems . . . Vol. I*
378²	PURCELL (D.), *Judgment of Paris*		
379	PURCELL (H.), *The Prophetess, or . . . Dioclesian*	397	*L'Allegro, il Penseroso, ed il Moderato*
		398	*[Utrecht Te Deum]. Te Deum et Jubilate . . . perform'd before the sons of the clergy . . . Vol. III*
380 A	HINE, *[Harm]onia Sacra Glocestriensis*		
380 B	PARRY, *British Harmony*		
380 C	*[Le Mariage Mexicain]. Favorite pas de trois*	399	*Messiah*
		400	*Choice of Hercules*
380 D¹	WESLEY (C.), *Now I know what it is to have strove*	401	*Saul*
		402	*Joshua*
380 D²	SMITH (C.), *Old England for ever & God save the King*	403	*Israel in Egypt*
		404	*Samson*
380 E¹	MUGNIÉ, *Le Papillon*	405	*Judas Macchabaeus*
380 E²	*La Colombe reperdue*	406	*Ode for St Cecilia's Day*
380 E³	*A Grand military divertimento*	407	*Acis and Galatea*
380 E⁴	*L'Amour piqué par une abeille*	408	*[Serse]. Xerxes*
381 A	HANDEL, *[Lotario]. Lotharius*	409	MARCELLO, *Estro poetico-armonico*
381 B	*[Riccardo Primo]. Richard ye Ist*	410	NOVELLO, *Fitzwilliam Music*
381 C	*[Scipione]. Scipio*	411 A–C	BOYCE, *Cathedral Music*
381 D	*Siroe*	412	CROFT, *Musicus apparatus academicus*
382 A	*[Arianna]. Ariadne*	413 A–B	MORLEY, *Triumphs of Oriana*
382 B	*Rodelinda*	[414]	
383 A	*Giulio Cesare*	415	KEEBLE, *Select pieces ⟨A second–fourth set of⟩ for the organ*
383 B	*[Tolomeo]. Ptolomy*		
384 A	*Faramondo*	416	CLEMENTI, *Selection of practical harmony*
384 B	*[Imeneo]. Hymen*		
384 C	*[Ottone]. Otho*	417	HART (P.), *Fugues . . . with lessons*
385 A	*Admeto*	418	SOLER (A.), *XXVII Sonatas para clave*
385 B	*[Arminio]. Arminius*		
385 C	*Deidamia*	419	PURCELL (H.), *Choice collection of lessons*
386 A	*Atalanta*		

420 A	CLARKE, *Choice lessons*	456	*Jephtha* [Arnold]
420 B	DIEUPART, *Select lessons*	457	*Triumph of Time and Truth* [Arnold]
421 A	MORLEY, *Six canzonets for two voices*		
421 B	NARES, *Treatise on singing*	458	*La Resurrezione* [Arnold]
421 C	KEEBLE AND KIRKMAN, *Forty interludes*	459	*L'Allegro, il Pensieroso, ed il Moderato* [Arnold]
422	SCARLATTI (D.), *Essercizi per gravicembalo*	460 A$^{1-6}$	*Anthem[s] . . . for . . . the Duke of Chandos* [nos. 1–6] [Arnold]
423	*Thirty sonatas, for the harpsichord*	460 B$^{1-6}$	*Anthem[s] . . . for . . . the Duke of Chandos* [nos. 7–12] [Arnold]
424	COUPERIN, *L'Art de toucher le clavecin*	461^1	*Te Deum . . . for . . . the Duke of Chandos (1720)* [Arnold]
425	*Pieces de clavecin . . . Premier livre*	461^2	*Te Deum . . . for . . . Queen Caroline* [Arnold]
426	*Second livre de pièces de clavecin*		
427	RAMEAU, *Pieces de clavecin en concerts*	461^3	*Te Deum . . . for . . . the Duke of Chandos (1719)* [Arnold]
428	PARADIES, *Sonate di gravicembalo*	461^4	*Te Deum . . . for the Peace of Utrecht* [Arnold]
429	DU PHLY, *Pieces ⟨second–quatrieme livre de pièces⟩ de clavecin*	461^5	*Jubilate . . . for the Peace of Utrecht* [Arnold]
430	CLEMENTI, *Introduction to . . . the piano forte*	461^6	*Te Deum . . . for the victory at Dettingen* [Arnold]
[431–2]			
433^1	HANDEL, *Sonata pour le clavecin . . . Opera seconda* (bound with MU. MS 78)	462^1	*[Op.2]. Six sonatas . . . 1731* [Arnold]
		462^2	*[Op.5]. Seven sonatas or trios . . . 1739* [Arnold]
433^2	*Capricio pour le clavecin . . . Opera terza* (bound with MU. MS 78)	462^3	*[Select Harmony. Fourth collection. No.1]. Concertante, in nine parts (1738)* [Arnold]
433^3	*Preludio et allegro pour le clavecin . . . Opera quarta* (bound with MU. MS 78)	462^4	*Water Musick* [Arnold]
433^4	*Fantasie pour le clavecin . . . Opera quinta* (bound with MU. MS 78)	462^5	*Musick for the royal fireworks* [Arnold]
434	*Music . . . for the harp*	463	*[Op.6]. Twelve grand concertos . . . 1737* [Arnold]
435	DIEUPART, *[Six suittes de clavessin]*		
436	ROGER, *VI Suittes . . . pour le clavessin*	464^1	*Ode for the birthday of Queen Ann* [Arnold]
437	BONONCINI (G.B.), *Cantate e duetti*	464^2	*Acis and Galatea* [Arnold]
		464^3	*Ode on St Cecilia's Day* [Arnold]
438	HARRISON, *Glee, 'Oh Nanny!'* (bound as MU. MS 166 C)	464^4	*Alexanders Feast* [Arnold]
		465^1	*[Alceste]. Alcides* [Arnold]
439–42	HANDEL, *Vocal works* [Clarke]	465^2	*Semele* [Arnold]
443	*Esther* [Arnold]	465^3	*Alchymist* [Arnold]
444	*Athalia* [Arnold]	466^1	*Choice of Hercules* [Arnold]
445	*Saul* [Arnold]	466^2	*[Il Pastor Fido]. Masque* [Arnold]
446	*Israel in Egypt* [Arnold]	467	*Agrippina* [Arnold]
447	*Messiah* [Arnold]	468	*Teseo* [Arnold]
448	*Samson* [Arnold]	469	*Giulio Cesare* [Arnold]
449	*Joseph* [Arnold]	470	*Sosarme* [Arnold]
450	*Belshazzar* [Arnold]	471	*Alexander Balus* [Arnold]
451	*Occasional Oratorio* [Arnold]	472^1	*Hercules* [Arnold]
452	*Judas Macchabaeus* [Arnold]	472^2	*Choice of Hercules* [Arnold]
453	*Solomon* [Arnold]	473	*Triumph of Time and Truth*
454	*Susanna* [Arnold]		
455	*Theodora* [Arnold]		

474¹   *Hercules*
474²   *Semele*
475¹   *[Radamisto]. Radamistus*
475²   *Rinaldo*
476¹   *[Utrecht Te Deum]. Te Deum et Jubilate . . . perform'd before the Sons of the Clergy*
476²   STEPHENSON, *Church harmony*
477 A¹   HANDEL, *Pastor Fido*
477 A²   *Ariodante*
477 B   HANDEL AND GEMINIANI, *Water Musick . . . two favourite minuets*
478   HANDEL, *Alexander Balus*
479   CLARI, *Sei madrigali . . . Parte prima*
480   MARTINI, *Duetti da camera*
481   MAZZAFERRATA, *Canzonette, e cantate a due voci . . . Opera terza*
482¹   BACH (J.S.), *Die Kunst der Fuge*
482²   *Exercices pour le clavecin . . . Œuv. III*
483¹   SMITH (J.C.), *Suites . . . pour le clavecin [Second book]*
483²⁻³   *Lessons for the harpsicord . . . Opera III ⟨IV⟩*
483⁴   *XII Sonatas for the harpsicord. Opera quinta*
484¹   ALBERTI, *VIII Sonate per cembalo. Opera prima*
484²   NUSSEN, *Musica di camera . . . Opera 3ᶻᵃ.*
484³   RAMEAU, *Lessons for the harpsicord . . . Opera seconda*
484⁴   *A 2ᵈ collection of lessons for the harpsicord . . . Opera 3ᶻᵃ.*
484⁵   ROSEINGRAVE, *Six double fugues . . . Scarlatti's celebrated lesson for the harpsicord*
484⁶   STANLEY, *Ten voluntarys . . . Opera 5ᵗʰ:*
484⁷   *Ten voluntarys . . . Opera sesta*
484⁸   *Ten voluntaries . . . Opera settima*
485¹   BURTON, *Ten sonatas for the harpsichord*
485²   GREENE, *Lessons for the harpsichord*
485³   *Lessons for the harpsichord . . . 2ᵈ. book*
485⁴   KELWAY, *Six sonatas for the harpsichord*
485⁵   NARES, *Lessons for the harpsichord . . . Opera II*
485⁶   WAGENSEIL, *Six sonatas for the harpsicord . . . Opera prima*
485⁷   *Six sonatas for the harpsichord . . . Opera III*

486¹   PARADIES, *A favorite concerto for the organ*
486²   RAMEAU, *Five concertos for the harpsicord*
486³   ROSEINGRAVE, *Voluntarys and fugues*
486⁴   SAN MARTINI, *Concertos for the harpsicord . . . Opera nona*
486⁵   SCARLATTI (D.), *Libro de XII sonatas modernas para clavicordio*
486⁶   STANLEY, *Six concertos set for the harpsicord*
486⁷   ZIPOLI, *A third collection of toccates, vollentarys and fuges*
486⁸   WAGENSEIL, *Six concertos for the harpsicord . . . with . . . two violins*
486⁹   *Six sonatas for the harpsichord . . . Opera 2ᵈᵃ.*
487   GALLIARD, *Six sonatas for the bassoon*
488¹⁻²   AVISON, *Twelve concertos . . . Opera nona. set I ⟨II⟩* (bound with MU. MS 208)
488³   BABELL, *Suits of the most celebrated lessons* (bound with MU. MS 208)
488⁴   DRAGHI, *Six select suites of lessons* (bound with MU. MS 208)
488⁵   JONES, *Suits or setts of lessons* (bound with MU. MS 208)
488⁶   KELLNER, *Six fugues for the organ* (bound with MU. MS 208)
488⁷   TARTINI, *Six solos for a violin . . . Opera seconda* (bound with MU. MS 208)
489   BERTON AND TRIAL, *Silvie*
490¹   RAMEAU, *Les Festes de l'Hymen et de l'Amour*
490²   *Les Fêtes de Polymnie*
491¹   PURCELL (H.), *Te Deum et Jubilate*
491²   BASSANI, *Harmonia festiva, being the thirteenth opera of divine mottetts*
491³   *Harmonia festiva, being the eighth opera of divine mottetts*
492   PRATT, *Collection of anthems*
493   PORPORA, *Opre di musica vocale*
494¹   GALLIARD, *Morning hymn*
494²   SMITH (J.S.), *Collection of English songs*
495   BONONCINI (G.B.), *Anthem . . . performed . . . at the funeral of . . . John, Duke of Marlborough*
[496]

497–8	WEBBE (S., the younger), *Convito armonico . . . Vol: 1⟨–2⟩*	882	SCHENCK, *Lessons for the bass viol*
499	HANDEL, *Fitzwilliam Music . . . Three hymns*	[883–1001]	
		1002–3	GORTON, *New ayres . . . for two bass-viols*
500	BONONCINI (G.B.), *Astartus*	[1004–168]	
501¹	HANDEL, *Messiah* [The Piano-Forte Magazine]	1169	MOZART, *Zwey Deutsche Arien . . . II^ter Theil*
501²	*Acis and Galatea* [The Piano-Forte Magazine]	1170	HUMPHRIES, *XII Sonatas, for two violins*
501³	*Judas Maccabaeus* [The Piano-Forte Magazine]	1171	ARNE (T.A.), *Rule Britannia*
501⁴	*L'Allegro, Il Penseroso, ed Il Moderato* [The Piano-Forte Magazine]	1172	*Aires & symphonys for ye bass viol*
		[1173]	
501⁵	*Coronation anthem* [The Piano-Forte Magazine]	1174¹⁻²	MUFFAT, *Componimenti musicali per il cembalo* (with separately bound modern MS notes)
501⁶	HAYDN, *The marvellous work, With verdure clad* [The Piano-Forte Magazine]	[1175]	
		1176	CARBONELLI, *Sonate da camera*
502–4	THOMSON, *Select melodies of Scotland*	1177¹	*The Summer's Tale*
[505]		1177²	ARNE (M.), *Almena*
506	HANDEL, *The Famous Water Piece*	1178	HANDEL, *[Op. 1]. Solos for a German flute*
507	PURCELL (H.), *Ten sonatas in four parts* [violin 1]	1179	*Messiah*
508	*Ten sonatas in four parts* [violin 2]	1180¹	BABELL, *The 3^d. book of the ladys entertainment . . . aires & duets in . . . Pyrrhus & Clotilda*
509	*Ten sonatas in four parts* [bass]		
510	*Ten sonatas in four parts* [bass continuo]	1180²	*The 3^d.* [altered in MS to 4th] *Book of the ladys entertainment in . . . Hydaspes & Almahide*
511–13	VALENTINE, *Six setts of aires and a chacoon*		
514	HANDEL, *Cecilia volgi un sguardo*	1180³	*Suits of the most celebrated lessons*
515¹	HASSE, *Salve Regina*	1181	ARNE (T.A.), *Judith*
515²	BONONCINI (G.B.), *Anthem . . . performed . . . at the funeral of . . . John, Duke of Marlborough*	1182¹	*Blind Beggar of Bethnal Green . . . Merchant of Venice*
		1182²	*[Vocal Melody. Book XIV]. A favourite collection of songs, with the dialogue in the Arcadian Nuptials . . . Book XIV*
515³	TRAVERS, *Eighteen canzonets*		
[516–20]			
521	ALBINONI, ⟨*Cantate . . . Opera quarta*⟩	1182³	*[Vocal Melody. Book XIII]. A Collection consisting of favourite songs and cantatas*
522	HANDEL, *[Poro]. Porus*		
523	GALLIARD, *Hymn of Adam and Eve*	1182⁴	*Six favourite concertos, for the organ, harpsichord, or piano forte*
524–7	WILLIAMS, *Six sonata's in three parts*		
528	PERGOLESI, *Stabat mater*	1183 A	LAMPE, *Pyramus and Thisbe*
[529–91]		1183 B	SMITH (J.C.), *The Fairies*
592	SHIELD, *When the rosy morn appearing . . . in . . . Rosina*	1183 C	*The Tempest*
		1184 A	ARNE (T.A.), *The Guardian Outwitted . . . No. 1*
[593–770]			
771 A	PLAYFORD (J.), *Select ayres and dialogues . . . second book*	1184 B	*Summer Amusement*
		1184 C	*The Syren*
[771 B–855]		1184 D	*The Vocal Grove*
856	HANDEL, *Messiah*	1184 E	*Thomas and Sally, or the Sailor's Return*
[857–81]			

1184 F	[Vocal Melody. Book XI]. No. XI, British Melody.	1189[19a]	DEFESCH, Polly of the Plain
1185[1]	HANDEL, Siroe	1189[20]	Thou rising sun whose gladsome ray
1185[2]	Rodelinda	1189[21]	HAWDOWN, So brightly sweet fair Nanny's eyes
1186[1]	KING, Oh this love! or the Masqueraders	1189[22]	JACKSON (J.), Sally of the dale
1186[2]	Plots, or the North Tower	1189[23]	You tell me I'm handsome
1186[3]	Turn out	1189[24]	LAMPE, The Parent Bird
1186[4]	Up All Night, or the Smugglers Cave	1189[25]	Silvia bright nymph who long had found
1186[5]	BRAHAM, The English Fleet	1189[26]	Come sweet lass, let's banish sorrow
1186[6]	REEVE, DAVY AND BRAHAM, Thirty Thousand, or Who's the Richest?	1189[27]	DEFESCH, Mutual Love
		1189[28]	Hark, hark o'er the plains
1187[1]	KELLY, The Africans	1189[29]	Near the side of a pond
1187[2]	Cinderella, or the Little Glass Slipper	1189[30]	HOWARD, The Generous Confession
1187[3]	The Gay Deceivers	1189[31]	That Jenny's my friend
1187[4]	Love Laughs at Locksmiths	1189[32]	To woo me and win me
1187[5]	The Peasant Boy	1189[33]	WORGAN, Miranda
1187[6]	Pizzarro	1189[34]	LONG, Of all my experience
1187[7]	The Royal Oak	1189[35]	Where the jessamine sweetens the bow'r
1187[8]	We Fly by Night, or Long Stories	1189[36]	P. (S.), The Rising Beauty
1187[9]	The Wood Daemon, or The Clock has Struck	1189[37]	A nymph there lives
		1189[38]	As Jockey was walking one midsummer morn
1187[10]	The Young Hussar, or Love & Mercy		
1188	DALAYRAC, La Soirée orageuse . . . Œuvre XII	1189[39]	HUDSON, The Impartial Lover
		1189[39a]	A dawn of hope my soul revives
1189[1]	Wou'd you taste ye noontide air	1189[40]	BRETT, A new song on Sadler's Wells
1189[2]	BOYCE, The Pleasures of the Spring Gardens at Vaux-hall	1189[41]	No more silly pipe
		1189[42]	ROZELLI, Cupid's Defeat
1189[3]	HOWARD, Myra	1189[43]	ARNE (T.A.), Lotharia
1189[4]	What Cato advises	1189[44]	Ye belles, and ye flirts
1189[4a]	The smiling morn, the breathing spring	1189[45]	CAREY (H.), In these groves
1189[5]	HOWARD, The lass of St. Osyth	1189[46]	HANDEL, When I survey Clarinda's charms
1189[6]	O lovely maid how dear's thy power		
1189[7]	GREENE, The Happy Shepherd	1189[47]	[The Contrivances]. The Maid's Husband
1189[8]	BAILDON, [The Laurel . . .]. If love's a sweet passion	1189[48]	CAREY (H.), The hunting song in Cephalus and Procris
1189[9]	[The Laurel . . .]. Beauty's bright standard	1189[49]	Thy vain pursuit fond youth give o'er
		1189[50]	MATTOX, Love's Victim
1189[10]	Forgive ye fair, nor take it wrong	1189[51]	The morning cloud was ting'd with gold
1189[11]	DAVIES, The Irish Lassie		
1189[12]	My soger laddie is over the seas	1189[52]	To an arbor of woodbine
1189[13]	DAVIES, Hobbinol, a new song	1189[53]	To Fanny fair I would impart
1189[14]	WEIDEMAN, When first by fond Damon	1190[1–5]	CAREY (H.), A choice collection of six favourite songs
1189[15]	DEFESCH, To Lysander	1190[5a]	[Jupiter and Europa]. ⟨This great world but a trouble⟩
1189[16]	HOWARD, The Lass of the Hill		
1189[17]	DEFESCH, To make me feel a virgins charms	1190[6]	[Myrtillo]. How happy are we. A song in . . . Martillo
1189[18]	A shape alone let others prize	1190[7]	MARCHANT, On a lady of quality
		1190[8]	PORTA, Strazo sempia furia
1189[19]	On the tays verdant banks	1190[9]	YOUNG, The Shy Shepherdess
		1190[10]	Cease my Cloe

1190^{11} A nymph of the plain

1190^{12} In summers solstace

1190^{13} HART (W.), My time, O ye muses

1190^{14} Ye circum and uncircumcis'd

1190^{15} RAVENSCROFT, Foolish woman fly mens charms

1190^{16} In London stands a famous pile

1190^{17} Lords and ladies, who deal in the sport

1190^{18} YOSLINGTON, O mine awn Jenny

1190^{19} Come let us prepare

1190^{20} POPELEY, Come Delia come, let's shun ye heat

1190^{21} GRANO, No more Florilla when I gaze

1190^{22} GALLIARD, Fairest if thou can'st be kind. A song . . . in . . . Circe

1190^{23} WEBBER, Inconstancy in woman

1190^{24} TURNER, On Mira's singing and beauty

1190^{25} Good wine in a morning

1190^{26} Dear Cupid smile thou god of love

1190^{27} WEBBER, Tell me, tell me, charming creature

1190^{28} Come follow follow me

1190^{29} Wine's a mistress gay and easy. Bass song . . . in . . . Love and Wine

1190^{30} Non e si vago e bello / I come my fairest treasure

1190^{31} M. (F.) The Constant Tarr

1190^{32} Sing ye muses praises sounding

1190^{33} ECCLES, O sleep why do'st thou leave me. Air in . . . Semele

1190^{34} Come dear Philada, let us haste away

1190^{35} Inspir'd with Venus sweet alarms

1190^{36} Late I came from roses on bushes

1190^{37} TURNER, On decanting a flask of Florence

1190^{38} A catch (a 4 voc.) in praise of claret

1190^{39} An Epigram. Gripe and Shifter

1190^{40} GRAVES, Tis he's an honest fellow

1190^{41} LEVERIDGE, The Wheel of Life

1190^{42} The Lass of Patties Mill

1190^{43} At Polwart on the green

1190^{44} Blest as th'immortal gods is he

1190^{45} There's auld Rob Moris

1190^{46} While some for pleasure waste their health

1190^{47} Happys the love that meets return

1190^{48} What beauties does Flora disclose?

1190^{49} Beneath a green shade

1190^{50} GRAVES, On His Majesty King George ye second

1190^{51} [Astianasse]. Observe, observe you tuneful charmer. Sung . . . in Astynax

1190^{52-4} Jupiter and Europa

1190^{55} ALBINONI, Under ye gloomy shade

1190^{56} [Arsaces]. Figurati estinte / My charmer! come bless me!. A favourite song in . . . Arsaces

1190^{57} Dear Cloe is my sole delight

1190^{58} When the hills and lofty mountains

1190^{59} HANDEL, [Giulio Cesare]. Venere bella per un instante

1190^{60} Tu mia speranza tu mio conforto / My hopes my pleasure

1190^{61} GAMBALL, Cynthia

1190^{62} Queen of citty's raise thy head

1190^{63} O lovely charmer. Favourite minuet in . . . Floridant

1190^{64} Love and wine by turns possess me

1190^{65} PEPUSCH, The God of love had lost his bow

1190^{66} Strech'd on the ground beneath an aged oake

1190^{67} ECCLES, Come zephyrs come. Air in . . . Semele

1190^{68} Toast about, to the church

1190^{69} Supine in Sylvia's snowy arms he lies

1190^{70} How charming Celia lookt last night

1190^{71} [Astarto]. Mio caro ben / Dear pritty maid. Mio caro ben . . . in Astartus

1190^{72} Restless to pass the tedious day

1190^{73} Gentle love this hour befriend me

1190^{74} The gay dragoons on Wellands banks

1190^{75} VANBRUGHE, Advice to a friend in love

1190^{76} [Dido and Eneas]. Hear me mourning princess

1190^{77} VANBRUGHE, Lesbia's reproach and denial

1190^{78} Much I love a charming creature

1190^{79} Great Cecil rais'd a stately pile

1190^{80} ECCLES, See after the toils of an amorous fight. Air in . . . Semele

1190^{81} VANBRUGHE, The Lovely Mourner

1190^{82} O my treasure, crown my pleasure

1190^{83} LULMAN, In vino veritas

1190^{84} HAWKINS, Whilst Strephon gaz'd on Cloe's eyes

1190^{85} Forbid me not enquire

1190^{86} Oh, thou connubial god . . . in . . . the Royal Revenge

1191¹	BICKHAM, *The musical entertainer ... Vol: I*	1197²⁹	*Fair Hebe I left with a cautious design*
[1191²]		1197³⁰	*When-e're I meet my Celia's eyes*
1192¹	BISCHOFF, *Six sonates à violoncelle, et basse ... Œuvre premiere*	1197³¹	*I have rambled I own it*
		1197³²	*[Arianna]. How is it possible ... in Ariadne*
1192²	MASCITTI, *Solos for a violin ... Opera 2ᵈᵃ.*	1197³³	ARNE (T.A.), *Cymon and Iphigenia*
1192³	HAYDN, *[Six sonates. Pour le clavecin ... Œuvre XIV]*	1197³⁴	*The morning is charming*
		1197³⁵	BOYCE, *Rail no more*
1193	BICKHAM, *The musical entertainer*	1197³⁶	*Where shall Celia fly for shelter*
1194	*The musical entertainer* [vol. 1]	1197³⁷	*[Artaxerxes]. Thy father, away*
1195–6	CORELLI, *The score of the four setts of sonatas ⟨twelve concertos⟩* [2 vols.]	1197³⁸	*Phoebus meaner themes disdaining*
		1197³⁹	*Ye ruling pow'rs attentive be*
1197¹	*Wou'd you taste yᵉ noontide air*	1197⁴⁰	GREENE, *Go Rose*
1197²	*[Apollo and Daphne]. The sun from the east tips the mountains with gold*	1197⁴¹	*Be hush'd ye rude tempests*
		1197⁴²	WORGAN, *The Thief*
1197³	PURCELL (H.), *Bess of Bedlam*	1197⁴³	*My dearest life were thou my wife*
1197⁴	*Forth from my dark and dismall cell*	1197⁴⁴	*My soger laddie is over the seas*
1197⁵	HANDEL, *Wise men flattring may decieve you*	1197⁴⁵	*If I live to grow old*
		1197⁴⁶	ARNE (T.A.), *Excuse for a love slip*
1197⁶	ARNE (T.A.), *Vain is beauty's gaudy flow'r ... in Judith*	1197⁴⁷	MOZART, *Within these sacred bowers*
		1197⁴⁸	*[Artaxerxes]. Adieu thou lovely youth*
1197⁷	HANDEL, *[Joshua]. O had I Jubal's lyre*	1197⁴⁹	GERARD, *On Friendship*
		1197⁵⁰	*[L'Allegro]. Let me wander not unseen ... in 'L'Allegro e Penseroso'*
1197⁸	RAYMOND, *Damon's Request*		
1197⁹	*[Hornpipe]. Miss Dawson's hornpipe*	1197⁵¹	HOWARD, *Why heaves my fond bosom?*
1197¹⁰	*In infancy our hopes & fears*		
1197¹¹	*To an arbor of woodbine*	1197⁵²	*Did you see e'er a shepherd*
1197¹²	*[The Sacrifice of Iphigenia]. How sweet are the flowers*	1197⁵³	W. (V.), *Nancy gay*
		1197⁵⁴	*Young Strephon once the blithest swain*
1197¹²ᵃ	WOOD, *The Landskip*	1197⁵⁵	*As blyth as the linnet*
1197¹³	JACKSON (W.), *Susannah*	1197⁵⁶	ARNE (M.), *Thro' the wood lassie*
1197¹⁴	*Fine songsters apologies too often use*	1197⁵⁷	CAREY (H.), *Stand by! Clear the way! ... in yᵉ Provok'd Husband*
1197¹⁵	HAYDEN, *As I saw fair Clora*		
1197¹⁶	*March of the thirty-fifth regiment*	1197⁵⁸	GIARDINI, *Voi amante*
1197¹⁷	ARNE (T.A.), *Ye fair marri'd dames ... in The Way to Keep Him*	1197⁵⁹	WEIDEMAN, *When first by fond Damon*
		1197⁶⁰	BARNARD, *In love shou'd there meet a fond pair ... in Love in a Village*
1197¹⁸	*No more my song*		
1197¹⁹	ARNE (M.), *The Lass with the delicate air*	1197⁶¹	*[The Way to Keep Him]. Attend all ye fair*
1197²⁰	*My mother wou'd fain have oblig'd me to wed*	1197⁶²	TENDUCCI, *In vain to keep my heart you strive*
1197²¹	ARNE (T.A.), *Thomas & Sally* [song]	1197⁶³	*A dawn of hope my soul revives*
1197²²	*Of all the various states of life*	1197⁶⁴	*From sweet bewitching tricks of love*
1197²³	*All hail to the King*	1197⁶⁵	*No nymph that trips the verdant plains*
1197²⁴	DEFESCH, *Hail England! Old England!*	1197⁶⁶	*How blest has my time been*
		1197⁶⁷	BAILDON, *The Union of love and wine*
1197²⁵	*By a pratt'ling stream*	1197⁶⁸	*To Caelia thus fond Damon said*
1197²⁶	*[Artaxerxes]. Fair Aurora prithee stay*	1197⁶⁹	*Some kind angel, gently flying*
1197²⁷	CAREY, *Sweet William's farewell*	1197⁷⁰	*[Thomas and Sally]. When I was a young one*
1197²⁸	*My banks they are furnish'd with bees*		

1197⁷¹   GEMINIANI, *The Tender Lover*
1197⁷²   SNOW, *The Bird*
1197⁷³   OSWALD, *The Wheel-Barrow*
1197⁷⁴   BOYCE, *The Song of Diana, in Mʳ. Dryden's Secular Masque*
1197⁷⁵   *Young Arabella Mamma's care*
1197⁷⁶   BRYAN, *Dorus & Cleora*
1197⁷⁷   *Of Linster fam'd for maidens fair*
1197⁷⁸   RILEY, *Roger of the Dale*
1197⁷⁹   *How can you lovely Nancy*
1197⁸⁰   *God save great George our King*
1197⁸¹   *[Minuet]. Lord How's new minuet*
1197⁸²   *In good King Charls' golden days*
1197⁸³   GRIFFES, *Arabel*
1197⁸³ᵃ   *[Pow'rful guardians]*
1197⁸⁴   ARNE (M.), *The Thrush*
1198¹   CORELLI, *The . . . four operas, containing 48 sonatas ⟨twelve concertos⟩ . . . Vol. I*
1198²   *XII Solos for a violin . . . Opera quinta*
1198³   *The . . . four operas, containing 48 sonatas ⟨twelve concertos⟩ . . . Vol. II*
1199   HELLENDAAL, *Tweedledum and Tweedledee*
1200   ROSS, *A First set of ten songs . . . Op. 2*
[1201 A–B]
1202   KENT, *Twelve anthems*
1203   ALCOCK (J., THE ELDER), *Six and twenty select anthems*
[1204¹⁻²]
1205   *Recueil d'airs*
1206   *The Irish Musical Repository*
1207   *The English Musical Repository*
1208 A–B   SIME, *The Edinburgh Musical Miscellany*
[1209¹⁻⁴–1210]
1211¹   ABRAMS, *Crazy Jane*
1211²   STORACE, *The jealous Don . . . in the Pirates*
1211³   SHIELD (arr.), *From night till morn I take my glass*
1211⁴   *Old women will you go a sheering*
1211⁵   MOORE, *Oh lady fair!*
1211⁶   WINTER, *Rest lady fair*
1211⁷   *Where ah where shall I my shepherd find*
1211⁸   *Cou'd a man be secure*
1211⁹   *[Comus]. O thou wert born to please me*
1211¹⁰   ARNOLD (S.), *Faint and wearily the way-worn traveller . . . in the Mountaineers*
1211¹¹   ATTWOOD, *O! Thou who thro' the silent air*
1211¹²   *Hook's Original Christmas Box . . . Vol. III . . . Op. 86*
1211¹³⁻¹⁴   HAYDEN, *Turn fair Clora . . . As I saw fair Clora*
1211¹⁵   *Since first I saw your face*
1211¹⁶   SUETT, *Soft, sensible and true*
1211¹⁷   *And must we part for ever*
1211¹⁸   JACKSON (W.), *Love in thine eyes*
1211¹⁹   ABRAMS, *The last time I came o'er the moor*
1211²⁰   KNYVETT, *Jesse*
1211²¹   ARNOLD (S.), *Pauvre Madelon . . . in the Surrender of Calais*
1211²²   STEVENS, *Sigh no more ladies*
1211²³   MAZZINGHI, *The Wreath*
1211²⁴   SHIELD, *Tho you think by this to vex me . . . in the Siege of Belgrade*
1211²⁵   STORACE, *Ah tell me softly . . . in the Prize*
1211²⁶   ATTWOOD, *In peace love tunes the shepherd's reed*
1211²⁷   STEVENS, *To what age must we live without love?*
1211²⁸   STEVENSON, *Tell me where is fancy bred*
1211²⁹   BIGGS, *Come my bonny love*
1211³⁰   *In airy dreams soft fancy flies*
1211³¹   MOZART, *The manly heart*
1211³²   STORACE, *A Plighted faith . . . in the Siege of Belgrade*
1211³³   CALLCOTT, *Thyrsis*
1211³⁴   *O say bonny lass*
1211³⁵   PURCELL (H.), *Come unto these yellow sands*
1211³⁶   GRÉTRY, *The favorite duett . . . in Richard Coeur de Lion*
1211³⁷   PURCELL (H.), *Full fathom five . . . in the Tempest*
[1212¹⁻³]
1213   JACKSON (W.), *Elegies . . . Opera terza*
1214   ROUSSEAU, *Le Devin du Village*
[1215–17²]
1218   WEBBE (S., THE ELDER), *A selection of glees, duetts, canzonets &c.*
1219 A–B   CALLCOTT, *A collection of glees, canons, and catches*

[1220–1]	
1222	HAGUE, *A collection of songs*
1223	BACH (J.S.), *Vierstimmige Choral-gesänge. [Erster] ‹–vierter› Theil*
1224 A–C	CORRI, *A select collection of the most admired songs*
[1225]	
1226	PICCINI, *Roland*
1227	STANLEY, *Twelve [4] cantatas*
1228	*Amusement for the ladies . . . Vol: II*
1229	STANLEY, *Eight solo's for a German flute*
1230¹	STEVENS, *Seven glees . . . Opera, 6*
1230²⁻³	*[Glees. Professional Collection of Glees]*
1230⁴	STEVENS, *Eight glees . . . Opera 3*
1230⁵	*Eight glees. Expressly composed for ladies . . . Op. IV*
1230⁶	*Ten glees . . . Op. V*
1230⁷	*Sigh no more ladies*
1230⁸	*O mistress mine*
1230⁹	*Ye spotted snakes!*
1230¹⁰	*What shall he have*
1230¹¹	*From Oberon in fairy land*
1230¹²	HOWARD, *Ye chearful virgins*
1230¹³	STEVENS, *Some of my heroes are low*
1230¹⁴	*When the toil of day is o'er*
1230¹⁵	*Crabbed age and youth*
1231¹⁻⁶	WARREN, *A [fifth] ‹–tenth› collection of catches, canons and glees . . . inscribed to . . . the Catch Club*
1230⁶	*Ten glees . . . Op. V*
1230⁷	*Sigh no more ladies*
1230⁸	*O mistress mine*
1230⁹	*Ye spotted snakes!*
1230¹⁰	*What shall he have*
1230¹¹	*From Oberon in fairy land*
1230¹²	HOWARD, *Ye chearful virgins*
1230¹³	STEVENS, *Some of my heroes are low*
1230¹⁴	STEVENS, *When the toil of day is o'er*
1230¹⁵	*Crabbed age and youth*
1231¹⁻⁶	WARREN, *A [fifth] ‹–tenth› collection of catches, canons and glees . . . inscribed to . . . the Catch Club*
1232–6	*Handel's songs, selected from his oratorios*
1237	*The Carman's Whistle. Then come kiss me now*
1238¹⁻³	MARPURG, *Clavierstücke*
1239–43	*Handel's songs selected from his latest ‹ › oratorios*
1244¹	SMITH (T.), *Six sonatas for the harpsichord . . . Opera VIII*

1244²	BACH (J.C.), *Six sonatas for the harpsichord . . . Opera XVII*
1244³	GLADWIN, *Eight lessons for the harpsichord*
1245	MUFFAT, *[72 Versetl sammt 12 Toccaten besonders beim Kirchen-Dienst]*
1246	HELLENDAAL, *Eight solos for the violoncello . . . Op. Vᵗᵃ.*
1247	LOCKE, *The English Opera; or . . . Psyche . . . To which is adjoyned . . . the Tempest*
1248¹	PEPUSCH, *The Beggars Opera*
1248²	*Polly*
1248³⁻⁴	ARNE (T.A.), *Lyric Harmony*
1249	WARREN, *A nineteenth collection of catches, canons and glees . . . inscribed to . . . the Catch Club*
1250¹	STEVENS, *Eight glees . . . Opera 3*
1250²	*Eight glees. Expressly composed for ladies . . . Op. IV*
1250³	*Blow blow thou winter wind*
1250⁴	*Ten glees . . . Op. V*
1250⁵	*Sigh no more ladies*
1250⁶	*O mistress mine*
1250⁷	*Ye spotted snakes!*
1250⁸	HOWARD, *Ye chearful virgins*
1250⁹	STEVENS, *What shall he have*
1250¹⁰	*From Oberon in fairy land*
1250¹¹	*Some of my heroes are low*
1250¹²	*When the toil of day is o'er*
1250¹³	*Crabbed age and youth*
1251¹	*Lionel & Clarissa*
1251²	*The Duenna*
1252¹	COOKE, *A collection of glees, catches and canons*
1252²	*Nine glees and two duets . . . Opera V*
1253	HANDEL, *Esther*
1254¹	DIBDIN, *The Padlock*
1254²	SHIELD, *The Poor Soldier*
1254³	ARNOLD (S.), *The Spanish Barber . . . Op. XVII*
1255	HAYES, *Sixteen psalms*
1256	BONONCINI (G.B.), *Divertimenti da camera*
1257¹	*The Summer's Tale*
1257²	*Midas*
1258¹	SHIELD, *Rosina*
1258²	*The Gentle Shepherd*
1259	*Talestri*
1260	ARNE (T.A.), *Elfrida*
1261	DURANTE, *‹Sonate per cembalo›*

1262	WHEELER, *Six glees*	1286 B³	CORELLI, *Concerti grossi ... da Francesco Geminiani composti delli sei soli della prima parte dell'opera quinta d'Arcangelo Corelli* [violin 2, concertino]
1263	WARREN, *An eighteenth collection of catches, canons and glees ... inscribed to ... the Catch Club*		
1264	*An eleventh collection of catches, canons and glees ... inscribed to ... the Catch Club*	1286 B⁴	*Concerti grossi ... composti della seconda parte dell'opera quinta d'Arcangelo Corelli per Francesco Geminiani* [violin 2, concertino]
1265	CORELLI, *Suonate ... Opera quarta. Prima parte.*		
1266	LULLI (G.B.), *Atys*	1286 C¹	GEMINIANI, *Concerti grossi ... Opera terza* [viola]
1267–9	*The Musical Miscellany*		
1270	ARNOLD (J.), *The Essex Harmony ... Volume I*	1286 C²	*Concerti grossi ... Opera seconda* [viola]
1271	*The Essex Harmony ... Vol. II*	1286 C³	CORELLI, *Concerti grossi ... da Francesco Geminiani composti delli sei soli della prima parte dell'opera quinta d'Arcangelo Corelli* [viola]
1272	*Psalms, hymns and anthems; for ... the hospital for ... deserted young children*		
1273	*Handel's favourite minuets*	1286 C⁴	*Concerti grossi ... composti della seconda parte dell'opera quinta d'Arcangelo Corelli per Francesco Geminiani* [viola]
1274	*A pocket companion for gentlemen and ladies ... Vol. II*		
1275	SCHMIDLIN, *Singendes und Spielendes Vergnügen reiner Andacht*	1286 D¹	GEMINIANI, *Concerti grossi ... Opera terza* [violoncello, concertino]
1276	HANDEL, *[Alessandro]. Alexander*	1286 D²	*Concerti grossi ... Opera seconda* [violoncello]
1277	*Almahide*		
1278	BONONCINI (M.A. [*sic, actually* G.B.]), *Camilla*	1286 D³	CORELLI, *Concerti grossi ... da Francesco Geminiani composti delli sei soli della prima parte dell'opera quinta d'Arcangelo Corelli* [violoncello]
1279	*Clotilda*		
1280	*[Pirro e Demetrio]. Pyrrhus and Demetrius*	1286 D⁴	*Concerti grossi ... composti della seconda parte dell'opera quinta d'Arcangelo Corelli per Francesco Geminiani* [violoncello, concertino]
1281	*[Idaspe]. Hydaspes*		
1282	*[Thomyris]. Thomiris*		
1283	CLAYTON, *Arsinoe*	1286 E¹	GEMINIANI, *Concerti grossi ... Opera terza* [violin 1, ripieno]
1284	*Rosamond*		
1285	GIBBS, *Eight solos for a violin*	1286 E²	*Concerti grossi ... Opera seconda* [violin 1, ripieno]
1286 A¹	GEMINIANI, *Concerti grossi ... Opera terza* [violin 1, concertino]		
1286 A²	*Concerti grossi ... Opera seconda* [violin 1, concertino]	1286 E³	CORELLI, *Concerti grossi ... da Francesco Geminiani composti delli sei soli della prima parte dell'opera quinta d'Arcangelo Corelli* [violin 1, ripieno]
1286 A³	CORELLI, *Concerti grossi ... da Francesco Geminiani composti delli sei soli della prima parte dell'opera quinta d'Arcangelo Corelli* [violin 1, concertino]		
1286 A⁴	*Concerti grossi ... composti della seconda parte dell'opera quinta d'Arcangelo Corelli per Francesco Geminiani* [violin 1, concertino]	1286 E⁴	*Concerti grossi ... composti della seconda parte dell'opera quinta d'Arcangelo Corelli per Francesco Geminiani* [violin 1, ripieno]
1286 B¹	GEMINIANI, *Concerti grossi ... Opera terza* [violin 2, concertino]	1286 F¹	GEMINIANI, *Concerti grossi ... Opera terza* [violin 2, ripieno]
1286 B²	*Concerti grossi ... Opera seconda* [violin 2, concertino]		

1286 F²   *Concerti grossi . . . Opera seconda* [violin 2, ripieno]

1286 F³   CORELLI, *Concerti grossi . . . da Francesco Geminiani composti delli sei soli della prima parte dell'opera quinta d'Arcangelo Corelli* [violin 2, ripieno]

1286 F⁴   *Concerti grossi . . . composti della seconda parte dell'opera quinta d'Arcangelo Corelli per Francesco Geminiani* [violin 2, ripieno]

1286 G¹   GEMINIANI, *Concerti grossi . . . Opera terza* [bass, ripieno]

1286 G²   *Concerti grossi . . . Opera seconda* [bass, ripieno]

1286 G³   CORELLI, *Concerti grossi . . . da Francesco Geminiani composti delli sei soli della prima parte dell'opera quinta d'Arcangelo Corelli* [bass, ripieno]

1286 G⁴   *Concerti grossi . . . composti della seconda parte dell'opera quinta d'Arcangelo Corelli per Francesco Geminiani* [bass, ripieno]

1287¹   STEVENS, *He may come if he dare*

1287²   *Our tars so fam'd in story*

1287³   CAREY (G.S.), *The Sailor's Allegory*

1287⁴   KELLY, *The Wife's Farewell . . . in . . . of Age To-morrow*

1287⁵   PIERCY, *The Beggar Girl*

1287⁶   SHIELD, *Sally Roy . . . in . . . the Wandering Melodist*

1287⁷   KREUTZER, *Adieu! my Fernando . . . in . . . Lodoiska*

1287⁸   *[Inkle and Yarico]. Ah will no change of clime*

1287⁹   SHIELD, *The Plough Boy . . . in the Farmer*

1287¹⁰   MOULDS, *Down in a valley where sweet violets grew*

1287¹¹   CARTER, *Oh Nanny wilt thou fly with me*

1287¹²   FISIN, *Only tell him that I love*

1287¹³   HAIGH, *Ah! prithee ask me not*

1287¹⁴   CAVENDISH, *I have a silent sorrow here . . . in the Stranger*

1287¹⁵   WEBBE (S., THE ELDER), *The Traveller*

1287¹⁶   SHIELD, *The Billet Doux*

1287¹⁷   CORRI, *Donald*

1287¹⁸   *Since, then I'm doom'd. I am a brisk and sprightly lad . . . in the Spoil'd Child*

1287¹⁹   *[The Wedding Day]. In the dead of the night*

1287²⁰   *My lodging is on the cold ground*

1287²¹   GIORDANI, *Queen Mary's Lamentation*

1287²²   *O say bonny lass*

1287²³   PLEYEL, *Henry's Cottage Maid*

1287²⁴   ARNOLD (S.), *Little Bess the ballad singer*

1287²⁵   DIGNUM, *Fair Rosale*

1287²⁶   STORACE, *Toll toll the knell . . . in Mahmoud*

1287²⁷   SHIELD, *The streamlet that flow'd round her cot . . . in the Woodman*

1287²⁸   LINLEY (T., THE ELDER), *In my pleasant native plains . . . in the Carnival of Venice*

1287²⁹   BOYCE, *Tell me, lovely shepherd, where*

1287³⁰   MOORE, *When time who steals our years away*

1287³¹   BARTHELEMON, *Durandarte and Belerma*

1287³²   MAZZINGHI, *The Captive to his Bird . . . in . . . Variety*

1287³³   *Sleep poor babe*

1288 A¹   STEVENS, *O mistress mine*

1288 A²   *Sigh no more ladies*

1288 A³⁻⁴   *Doubt thou the stars are fire* [2 copies]

1288 A⁵   *Charming to love*

1288 A⁶   *[Glees. Professional Collection of Glees]*

1288 A⁷   STEVENS, *Some of my heroes are low*

1288 A⁸   *[Another issue]*

1288 A⁹   *Sir, what's o'clock?*

1288 B¹⁻⁷   STEVENS, *He may come if he dare* [7 copies]

1288 B⁸   *To what age must we live without love?*

1288 B⁹   *Bragela*

1288 B¹⁰⁻¹²   *Sober lay and mirthful glee* [3 copies]

1288 B¹³   *Floreat Aeternum*

1288 B¹⁴   *Who is Sylvia?*

1288 B¹⁵⁻²⁰   *All in the downs* [6 copies]

1288 B²¹⁻²   *Unfading Beauty* [2 copies]

1288 B²³   *Our tars so fam'd in story*

1288 B²⁴   *What's this dull town to me*

[1288 B²⁵]

1288 B²⁶   KILLICK, *The morning & evening hymns*

1288 B²⁷   FORD, *There is a lady sweet & kind*

1288 C	SMITH (T.), *Three favourite duets, for two performers on one harpsichord*	[1326¹]	
1289 A	STEVENS, *What shall he have*	1326²	HASSE, *Concerto . . . for the harpsichord* [Op. 4. No. 1]
1289 B–F	*Eight glees. Expressly composed for ladies . . . Op. IV*	1327	PLAYFORD (J.), *Select musicall ayres and dialogues*
[1289 G]		1328	*Select ayres and dialogues for one, two, and three voyces*
1289 H	*When Chloris, like an angel, walks*	1329	*Calliope, or English Harmony*
1289 I	STEVENS, *To banish life's troubles*	1330	*Universal Harmony*
1290 A–C	*Sacred music*	1331	*[Another issue]*
1291	*Ten songs . . . Opera II*	1332	B. (R.), *A collection of duets, rotas, canons, catches & glees*
1292	*Three sonatas for the harpsichord . . . Opera prima*	[1333]	
1293	*Who is it that this dark night*	1334¹⁻²	BANISTER, *A ⟨2ᵈ.⟩ collection of the most celebrated song tunes . . . fitted to the violin*
1294	HANDEL, *Eight anthems . . . with an accompaniment for the organ*	1334³	*Select preludes [& vollentarys] for the violin*
[1295]		[1335]	
1296	KILLICK, *Concerto, for the piano forte*	1336	STARTER, *Friesche Lust-Hof*
1297	MILLER, *The psalms of David*	[1337–45]	
1298	*[Scots]. A selection of the most favourite Scots-songs*	1346¹	HANDEL, *Theodora*
		1346²	*Solomon*
1299	TATTERSALL, *Improved Psalmody. Vol. 1*	1347	*Susanna*
		1348	*Samson*
[1300]		1349¹	*Judas Macchabaeus*
1301	WEBBE (S., THE ELDER), *A collection of masses*	1349²	*Occasional Oratorio*
		1350¹	*Deborah*
1302	WEBER, *Der Freischütz*	1350²	*Athalia*
1303	*Oberon*	1351	*Belshazzar*
[1304]		1352	*Alexander's Feast*
1305	BLOW, *Amphion Anglicus*	1353¹	*[Op. 4]. Six concertos for the harpsicord or organ*
1306	PURCELL (H.), *Orpheus Britannicus*	1353²	*L'Allegro, il Penseroso, ed il Moderato*
1307	*A collection of ayres* [violin 1]		
1308	*A collection of ayres* [violin 2]	1354	*Acis and Galatea*
1309	*A collection of ayres* [tenor]	1355	*[Giulio Cesare]. Julius Caesar*
1310	*A collection of ayres* [bass]	1356¹	*[Imeneo]. Hymen*
1311	*Sonnata's of III parts* [violin 1]	1356²	*[12 arias]*
1312	*Sonnata's of III parts* [bass]	1356³	*[Ottone]. Otho*
1313	*Sonnata's of III parts* [continuo]	1356⁴	*[Aditional celebrated aires in . . . Floridante]*
1314	*Sonnata's of III parts* [violin 2]		
1315	*Amphitryon*	1357	ARNE (T.A.), *Artaxerxes*
[1316]		1358	MARTINI, *Sonate per l'organo*
1317	PLAYFORD (J.), *Musick's Delight on the cithren*	[1359]	
		1360¹	PARADIES, *Sonate di gravicembalo*
[1318–19]		1360²	*A favourite minuet*
1320	SIMPSON, *Chelys . . . The division-viol*	1360³	*A favorite concerto for the organ*
1321	GALILEI, *Fronimo*	1361	TRAVERS, *Eighteen canzonets*
[1322¹–4¹]		1362	*Psalms*
1324²	WHALLEY, *O give thanks*	1363	ARNE (T.A.), *Judith*
1324³	KENT, *Hear my prayer*		
1325	MILLER, *Elements of thorough bass and composition . . . Opera quinta*		

1364	GRÉTRY, *Richard Coeur de Lion . . . Oeuvre XXIV*	1400¹	BACH (J.C.), *Six overtures . . . addapted for the harpsichord*
1365¹	ARNE (T.A.), *Judgment of Paris . . . Rule Britannia, and Sawney & Jenney . . . Opera sesta*	1400²	PICCINI, *La Buona Figliuola. [Overture]*
		1400³	*La Buona Figliuola Maritata. [Overture]*
1365²	*Elegy on the death of M'. Shenstone*	1400⁴	*La Schiava. [Overture]*
1366	*Comus*	1400⁵	SACCHINI, *Il Cid. Overture*
1367	*Eliza*	1400⁶	*Motezuma. Overture*
1368	KELLY, *Of Age Tomorrow*	1400⁷	*Tamerlano. Overture*
1369	MARTYN, *Fourteen sonatas*	1400⁸	GUGLIELMI, *Il Desertore. Overture*
1370	ALCOCK (J., THE YOUNGER), *Eight easy voluntarys*	1400⁹	TRAETTA, *Antigono. Overture*
		1400¹⁰	*Demetrio. Overture*
1371	FISHER, *Six sonatas . . . Opera prima*	1401	*Tenducci's new rondeau* [Song]
[1372–3]		1402	ARNOLD (S.), *Peeping Tom of Coventry*
1374	ABEL, *Sei sonate . . . per il flauto . . . Opera sesta*	1403	*[Twelve sonatas. Op. XII, part 2]*
1375	HOWARD, *The Amorous Goddess*	1404¹	DIETZ, *XII Variations . . . sur le rondeau favori de M': Fischer*
1376	WANHAL, *Six trios . . . Œvre premiere*	1404²	HOOK, *A favourite concerto for the harpsichord with twelve variations to Lovely Nancy*
1377¹	WEBBE (S., THE ELDER), *The Ladies' Catch Book*		
1377²	*A second book of catches, canons and glees*	1404³	WAGENSEIL, *A lesson for the harpsichord . . . To which is added . . . Gramachee Molly*
1377³	*A third book of catches, canons and glees*		
1377⁴	*A fourth book of catches, canons and glees*	1405¹	WEBBE (S., THE ELDER), *A V book of catches, canons & glees*
1377⁵	*A Vth. book of catches, canons & glees*	1405²	*A VI book of catches, canons & glees*
1377⁶	*A VIth. book of catches, canons & glees*		
1377⁷	*A seventh book of catches, canons & glees*	1406	*[A second book of catches,] canons [and glees]*
1377⁸	*An eighth book of glees, canons, and catches*	1407	*The Ladies' Catch Book*
		1408	WEBBE (S., THE ELDER, AND S., THE YOUNGER), *A collection of vocal music . . . ⟨Ninth book⟩*
1377⁹	WEBBE (S., THE ELDER, AND S., THE YOUNGER), *A collection of vocal music . . . ⟨Ninth book⟩*		
[1378]		1409	WEBBE (S., THE ELDER), *An eighth book of glees, canons, and catches*
1379	HUMMEL, *[Op. 83]. Grand trio*		
1380	*[Op. 12. No. 1]. Grand trio concertante*	1410	DITTERSDORF, *The favorite sinfonie . . . Disposed for the piano forte*
1381	HANDEL, *Joshua*		
1382	*Messiah*	1411	TENDUCCI, *The overture to the Revenge of Athridates*
1383	HARMONIC SOCIETY OF CAMBRIDGE, *A collection of glees and rounds*		
		1412 A	*Vivaldi's most celebrated concertos . . . Opera terza*
1384	STEVENS, *The collect for the first Sunday in Advent*	1412 B	*The second part . . . parti 2ᵈ.*
		1413	*Select Harmony*
[1385–96]		1414	*La Stravaganza . . . Opera 4ᵗᵃ.*
1397	WANHAL, *Two favorite lessons for the harpsicord*	1415	*VI Concerti . . . Opera decima*
		1416	*Sei concerti . . . Opera undecima*
[1398]		1417	*Sei concerti . . . Opera duodecima*
1399	PARKE, *Overture to Netley Abbey*	1418	*La Cetra . . . Opera nona*

1419	Two celebrated concertos ... the Cuckow, and the ... Extravaganza	1436	Anthem. For the coronation of George II^D. ['Zadok the priest'] [Arnold]
1420	Il Cimento dell' Armonia e dell' Inventione ... Opera ottava	1437	Anthem. For the coronation of George II^D. ['The King shall rejoice'] [Arnold]
1421 A	Camilla	1438	Anthem. For the coronation of George II^D. ['My heart is inditing'] [Arnold]
1421 B	Six overtures ... in ... Astartus, Croesus, Camilla, Hydaspes, Thomyris, Rinaldo [Camilla only]	1439	DEFESCH, X. Sonata's for two German flutes ... Opera settima
1422 A	[Idaspe]. The instrumental musick in ... Hydaspes	1440^1	PAER, La Nouvelle Valentine
1422 B	Six overtures ... in ... Astartus, Croesus, Camilla, Hydaspes, Thomyris, Rinaldo [Hydaspes only]	1440^2	GUIGOU, La nouvelle Valentine
		1440^3	PACINI, Imite le mon fils
		1440^4	SPONTINI, La nouvelle Valentine
1423 A	The symphonys ... in ... Thomyris	1440^5	[French songs, c. 1820]
1423 B	Six overtures ... in ... Astartus, Croesus, Camilla, Hydaspes, Thomyris, Rinaldo [Thomyris only]	[1441–5]	
		1446–7	BLAKE, Six duets. For a violin, and tenor
[1424]		[1448–53]	
1425	Periodical overture for the harpsicord [Nos. 1–12]	1454	STEINER, [Neues Gesang-Buch]
		[1455–6]	
[1426–8]		1457^1	WARREN, Index to a collection of vocal harmony ... Arranged by G. Gwilt
1429^1	Royal Merchant. Overture		
1429^2	Peep behind the Curtain. Overture	1457^2	A general index to Warren's collection of catches, canons, and glees ... Arranged by ... G. Gwilt
1430	DEFESCH, VIII Concerto's in seven parts		
[1431–2]		1458–60	Apollo's Feast
1433^1	HANDEL, Te Deum ... for ... Queen Caroline [Arnold]	[1461–2]	
		1463–7	NOVELLO, Fitzwilliam Music
1433^2	Anthem. For the victory at Dettingen [Arnold]	1468	DAMON, Second booke [altus]
		1469	[Harpsichord Master]. The second book of the harpsichord master
1434	Anthem. For the funeral of Queen Caroline [Arnold]		
		1470	[Anthems]. Six select anthems
1435	Anthem. For the coronation of George II^D. ['Let thy hand be strengthened'] [Arnold]		

CHRONOLOGICAL LIST OF THE FOUNDER'S COLLECTION OF PRINTED MUSIC

IT WAS THE Founder's practice to inscribe his books with his name ('R. Fitzwilliam' until 1776, when on becoming 7th Viscount he signed simply 'Fitzwilliam') and the date (presumably either the date of purchase or of formal accession to his collection).

In the case of a few groupings (either volumes or in some cases groups of volumes) where only the first item is inscribed, but where binding or annotation shows clearly that all the items belonged to the Founder, the fact is briefly noted in the entry for the first item. The uninscribed items may then be traced through the numerical list.

There is, however, a problematic category of items not inscribed and not definitely associated with the Founder by other evidence, but which have at various times been grouped in sequence following an inscribed item. Where this is clearly the case the fact is noted in the present list, in the entry for the first item in the grouping, and the other items in question can then be located from the numerical list. Readers interested in this aspect of the collection are strongly advised to make their own detailed inspection, as the hints offered in this list are for guidance only. Moreover, the suggestions made below regarding uninscribed items possibly associated with the Founder are not to be regarded as in any way exhaustive.

Where an item contains a subscribers' list which includes the Founder, an asterisk represents each copy subscribed for.

1763

BONONCINI (G.B.), *Cantate e duetti*
Inscribed 'R. Fitzwilliam 1763'.
MU. 437

GEMINIANI, *[Sonatas Op. 1]. Le prime sonate*
Inscribed 'R. Fitzwilliam 1763'. This is the first item in a volume assembled by the Founder (see 'Numerical list').
MU. 304[1]

1764

HANDEL, *Suites de pieces . . . Premier livre*
Inscribed 'R. Fitzwilliam 1764'. This is the first item in a volume assembled by the Founder (see 'Numerical list').
MU. 317[1]

1765

BONONCINI (G.B.), *Anthem . . . performed . . . at the funeral of . . . John, Duke of Marlborough*
Inscribed 'R. Fitzwilliam 1765'.
MU. 495

CORELLI, *The . . . four operas, containing 48 sonatas ⟨twelve concertos⟩ . . . Vol. I. ⟨II⟩*
Both volumes inscribed 'R. Fitzwilliam 1765'.
MU. 305–6

CORELLI, *XII Solos for a violin . . . Opera quinta*
Inscribed 'R. Fitzwilliam 1765'.
MU. 307

RAMEAU, *Pigmalion*
Inscribed 'Fitzwilliam 1765'.
MU. 359

ROGER, *VI Suittes . . . pour le clavessin*
Inscribed 'R. Fitzwilliam 1765'.
MU. 436

1766

DIEUPART, *[Six suittes de clavessin]*
Inscribed 'R. Fitzwilliam 1766'.
MU. 435

ECCLES AND PURCELL (D.), *Collection of lessons and aires*
Inscribed 'R. Fitzwilliam 1766'.
MU. 361 C

PURCELL (H.), *Choice collection of lessons*
Inscribed 'R. Fitzwilliam 1766'.
MU. 419

PURCELL (H.), *Orpheus Britannicus*
Both volumes inscribed 'R. Fitzwilliam 1766'. Vol I is bound with Blow's *Ode on the death of Mr. Henry Purcell*. The binding apparently dates from before or during the Founder's lifetime.
MU. 375^1, 376

1767

BOYCE, *Cathedral Music*
* Inscribed 'R. Fitzwilliam 1767' (vol. I), 'R. Fitzwilliam 1768' (vol. II), 'R. Fitzwilliam 1773' (vol. III).
MU. 411 A–C

CHARPENTIER, *Medée*
Inscribed 'R. Fitzwilliam 1767'.
MU. 339

CLARKE, *Choice lessons*
Inscribed 'R. Fitzwilliam 1767'. The two items in MU. 420 were at one time bound together, probably after their arrival in the Museum, and the

second may or may not have been the Founder's (see 'Numerical list').
MU. 420 A

COLASSE, *Achille et Polixene*
Inscribed 'R. Fitzwilliam 1767'.
MU. 328

COLASSE, *Enée et Lavinie*
Inscribed 'R. Fitzwilliam 1767'.
MU. 338

COLASSE, *Thetis et Pelée*
Inscribed 'R. Fitzwilliam 1767'.
MU. 337

DESMARETS, *Circé*
Inscribed 'R. Fitzwilliam 1767'.
MU. 329

GALLIARD, *Six sonatas for the bassoon*
Inscribed 'R. Fitzwilliam 1767'.
MU. 487

HANDEL, *Admeto*
Inscribed 'R. Fitzwilliam 1767'.
MU. 385 A

HANDEL, *Alcina*
Inscribed 'R. Fitzwilliam 1767'.
MU. 391 A

HANDEL, *[Alessandro]. Roxana, or Alexander*
Inscribed 'R. Fitzwilliam 1767'.
MU. 386 B

HANDEL, *[Arianna]. Ariadne*
Inscribed 'R. Fitzwilliam 1767'.
MU. 382 A

HANDEL, *[Arminio]. Arminius*
Inscribed 'R. Fitzwilliam 1767'.
MU. 385 B

HANDEL, *Atalanta*
Inscribed 'R. Fitzwilliam 1767'.
MU. 386 A

HANDEL, *Berenice*
Inscribed 'R. Fitzwilliam 1767'.
MU. 391 B

HANDEL, *Deidamia*
Inscribed 'R. Fitzwilliam 1767'.
MU. 385 C

HANDEL, *[Ezio]. Aetius*
Inscribed 'R. Fitzwilliam 1767'.
MU. 390 A

HANDEL, *Faramondo*
Inscribed 'R. Fitzwilliam 1767'.
MU. 384 A

HANDEL, *[Flavio]. Flavius*
Inscribed 'R. Fitzwilliam 1767'.
MU. 390 B

HANDEL, *[Floridante]. Floridant*
Inscribed 'R. Fitzwilliam 1767'.
MU. 388 A

HANDEL, *Giulio Cesare*
Inscribed 'R. Fitzwilliam 1767'.
MU. 383 A

HANDEL, *[Giustino]. Justin*
Inscribed 'R. Fitzwilliam 1767'.
MU. 387 B

HANDEL, *[Imeneo]. Hymen*
Inscribed 'R. Fitzwilliam 1767'.
MU. 384 B

HANDEL, *[Lotario]. Lotharius*
Inscribed 'R. Fitzwilliam 1767'.
MU. 381 A

HANDEL, *Orlando*
Inscribed 'R. Fitzwilliam 1767'.
MU. 389 A

HANDEL, *[Ottone]. Otho*
Inscribed 'R. Fitzwilliam 1767'.
MU. 384 C

HANDEL, *[Partenope]. Parthenope*
Inscribed 'R. Fitzwilliam 1767'.
MU. 389 B

HANDEL, *Radamisto*
Inscribed 'R. Fitzwilliam 1767'.
MU. 388 B

HANDEL, *[Riccardo Primo]. Richard ye I^{st}*
Inscribed 'R. Fitzwilliam 1767'.
MU. 381 B

HANDEL, *Rinaldo*
Inscribed 'R. Fitzwilliam 1767'.
MU. 388 C

HANDEL, *[Scipione]. Scipio*
Inscribed 'R. Fitzwilliam 1767'.
MU. 381 C

HANDEL, *[Serse]. Xerxes*
Inscribed 'R. Fitzwilliam 1767'.
MU. 408

HANDEL, *Siroe*
Inscribed 'R. Fitzwilliam 1767'.
MU. 381 D

HANDEL, *[Sosarme]. Sosarmes*
Inscribed 'R. Fitzwilliam 1767'.
MU. 390 C

HANDEL, *Suites de pieces . . . [Vol. I]*
Inscribed 'R. Fitzwilliam 1767'. This is the first item
in a volume assembled by the Founder (see 'Numerical list').
MU. 316^1, bound with MU. MS 79

HANDEL, *[Tamerlano]. Tamerlane*
Inscribed 'R. Fitzwilliam 1767'.
MU. 386 C

HANDEL, *[Tolomeo]. Ptolomy*
Inscribed 'R. Fitzwilliam 1767'.
MU. 383 B

JACQUET DE LA GUERRE, *Cephale et Procris*
Inscribed 'R. Fitzwilliam 1767'.
MU. 340

LULLI (G.B.), *Acis et Galatée*
Inscribed 'R. Fitzwilliam 1767'.
MU. 326

LULLI (G.B.), *Bellerophon*
Inscribed 'R. Fitzwilliam 1767'. This is the first of a
pair of items apparently bound together in the
Founder's lifetime (see 'Numerical list').
MU. 321^1

LULLI (G.B.), *Persée*
Inscribed 'R. Fitzwilliam 1767'.
MU. 323

LULLI (G.B.), *Proserpine*
Inscribed 'R. Fitzwilliam 1767'.
MU. 322

LULLI (G.B.), *Roland*
Inscribed 'R. Fitzwilliam 1767'.
MU. 324

LULLI (G.B.), *Temple de la paix*
Inscribed 'R. Fitzwilliam 1767'.
MU. 325

LULLY (L. de), *Orphée*
Inscribed 'R. Fitzwilliam 1767'.
MU. 327

MAZZAFERRATA, *Canzonette, e cantate a due voci*
. . . Opera terza
Inscribed 'R. Fitzwilliam 1767'.
MU. 481

WAGENSEIL, *Six concertos for the harpsicord . . .*
with . . . two violins
Inscribed 'R. Fitzwilliam 1767'.
MU. 486[8]

WAGENSEIL, *Six sonatas for the harpsicord . . .*
Opera prima
Inscribed 'R. Fitzwilliam 1767'.
MU. 485[6]

WAGENSEIL, *Six sonatas for the harpsichord . . .*
Opera 2da.
Inscribed 'R. Fitzwilliam 1767'.
MU. 486[9]

WAGENSEIL, *Six sonatas for the harpsicord . . .*
Opera III
Inscribed 'R. Fitzwilliam 1767'.
MU. 485[7]

1768

ALBERTI, *VIII Sonate per cembalo. Opera prima*
Inscribed 'R. Fitzwilliam 1768'. This is the first item
in a Museum binding most of whose contents are
inscribed by the Founder (see 'Numerical list').
MU. 484[1]

BABELL, *Suits of the most celebrated lessons*
Inscribed 'R. Fitzwilliam 1768'.
MU. 488[3], bound with MU. MS 208

BACH (J.C.), *Six sonatas for the piano forte . . .*
Opera 5
Inscribed 'R. Fitzwilliam 1768. From the author'.
MU. 362 E

ECCLES, *Iudgment of Paris*
Inscribed 'R. Fitzwilliam 1768'. This is the first of a
pair of settings of the text apparently bound
together in or before the Founder's lifetime (see
'Numerical list').
MU. 378[1]

GALLIARD, *Hymn of Adam and Eve*
* Inscribed 'R. Fitzwilliam 1768'.
MU. 523

GREENE, *Forty select anthems*
* Inscribed 'R. Fitzwilliam 1768'.
MU. 368

GREENE, *Lessons for the harpsichord*
Inscribed 'R. Fitzwilliam 1768'.
MU. 485[2]

GREENE, *Lessons for the harpsichord . . . 2d. book*
Inscribed 'R. Fitzwilliam 1768'.
MU. 485[3]

HANDEL, *[Op.4]. Six concertos for the harpsicord*
Inscribed 'R. Fitzwilliam 1768'. This is the first item
in a volume assembled by the Founder (see 'Numerical list').
MU. 319[1]

JONES (R.), *Suits or setts of lessons*
Inscribed 'R. Fitzwilliam 1768'.
MU. 488[5], bound with MU. MS 208

KELWAY, *Six sonatas for the harpsicord*
Inscribed 'R. Fitzwilliam 1768'.
MU. 485[4]

NARES, *Lessons for the harpsicord . . . Opera II*
Inscribed 'R. Fitzwilliam 1768'.
MU. 485[5]

PLAYFORD (H.), *Harmonia sacra . . . first book*
Inscribed 'R. Fitzwilliam 1768'. This is the first item
of a volume apparently bound in or before the
Founder's lifetime (see 'Numerical list').
MU. 372[1]

PLAYFORD (J.), *Select ayres and dialogues to sing to*
the theorbo-lute
Inscribed 'R. Fitzwilliam 1768'. This is the first item
of a volume apparently bound in or before the
Founder's lifetime (see 'Numerical list').
MU. 377[1], bound with MU. MS 118

ROSEINGRAVE, *Voluntarys and fugues*
Inscribed 'R. Fitzwilliam 1768'.
MU. 486[3]

SYMONDS, *Six sets of lessons for the harpsicord*
Inscribed 'R. Fitzwilliam 1768'.
MU. 362 B

1769

BONONCINI (G.B.), *[Cantate e duetti]*
Inscribed 'R. Fitzwilliam 1769'.
MU. 302

BURTON, *Ten sonatas for the harpsichord*
Inscribed 'R. Fitzwilliam 1769'.
MU. 485[1]

COUPERIN, *L'Art de toucher le clavecin*
Inscribed 'R. Fitzwilliam 1769'.
MU. 424

COUPERIN, *Pieces de clavecin . . . Premier livre*
Inscribed 'R. Fitzwilliam 1769'.
MU. 425

COUPERIN, *Second livre de pièces de clavecin*
Inscribed 'R. Fitzwilliam 1769'.
MU. 426

DU PHLY, *Pieces ⟨second–quatrieme livre de pieces⟩ de clavecin*
Vol. I inscribed 'R. Fitzwilliam 1769 – de la part de l'auteur'. Vols. II–IV have the same inscription except that the dates are respectively 1769, 1771 and 1772.
MU. 429

LALANDE, *Motets*
Inscribed 'R. Fitzwilliam 1769'.
MU. 330–6

LE ROUX, *Pieces de clavessin*
Inscribed 'R. Fitzwilliam 1769'.
MU. 360

PARADIES, *A favorite concerto for the organ*
Inscribed 'R. Fitzwilliam 1769'.
MU. 486^1

RAMEAU, *Pieces de clavecin en concerts*
Inscribed 'R. Fitzwilliam 1769'.
MU. 427

SCARLATTI (D.), *Essercizi per gravicembalo*
Inscribed 'R. Fitzwilliam 1769'.
MU. 422

1770

DUPORT, *Six sonatas . . . dediées à Messire Fitzwilliam*
Inscribed 'R. Fitzwilliam 1770'.
MU. 308

HANDEL, *L'Allegro, il Penseroso, ed il Moderato*
Inscribed 'R. Fitzwilliam 1770'.
MU. 397

PARADIES, *Sonate di gravicembalo*
Inscribed 'RICHARD FITZWILLIAM London 27^d Dec^r: 1770'.
MU. 428

RAMEAU, *Lessons for the harpsicord . . . Opera seconda*
Inscribed 'R. Fitzwilliam 1770'.
MU. 484^3

SAN MARTINI, *Concertos for the harpsicord . . . Opera nona*
Inscribed 'R. Fitzwilliam 1770'.
MU. 486^4

1771

AVISON, *Twelve concertos . . . Opera nona. Set I ⟨II⟩*
* Each set inscribed 'R. Fitzwilliam 1771'. This is the first item in a Museum binding most of whose contents are inscribed by the Founder (see 'Numerical list').
MU. 488$^{1–2}$, bound with MU. MS 208

BERTON AND TRIAL, *Silvie*
Inscribed 'R. Fitzwilliam 1771'.
MU. 489

BOYCE, *Ode [for the] installation of . . . [the] Chancellor of the University*
Inscribed 'R. Fitzwilliam 1771'.
MU. 363 A

BOYCE, *Solomon*
Inscribed 'R. Fitzwilliam 1771'.
MU. 363 B

CROFT, *Musicus apparatus academicus*
Inscribed 'R. Fitzwilliam 1771'.
MU. 412

HART, *Fugues . . . with lessons*
Inscribed 'R. Fitzwilliam 1771'.
MU. 417

HINE, *[Harm]onia Sacra Glocestriensis*
Inscribed 'R. Fitzwilliam 1771'. All the items in MU. 380 were at one time uniformly bound, probably after their arrival in the Museum, and most are inscribed by the Founder (see 'Numerical list').
MU. 380 A

PURCELL (H.), *Harmonia sacra*
Inscribed 'R. Fitzwilliam 1771'.
MU. 366^2

PURCELL (H.), *Te Deum et Jubilate*
Inscribed 'R. Fitzwilliam 1771'.
MU. 366^3

RAMEAU, *Five concertos for the harpsicord*
Inscribed 'R. Fitzwilliam 1771'.
MU. 486^2

RAMEAU, *A 2ᵈ collection of the lessons for the harpsi-cord . . . Opera 3ᶻᵃ.*
Inscribed 'R. Fitzwilliam 1771'.
MU. 484⁴

SCARLATTI (D.), *Libro de XII sonatas modernas para clavicordio*
Inscribed 'R. Fitzwilliam 1771'.
MU. 486⁵

TARTINI, *II Concerti . . . accommodati per il cembalo*
Each vol. inscribed 'R. Fitzwilliam 1771'. All the items in MU. 361 were at one time uniformly bound, probably after their arrival in the Museum, and most are inscribed by the Founder (see 'Numerical list').
MU. 361 A¹⁻²

VERACINI, *Sonate accademiche . . . Opera seconda*
Inscribed 'R. Fitzwilliam 1771'.
MU. 312

ZIANI, *XVII Sonates da organo*
Inscribed 'R. Fitzwilliam 1771'. All the items in MU. 362 were at one time uniformly bound, probably after their arrival in the Museum, and most are inscribed by the Founder (see 'Numerical list').
MU. 362 A

1772

BURNEY, *La musica . . . della settimana santa*
Inscribed 'R. Fitzwilliam 1772'.
MU. 366¹

HANDEL, *Alexander's Feast*
Inscribed 'R. Fitzwilliam 1772'.
MU. 392

PEPUSCH, *XXIV Solos*
Inscribed 'R. Fitzwilliam 1772'.
MU. 313

ROSEINGRAVE, *Six double fugues . . . Scarlatti's celebrated lesson for the harpsichord*
Inscribed 'R. Fitzwilliam 1772'.
MU. 484⁵

1774

KELLNER, *Six fugues for the organ*
Inscribed 'R. Fitzwilliam 1774'.
MU. 488⁶, bound with MU. MS 208

PURCELL (H.), *The Prophetess, or . . . Dioclesian*
Inscribed 'R. Fitzwilliam 1774'.
MU. 379

1775

HANDEL, *Twelve duets . . . trio in . . . Alcina*
Inscribed 'R. Fitzwilliam 1775'.
MU. 354 B

MORLEY, *Six canzonets for two voices*
Inscribed 'R. Fitzwilliam 1775'.
MU. 421 A

NARES, *A treatise on singing*
Inscribed 'Fitzwilliam 1775'.
MU. 421 B

STANLEY, *Six concertos set for the harpsicord*
Inscribed 'R. Fitzwilliam 1775'.
MU. 486⁶

STANLEY, *Ten voluntarys for the organ or harpsicord . . . Opera 5ᵗʰ:*
Inscribed 'R. Fitzwilliam 1775'.
MU. 484⁶

1778

MARCELLO, *Estro poetico-armonico*
Inscribed 'Fitzwilliam 1778'.
MU. 409

1781

HANDEL, *Suites de pieces . . . Premier volume*
Inscribed 'Fitzwilliam 1781'.
MU. 315

1782

GALLIARD, *Morning hymn*
Inscribed 'Fitzwilliam 1782'.
MU. 494¹

RAMEAU, *Les Festes de l'Hymen et de l'Amour*
Inscribed 'Fitzwilliam 1782'.
MU. 490¹

RAMEAU, *Les Fêtes de Polymnie*
Inscribed 'Fitzwilliam 1782'.
MU. 490²

RAMEAU, *Pigmalion*
Inscribed 'Fitzwilliam 1782'.
MU. 358

RAMEAU, *Les Surprises de l'Amour*
Inscribed 'Fitzwilliam 1782', and on a preliminary blank, apparently in the same hand, '6.2 Livres Paris 20 Jul 1781'.
MU. 303

SMITH (J.C.), *Suites . . . pour le clavecin. [Second book]*
Inscribed 'Fitzwilliam 1782'. This is the first item in a Museum binding whose other contents may or may not have belonged to the Founder (see 'Numerical list').
MU. 483¹

ZIPOLI, *A third collection of toccates, vollentarys and fuges*
Inscribed 'Fitzwilliam 1782'.
MU. 486⁷

1787

[The Works of Handel, in score . . . under the immediate direction and inspection of Dr. [Samuell] Arnold]
** This edition appeared between 1787 and 1797. Only a few volumes bear Fitzwilliam's inscription (see separate entries in main catalogue), and it is clear that not all the volumes in the present collection were his.
MU. 345, 352, 443–72, 1433–8

1788

AYRTON, *Anthem [written for] the degree of Doctor in Music*
Inscribed 'R. Fitzwilliam 1788'.
MU. 369

KEEBLE, *Select pieces ⟨A second–fourth set of⟩ for the organ*
Inscribed 'Fitzwilliam 1788'.
MU. 415

1790

PARRY, *British Harmony*
* Inscribed 'Fitzwilliam 1790'.
MU. 380 B

1791

CLARI, *Sei madrigali . . . Parte prima*
* Inscribed 'R. Fitzwilliam 1791'.
MU. 479

WARREN, *A twenty sixth collection of catches*
Inscribed 'Fitzwilliam 1791'.
MU. 357 C

1792

NARES, *Morning and evening service . . . with six anthems*
Inscribed 'Fitzwilliam 1792'.
MU. 365¹

1793

KEEBLE AND KIRKMAN, *Forty interludes*
Inscribed 'Fitzwilliam 1793'.
MU. 421 C

MARTINI, *Duetti da camera*
Inscribed 'Fitzwilliam 1793'.
MU. 480

SMITH (J.S.), *Collection of English songs*
* Inscribed 'Fitzwilliam 1793'.
MU. 494²

1796

SOLER (A.), *XXVII Sonatas para clave*
Inscribed 'Fitzwilliam 1796'. Facing the title the Founder has written, 'The originals of these harpsichord lessons were given to me by Father Soler, at the Escurial, the 14ᵗʰ. February, 1772. Father Soler had been instructed by Scarlatti'. There is no record of such MSS in the Museum.
MU. 418

1799

BONONCINI (G.B.), *Divertimenti da camera*
Inscribed 'R. Fitzwilliam 1799'.
MU. 361 F

BOYCE, *Fifteen anthems . . . Te Deum, and Jubilate*
* Inscribed 'R. Fitzwilliam 1799'.
MU. 364

Catch Club . . . Book I
Inscribed 'R. Fitzwilliam 1799'.
MU. 357 D

HANDEL, *Acis and Galatea*
Inscribed 'Fitzwilliam 1799'.
MU. 407

HANDEL, *Anthems . . . for . . . James Duke of Chandos . . . Vol. I ⟨–III⟩*
Each volume inscribed 'Fitzwilliam 1799'.
MU. 351 A–C

Handel's celebrated Coronation Anthems . . . Vol. I
Inscribed 'Fitzwilliam 1799'.
MU. 396

HANDEL, *Anthem . . . perform'd . . . at the funeral of Queen Caroline . . . Vol. II*
Inscribed 'Fitzwilliam 1799'.
MU. 393

HANDEL, *Choice of Hercules*
Inscribed 'Fitzwilliam 1799'.
MU. 400

HANDEL, *Six grand chorusses*
Each volume inscribed 'Fitzwilliam 1799'.
MU. 354 A$^{1-3}$

HANDEL, *Concerti grossi . . . Opera terza*
Inscribed 'Fitzwilliam 1799' in violin 2 only.
MU. 320 E^1, 320 F^1, 320 G^3, 320 H^3, 320 I^3, 320 J^3, 320 K^3, 320 M^3, 320 N^3

HANDEL, *Thirteen celebrated Italian duets*
** Inscribed 'Fitzwilliam 1799'.
MU. 395

HANDEL, *Esther*
* Inscribed 'Fitzwilliam 1799'.
MU. 343

HANDEL, *Israel in Egypt*
* Inscribed 'Fitzwilliam 1799'.
MU. 403

HANDEL, *Jephtha*
* Inscribed 'Fitzwilliam 1799'.
MU. 394

HANDEL, *Joshua*
* Inscribed 'Fitzwilliam 1799'.
MU. 402

HANDEL, *Judas Macchabaeus*
* Inscribed 'Fitzwilliam 1799'.
MU. 405

HANDEL, *Messiah*
* Inscribed 'Fitzwilliam 1799'.
MU. 399

HANDEL, *Ode for St Cecilia's Day*
Inscribed 'Fitzwilliam 1799'.
MU. 406

Handel's overtures
Inscribed 'Fitzwilliam 1799'. This would originally have been the first item in a large set of orchestral music assembled by the Founder, although rebinding has partially concealed his sequence (see 'Numerical list' for details of the other items in MU. 320).
MU. 320 G^1, 320 H^1, 320 I^1, 320 J^1, 320 K^1, 320 L^1, 320 M^1, 320 N^1

HANDEL, *Samson*
Inscribed 'Fitzwilliam 1799'.
MU. 404

HANDEL, *Saul*
* Inscribed 'Fitzwilliam 1799'.
MU. 401

HANDEL, *Solomon*
Inscribed 'Fitzwilliam 1799'.
MU. 348

HANDEL, *VI Sonates . . . Second ouvrage*
Inscribed 'Fitzwilliam 1799' in violin 1. This is the first item in a collection assembled by the Founder (see 'Numerical list').
MU. 318 A^1, 318 B^1, 318 D^1

HANDEL, *[Utrecht Te Deum]. Te Deum et Jubilate . . . perform'd before the sons of the clergy . . . Vol. III*
Inscribed 'Fitzwilliam 1799'.
MU. 398

MARCHAND, *Pieces de clavecin*
Inscribed 'Fitzwilliam 1799'.
MU. 361 D

NUSSEN, *Musica di camera . . . Opera 3^{za}*
Inscribed 'Fitzwilliam 1799'.
MU. 484^2

PEPUSCH, *Six English cantatas [2 vols.]*
Each vol. inscribed 'Fitzwilliam 1799'.
MU. 366$^{4-5}$

PEREZ, *Mattinuto de' Morti*
Inscribed 'Fitzwilliam 1799'.
MU. 309

PORPORA, *Opre di musica vocale*
Inscribed 'Fitzwilliam 1799'.
MU. 493

The Works of Henry Purcell, in five classes, edited by Benjamin Goodison
* Inscribed 'Fitzwilliam 1799'. Includes works by other composers.
MU. 341 A$^{1-4}$, 341 B$^{1-9}$

SCARLATTI (D.), *Forty two suits of lessons for the harpsicord [vol. I]*
Inscribed 'Fitzwilliam 1799'.
MU. 362 C

TARTINI, *XII Solos for a violin*
Inscribed 'Fitzwilliam 1799'.
MU. 310

WARREN, *Collection of catches*
Inscribed 'Fitzwilliam 1799'.
MU. 357 A

WARREN, *A second ⟨–fourth⟩ collection of catches*
Each inscribed 'Fitzwilliam 1799'.
MU. 357 B$^{1-3}$

WOODWARD, *Cathedral music . . . Opera terza*
Inscribed 'Fitzwilliam 1799'.
MU. 365^2

1800

HANDEL, *Agrippina*
Inscribed 'Fitzwilliam 1800'.
MU. 467

Music . . . for the harp
Inscribed 'This Copy is most respectfully presented to Lord Viscount Fitzwilliam by the Author Thomas Jones, Wigmore Street, 30th March 1800'.
Also inscribed 'Fitzwilliam 1800'.
MU. 434

SCARLATTI (D.), *Thirty sonatas, for the harpsichord or piano-forte; publish'd (by permission) from manuscripts in the possession of Lord Viscount Fitzwilliam*
Inscribed 'Fitzwilliam 1800'.
MU. 423

1801

HANDEL, *Anthem. For the wedding of Frederick Prince of Wales*
Inscribed 'Fitzwilliam 1801'.
MU. 352

HANDEL, *Belshazzar*
* Inscribed 'Fitzwilliam 1801'.
MU. 346

HANDEL, *Cecilia volgi un sguardo*
Inscribed 'Fitzwilliam 1801'.
MU. 514

HANDEL, *Deborah*
Inscribed 'Fitzwilliam 1801'.
MU. 342

HANDEL, *Dettingen Te Deum*
Inscribed 'Fitzwilliam 1801'.
MU. 353

HANDEL, *Joseph*
* Inscribed 'Fitzwilliam 1801'.
MU. 344

HANDEL, *Occasional Oratorio*
* Inscribed 'Fitzwilliam 1801'.
MU. 347

Handel's overtures
Inscribed 'Fitzwilliam 1801'.
MU. 355^1

HANDEL, *Overtures to . . . anthems . . . for James Duke of Chandos*
Inscribed 'Fitzwilliam 1801'.
MU. 355^2

HANDEL, *Semele*
Inscribed 'Fitzwilliam 1801'.
MU. 345

HANDEL, *Susanna*
Inscribed 'Fitzwilliam 1801'.
MU. 349

HANDEL, *Theodora*
* Inscribed 'Fitzwilliam 1801'.
MU. 350

1803

HARRISON, *Glee, 'Oh Nanny!'*
Inscribed 'Fitzm. 1803. from the Author'.
MU. 438, bound as MU. MS 166 C

LOCKE, *Modern church-musick pre-accus'd*
Inscribed 'Fitzwilliam 1803'.
MU. 367, bound with MU. MS 117 B

1805

CLEMENTI, *Introduction to . . . the piano forte*
Inscribed 'Fitzwilliam 1805'.
MU. 430

CLEMENTI, *Selection of practical harmony*
Inscribed 'Fitzwilliam 1805'.
MU. 416

Handel's songs, selected from his oratorios
Inscribed 'Fitzwilliam 1805'.
MU. 1232–6

MUGNIÉ, *L'Amour piqué par une abeille*
Inscribed 'Fitzwilliam 1805. De la part de l'auteur'.
MU. 380 E^4

MUGNIÉ, *A Grand military divertimento*
Inscribed 'Fitzwilliam 1805. De la part de l'auteur'.
MU. 380 E^3

MUGNIÉ, *Le Papillon*
Inscribed 'Fitzwilliam 1805. De la part de l'auteur'.
MU. 380 E^1

1807

WESLEY (C.), *Now I know what it is to have strove*
Inscribed, apparently in Lord Fitzwilliam's hand,
'From the author. 1807'.
MU. 380 D^1

1808

PLAYFORD (H.), *Harmonia sacra . . . first book*
Inscribed 'Fitzwilliam 1808'. This is the first item in
a volume apparently assembled in or before the
Founder's lifetime (see 'Numerical list').
MU. 373^1

1814

MORLEY, *Triumphs of Oriana*
The name of the original subscriber has been
deleted and 'Earl Fitzwilliam' substituted, probably
the bookseller's mistake for the Founder, although
neither part bears his usual inscription.
MU. 413 A–B

1815

PORTER, *Cathedral music*
Inscribed 'Fitzwilliam 1815'. W.J. Porter, son of the
composer, was Fitzwilliam's chaplain.
MU. 370